THE CRIMSON
TIDE

An Illustrated History of Football at The University of Alabama

THE CRIMSON TIDE

An Illustrated History of Football at The University of Alabama

WINSTON GROOM

THE UNIVERSITY OF ALABAMA PRESS
Tuscaloosa and London

Published in Cooperation with the
PAUL W. BRYANT MUSEUM

"Goodbye to the Bear" by Howell Raines was adapted from an article in
The New Republic.

"Deacon Blues"
Words and music by Walter Becker and Donald Fagan
Copyright © 1977 Universal-MCA Music Publishing, Inc.,
a division of Universal Studios, Inc. (ASCAP)
International Copyright Secured. All Rights Reserved.
Used by Permission.

Full picture credits appear on page 277.

Manufactured in Hong Kong by C&C Offset Printing Company, Ltd.

1 2 3 4 5 6 7 8 9 . 07 06 05 04 03 02 01 00

DESIGNED BY ROBIN MCDONALD

Text set in Century Old Style; headings and titles set in Cushing.

Library of Congress Cataloging-in-Publication Data

Groom, Winston, 1943-
  The Crimson Tide : an illustrated history of football at the
University of Alabama / Winston Groom.
    p. cm.
Includes index.
  ISBN 0-8173-1051-7 (alk. paper)
 1. Alabama Crimson Tide (Football team)—History. 2. University of
Alabama—Football—History. 3. Alabama Crimson Tide (Football
team)—History--Pictorial works. 4. University of
Alabama—Football—History—Pictorial works. I. Title.
  GV958.A4 G76 2000
  796.332'63'0976184--dc21
                    00-008871

British Library Cataloguing-in-Publication Data available

The Crimson Tide

CONTENTS

FOREWORD

Keith Jackson has announced college football games since 1952. He was the ABC television network's lead play-by-play announcer for college football from 1966 to 1999 and has won four Emmy Awards—three for best play-by-play commentator and a Lifetime Achievement in Sports award. The "Voice of College Football" called dozens of Alabama games over the last four decades of the twentieth century.

HERE IS NOTHING IN THIS WORLD more certain to jar a Southerner from the apathy of dog days than the thump of a football being hammered with a size eleven foot.

I mean it's like a bucket of cold water at Labor Day noon in the bottomland.

And if your druthers are colored red and white down by the Black Warrior River the thump of that ole football sets your motor running all the way through December.

By the time I reached awareness the Crimson Tide of Alabama had already claimed two national championships and we had the mind-boggling experience of having a former Notre Dame quarterback, Frank Thomas, as head coach. I'm not sure I'm over that yet! But he was a long-time winner and we all know how medicinal winning can be.

Across the years the legends (some mythical) accumulated with highs and lows and then one magic day—Mama called! Tuscaloosa hasn't been the same since and that's just fine. Paul William Bryant would have been wasted doing anything other than coaching Alabama football.

And it would have been a pity if Winston Groom hadn't taken the time to wrap his marvelous imagination around the stories and pictures of Alabama football history.

This is no Forrest Gump spring—this is a slow wonderful stroll across the history and tradition of a people and a place where so many feel right at home.

Enjoy!

ROLL TIDE!

Paul Bryant wanted to honor his
in any recognition given to his ca
Here, representing four universities
teams he coached to 323 victories in 3

ACKNOWLEDGMENTS

THIS BOOK IS A HISTORY OF FOOTBALL at The University of Alabama, but anyone reading it will soon discover that the historian is not entirely dispassionate. It is not the kind of story that a dispassionate person ought to write.

An undertaking of this sort requires the help of many people, not only to assemble more than a hundred years of historical information but to select hundreds of photographs out of thousands, properly identify them, find negatives or prints, and lay them all out in the text so that they not only make sense but look good. As for the last, designer Robin McDonald did a masterful job.

My writing of this book was the idea of Dr. Culpepper Clark, dean of the College of Communication and Information Sciences and one of the University's most avid football fans. Nicole Mitchell, director of The University of Alabama Press, and Curtis Clark, its assistant director and editor-in-chief, were enthusiastic about the idea and thus a book was born.

Ken Gaddy, director of the Paul W. Bryant Museum, agreed to co-sponsor the project, and Steve Townsend, who was with the athletic department at the time the book was started, offered cooperation. But the thing took longer and was more complicated than anyone thought.

Taylor Watson, curator of the Bryant Museum, provided invaluable research and labored long and hard to cull through thousands of photos dating back to the nineteenth century. Student assistants to Mr. Watson were C. J. Guercio, Kevin Nunnally, Jim Smith, and Amber Watson. Coach Clem Gryska of the museum was indispensible in helping to identify players, games, and scores in many of the photos. Mindy Wilson, an editor at the University Press, organized the whole book and, serving as photo editor, spent hours tracking down photographs and permissions from The University of Alabama library's Special Collections division, the athletic department, and various sources throughout the state. Rebecca Roberts and Lisa Speer of the Special Collections division also helped find and gather photographs. Neil Brake of the *Tuscaloosa News* and Kent Gidley from the University's Intercollegiate Athletics Media Relations department provided photos and expertise. *The University of Alabama: A Pictorial History*, by Suzanne Wolfe, and *Alabama Heritage* magazine were excellent sources for photographs and information about the early days of the University. Debbie Purifoy, Alabama Cheerleader Coach, helped with information on the history of cheerleading at Bama. I'd also like to note the dogged work of football historian James S. Edson in chronicling the history of Alabama football through the first half of the century, in *Alabama's*

FOOTBALL GAME
ROSE BOWL
PASADENA
JANUARY 1ST 1931

Crimson Tide: A History of Football at the University of Alabama for the Period of 1892 through 1945. Roses of Crimson, a documentary produced by Tom Rieland at UA's Center for Public Television, was also immensely helpful on the Tide's first Rose Bowl appearance in 1926.

Former university president David Mathews generously massaged his recollections of how black players were finally accepted onto the football team and so did former university attorney Rufus Bealle.

Jennifer Horne, managing editor of the Press, and copyeditor of the manuscript, saved me from myself more than once.

Lee Davis, freelance writer and sportscaster for WERC 90.6 AM radio in Birmingham, generously agreed to give the entire manuscript a final read-through.

ABC's Keith Jackson was gracious enough to write a fine introduction and Phil Beidler, Clyde Bolton, Scott Hunter, the late Willie Morris, Howell Raines, Gay Talese, and Sela Ward contributed invaluable and fascinating sidebars to enhance the main text.

Larry Wells kindly gave help locating photos and permission for us to scan his own book on Bama Ball for pictures. John Logue, former editor of *Southern Living,* former sportswriter (and former Auburn man!) took time to read the manuscript and give valuable advice.

President Andrew Sorensen and Board of Trustees member Frank Bromberg have been grand in their support of the project.

A special note of thanks to the John Forney family for allowing us permission to use quotes from his oral history *The Talk of the Tide*—and to professor Don Noble of the English Department for permission to quote from his introduction to *Mud on the Stars* by William Bradford Huie.

And finally, two people who worked on this about as hard as I did: my wife, Anne-Clinton Groom, and her mother, Wren Murphy, spent countless hours typing manuscripts, finding research materials, copying and express mailing to the editors all the various segments of the book, as well as reading the copy and rendering good and honest evaluations of it.

To each and every one of these fine people is owed a tremendous debt of gratitude.

—Winston Groom
Point Clear, Alabama, January 15, 2000

~

THIS BOOK IS DEDICATED to everybody who ever played any part in

the illustrious history of the University of Alabama football program. And

most especially it is dedicated to one of the Tide's greatest football fans,

the late, and great, John Forney, who coined the exhilarating echo heard

by millions over and over again on the radio, "TOUCHDOWN, ALABAMA!"

~

THE CRIMSON TIDE

Chapter One

GENESIS

1892 ~ 1918

IME WAS, THERE WAS NO FOOTBALL AT ALABAMA.
In the autumn of 1892 the University was celebrating its sixty-first year. A quarter century earlier, in the waning days of the Civil War, most of the campus had been burned to the ground by federal troops even as the student Corps of Cadets made a valiant but futile attempt to defend it. Aside from the task of rebuilding the school, little had changed in those twenty-seven years; the University was still a small military college, along the lines of the Virginia Military Institute. There were no women students. There was no such game as football.

But within a few years much of the old system was swept away. The military order would be abolished. Women would become a major part of the school. And there would be football and the building of glorious dynasties of that game until the name of The University of Alabama became synonymous with the sport.

There are still a skulking few who say this denigrates the University. They would argue it's not the aim of a great college; football detracts from the academic mission, siphons off critical resources, distracts students from their intended goals, makes a mockery of higher education, and so on. That is all hogwash, as we shall see ...

~

OVER THE LAST CENTURY, Alabama's football teams have played over one hundred opponents in more than one thousand games and won nearly 75 percent of them, a phenomenal and proud record. The Crimson Tide is the third winningest major college team in the nation. It has outscored its opposition more than two to one. It has won twelve national championships and leads the Southeastern Conference with twenty-one SEC championships. Its nearest rival in conference championships, Tennessee, has won thirteen. More than 100 Bama players have made First Team All-America and 250 First Team

The University of Alabama football squad of 1910, posed on the quad during "Mule-and-Buggy-Days."

All-SEC. Alabama has sent 175 players on to the National Football League, including such all-time greats as Bob Baumhower, John Hannah, Don Hutson, Lee Roy Jordan, Joe Namath, Ozzie Newsome, Kenny Stabler, Bart Starr, and Dwight Stephenson. Its team members have gone on to become judges, lawyers, doctors, prominent businessmen, and stellar football coaches—as well as governors and congressmen. A number of Alabama players have been elected Phi Beta Kappa. Over the years The University of Alabama football team has elated millions of fans. There is no finer football program in the country and it is a splendid credit to the University, to the state, and to the nation. But to understand how all this came about, we must turn back to the beginning, many years ago.

〜

THE UNIVERSITY OF ALABAMA HAD ITS ORIGIN as a land grant college only a few years after the Creek Indian Nation was ousted from the central part of the state. Congress in 1818 set aside thousands of what had now become federal

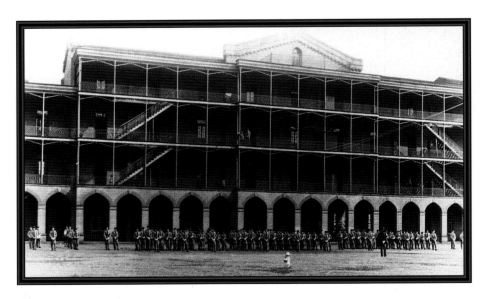

acres for the purpose of establishing a university, but thirteen more years would pass before buildings were erected and the school opened its doors to a class of fifty-two freshmen. Organized physical sports were virtually unknown in those days; the games of baseball, basketball, and football were yet to be invented, and students took their solace at the card table, the racetrack, the saloon, and in some instances, the church.

In 1860, as the cataclysm of civil war loomed near, the University was set up as a military college—but for reasons of discipline, not impending

Above: *In the early days of Bama football, the University was a military college, modeled after the Virginia Military Institute. This was the Corps of Cadets in the 1890s.* **Opposite page:** *The man who started it all: William Gray Little, father of Alabama football, organized what was to become the Crimson Tide in 1892 after playing the sport at an eastern prep school.*

war—and remained so until almost the turn of the century. After the war, athletics gradually became part of the program. Baseball was the first organized team sport, and among other activities were gymnastics, track and field, fencing, and tennis.

Then in 1892 a young man named William G. Little arrived on the scene. A native of Livingston, Alabama, Little had attended Phillips-Exeter Academy in Andover, Massachusetts, in hopes of going on to an Ivy League college. But the death of his brother brought him closer to home at The University of Alabama and he enrolled in the fall of 1892 with a pair of cleats, a leather football, and tales of the new sport that had captured the imagination of the Northeast and Middle West.

Something called football had been played in America since the early 1800s, but it was more closely akin to soccer in that the ball could only be kicked or batted, not carried, and later evolved into a rugby-style game in which the ball could be kicked on the ground, batted, *or* carried, and tack-

ling was permitted to keep an opponent from scoring. But this early version more resembled an uncouth brawl than a sport and was banned on many college campuses before the Civil War. Nevertheless, on Saturday, November 6, 1869, the first intercollegiate football game was played between Princeton and Rutgers before one hundred spectators in New Brunswick, New Jersey. There were twenty-five players to a side. One Rutgers professor was so appalled at what he saw, he stormed off shouting, "You men will come to no Christian end!"

Harvard had another version of the game, allowing the ball to be carried, and eventually it was agreed among football-playing schools that touchdowns (a rugby term meaning that if the ball was carried it must be physically "touched down" on the ground inside the goal line) would be permitted. Other refinements quickly followed. Team sizes were reduced to fifteen men (a standard rugby team) and then to eleven. The dimensions of the playing field were reduced from 140 by 70 yards (a rugby field) to 110 by 53½. In 1880 a major change was instituted: the notion of continuous play was

Seen here in the Alabama-Auburn game is the infamous "Flying Wedge," a formation so dangerous that in a single season twenty-six deaths were recorded in the game nationwide. In the early 1900s President Theodore Roosevelt, a football fan, got all schools to agree to ban it.

replaced by the concept of continuous possession of the ball, meaning that the team having the ball when downed could stop, kick it forward, or give it to the quarterback rather than having to scuffle for it all the time, as in rugby.

Walter Camp, of Yale, regarded as the father of modern football, was active in the new Intercollegiate Football Association, precursor of the NCAA, and his innovations became the bedrock of what we now know as football. He inaugurated the notion of having downs in which a team could keep the ball continuously so long as they either gained five yards in three downs or lost ten yards in three downs. Otherwise, they had to give the ball up. It was an odd system compared with the modern game, but at least this allowed for the planning and setting up of individual plays.

At that point, manpower on the field was usually formed up into a notorious and sometimes deadly disposition called the "Flying Wedge." In this savage arrangement, the linemen either held hands or locked arms and charged at the opposing team in a "vee" configuration with the ball carrier in the pocket, colliding into each other full speed with heads and bodies. The idea on either side was to create something similar to what occurs in bowling alleys. In a single season twenty-six deaths and seventy crippling injuries nationwide were attributed to this cruel practice (there were of course few pads or headgear) and a movement was begun to outlaw the game entirely. But this was finally headed off by none other than President Theodore Roosevelt, who got all teams to agree that henceforth such mass formations would be illegal.

Meantime, football was quickly sweeping into the Midwest, West, and upper South and rules were further refined to include forward passing, tackling below the waist, and a fixed system of timed quarters and halves.

Back at Alabama, young, sturdy William Little persuaded a score of his classmates to organize a football squad. Of the new game, Little declared, "Football is the game of the future in college life. Players will be forced to live a most ascetic life, on a diet of rare beef and pork, to say nothing of rice pudding for dessert, for additional courage and fortitude, to stand the bumps and injuries." Little was elected captain, and a man named Eugene Beaumont, who had learned something about football at the University of Pennsylvania, was selected as coach. Felix Tarrant Bush was manager. Thus was The University of Alabama athletic department born.

Program and ticket for Alabama's first game against a "real" opponent, on display in the Bryant Museum. On November 12, 1892, the team played the Birmingham Athletic Club at Lakeview Park and lost, 5-4.

Football was not unknown below the Mason-Dixon Line at this time. The first game to be played in the Southeast was in Kentucky in 1880. In Alabama, Auburn had fielded a team the year previous in 1891. But the game for the most part was still a club sport, like rugby. Students were in charge and the senior class was responsible for uniforms, coach's pay, and traveling expenses. To offset this, they sold tickets to the games.

The uniform of Alabama's first team was white with crimson stockings and the big letters U of A on the chest. It had some cotton padding at the knees and elbows but there were no shoulder pads or helmets. The basic football play during this period was still the Flying Wedge. Alabama opened its debut football season November 11, 1892, with what amounted to a practice game, played against an inauspicious opponent—a team picked from various Birmingham schools, and calling itself Birmingham High School. Alabama won the game handily, 56-0.

Flushed with this initial victory, the Cadets of Alabama, as they were known, played on the following day their first real opponent, the Birmingham Athletic Club, at Lakeview Park. Under intercollegiate rules of the period, a touchdown counted for four points, an after-touchdown conversion two points, and a field goal five. Newspaper accounts say the grandstand was

The first team. One player rose to become Speaker of the U.S. House of Representatives, another a two-term governor of Alabama, three became lawyers, another was a judge, one became a physician, another a state senator and the rest prominent businessmen. The man in the derby is the coach, Eugene Beaumont.

filled with gaily dressed men and women and the bleachers were decorated with colored bunting.

When the Cadets of Alabama took the field it was apparent they were woefully outweighed by their more mature opponents, many of whom had played college football back east. Accounts state that the Alabama players "looked like boys" compared to the Athletic Club team. In fact, Little, a guard, was one of the heavier players for Alabama, at 173 pounds. Alabama scored on a "guard around" play by Little in the first half, but missed the try for extra points. Toward the end of the fourth quarter Alabama still led 4-0, but in the waning moments an Athletics player named J. P. Ross, who had played rugby football in Ireland, put an astonishing 63-yard dropkick through the uprights to win the game. To demonstrate the innocence which marked that gilded age, the referee of the game was none other than the Alabama coach, Eugene Beaumont.

A month later, Alabama, "showing a decided improvement," beat the Birmingham Athletic Club on the same site 14-0, and in February 1893 played its first game against Auburn before four thousand fans at Lakeview Park. Football was so new that most of the spectators did not understand it, and

Left: *The first Alabama-Auburn game, Lakeview Park, Birmingham, February 1893. Auburn won it 32-22. Note the number of players milling about the scrimmage while the play is still alive. This practice was discouraged by later coaches, particularly Paul "Bear" Bryant.* **Opposite page, below:** *Auburn kicks an extra point for two. A field goal in those days, however, counted for five points! Note referees dressed in cutaway coats and one carrying a cane, possibly for self-protection.* **Below:** *An early Alabama-Auburn ticket on display in the Bryant Museum, probably printed at Auburn.*

Student Ticket
RESERVED SEAT. GRAND STAND.
WEDNESDAY, FEB. 22D.
TUSKALOOSA vs. AUBURN
ADMIT ONE.   ROW
PRICE TWENTY-FIVE CENTS.

the programs of the day contained elaborate explanations of how the game was played. Alabama lost, 32-22, but a magnificent tradition had been set into motion that would carry the University on to glory for a hundred and more years. Of that original little team of Cadets in 1892, much was promised. Of its number, one rose to become Speaker of the U.S. House of Representatives, another two-term governor of Alabama, three became lawyers, another was a judge, one became a physician, another a state senator, and the rest prominent businessmen. Though they hardly could have known it at the time, they were the vanguard of the Crimson Tide.

≈

THE FOLLOWING YEAR, 1893, the Cadets had lost most of their star players, including team captain Little, to graduation. They had such an unfavorable season that one player, Hill Ferguson, who went on to serve on the University's Board of Trustees for forty years, remarked that "nobody seemed to have enough interest to take a picture of the team." They won no games and were even beaten by Sewanee, 20-0. It must be noted, though, that during these years the total enrollment at Alabama was less than two hundred men, and in

Top: *The varsity of 1895 seems quite relaxed compared with team pictures of today.* Above: *Alabama-Auburn game ball from 1894, on display in the Bryant Museum. Bama won it, 18-0.* Opposite page: *A game uniform for the Crimson Tide, ca. 1890s. On display at the Bryant Museum.*

terms of available manpower, the University was not yet superior to colleges like Sewanee, Centre of Kentucky, or others now thought of as "small schools." The *Corolla,* then in its first year as Bama's official yearbook, tersely observed in respect to Coach Beaumont: "We were unfortunate in securing a coach. After keeping him for a short time, we found that his knowledge of the game was very limited. We therefore got rid of him."

In 1893 Bama had a new coach, Eli Abbott. Abbott had been a tackle and fullback on the inaugural team of 1892 after being solicited away from his job as foreman on Warrior River Lock 17—under construction at the time—by then coach Beaumont, who had known him at Penn. Abbott was sort of a wandering football player, having played at Penn and Mississippi A&M before landing the job at the lock. At the urging of Beaumont and others he enrolled at Alabama to get a degree in engineering. Fortunes began to improve under Abbott. Alabama lost the opener to Ole Miss 6-0 but, with the 155-pound Coach Abbott himself playing fullback, the team roared back to defeat Tulane 18-6. When they next encountered Sewanee they beat them, too, even though Abbott was ejected from the game for fighting. In the final match against Auburn, Coach Abbott again became the center of controversy when the Auburnites complained that he was being paid a salary. The objection was denied and Alabama went on to win 18-0.

The next season, 1895, Alabama resumed its seesaw reputation, losing all of its games to Georgia, Tulane, LSU, and Auburn by a combined point score of 112-12. But sixty more years would pass before an Alabama football team had a season as wretched as that.

In 1896, while the Olympic Games were being renewed in Paris after a lapse of fifteen hundred years, the University's Board of Trustees for some odd reason concluded it was undignified for its athletic teams to play games off campus, and Alabama had a terrible time finding opponents. They played only three football games that year but won two of them, including a 20-0 victory against a new opponent, Mississippi State. It then went from bad to worse: in 1897 only one game was played, in which Alabama beat the Tuscaloosa Athletic Club 6-0—on campus, of course. And the next year, with the outbreak of the Spanish-American War, there was no team at all, due to lack of opposition. The *Corolla* sourly noted: "In reviewing our past athletic season, we find very little to be proud of . . . handicapped by the stringent law of the Trustees, which prevented our traveling. . . ."

But in 1899 things changed for the better. According, again, to the *Corolla*, "For the past four years our teams have been kept at home like children, but this year the guardians of the University have allowed them to visit twice a year in charge of a nurse to keep them from harm." This intended protection was not always accomplished, however, according to the description of the Tulane game that year by Alabama guard Thomas M. Wert, who testified afterward: "They had prizefighters, dockhands on their team. I don't know if they had any students. They kicked me, trampled me, and sometimes bit me, all at the same time."

The Corolla *commissioned an artist to decorate the sports sections of its various issues with football related drawings, this in 1901.*

As the century turned with the soon-to-be-assassinated President William McKinley in the White House, the Alabama football team of 1900 compiled a measly 2-3 season, losing to Auburn in Montgomery by the humiliating score of 53-5. During halftime of that game a dispute broke out between an Alabama fan, Temple Seibels, the city solicitor, and Auburn tackle Michael H. Harvey. Seibels threw his hat into the air and when it landed on the field, Harvey mockingly kicked it as an imaginary field goal. Fans intervened in the ensuing altercation and next year, Harvey was named coach of The University of Alabama football team.

Harvey, however, only lasted a year. Alabama defeated Ole Miss and Mississippi State but lost to Auburn and tied with Georgia as well as a formidable new opponent, the University of Tennessee; the Tennessee game, held in Birmingham, was called on account of darkness after several thousand spectators rushed onto the field to protest an umpire's decision. Despite a decent season, Harvey had lost to Auburn and this spelled his demise.

For the next half decade, Alabama had a succession of coaches lasting but a year, including the ubiquitous Abbott, who returned in 1902 to lead the team to a 5-3 season. The team lost to another new opponent, the University of Texas, but defeated Marion Military Institute by a score of 81-0. Around this time a sportswriter used the term, "The Thin Red Line," to describe the Alabama team, a phrase no doubt borrowed from Rudyard Kipling's recent poem "Tommy," about the British soldier:

Then it's Tommy this, an' Tommy that,
An' Tommy, 'ow's your soul?
But it's "Thin red line of 'ero's,"
When the drums begin to roll—

In any event, Alabama again failed to win over Auburn and by next year Coach Abbott was no more.

In 1903, under the tutoring of coach W. B. Blount, a Yalie, the Alabama squad, averaging a mere 148 pounds per man, compiled a 3-4 season, losing to Vanderbilt, Mississippi State, Sewanee, and Cumberland. But it beat LSU, Tennessee, and, most importantly, Auburn, which meant that Coach Blount kept his job another year. The University's first ten-game season came in 1904, with seven wins and three losses. But the team failed to suppress Auburn that year and Coach Blount became history.

By now Henry Ford had just sold his first automobile, the Wright brothers had launched the first airplane, and the first World Series of baseball had been played. In football, certain improvements and changes were being made in equipment. A crude version of shoulder pads was coming into fashion, consisting of bulky wads of cotton sewn into the jersey. Some players had begun to wear thin leather helmets with flaps to protect the ears. The football itself was becoming less oval and more pointed at the ends, which made for better passing, but it did not kick as well. (There would be no more sixty-five-yard dropkicks for a field goal.) Alabama's game jersey was now crimson and the stockings crimson with white stripes. Also, with the admission of women to the University a decade earlier, the football squad began enlisting some of them as "sponsors," forerunners of the modern cheerleader.

The 1905 season opened under coach Jack Leavenworth, another Yalie, and Alabama ended up with a barely winning 6-4 season. They did, however,

Here was a typical Alabama offensive look in 1905—basically a "T" formation, but the quarterback assumed a sideways stance.

beat Auburn 30-0 before four thousand spectators in Birmingham, but an embarrassing 42-6 loss to Sewanee sent Coach Leavenworth packing.

There now arrived at Tuscaloosa John W. H. "Doc" Pollard, a Dartmouth man, to coach the 1906 team. During his four years at Alabama he compiled a 21-4-5 record. Pollard was not only innovative; he was ferocious. His players feared him, and with good reason. Following a listless 6-0 win over Maryville in the first game of the season, Pollard ordered his team straight onto the practice field and put it through a grueling hours-long scrimmage against the scrubs. His one loss that first year was a humiliating 78-0 defeat at the hands of Vanderbilt, which one observer described as "a farce." Fact was, injuries had taken seven of Pollard's starters out of the lineup and the substitutes averaged less than 145 pounds per man. Knowing this, Pollard tried to cancel the game but Vanderbilt, then the best team in the South, unchivalrously refused.

But when Auburn time rolled around, Pollard was ready. Before five thousand spectators—until that time the largest crowd in Alabama's history—Pollard's Thin Red Line defeated the Plainsmen 10-0. Before the game, Auburn's coach filed a protest, claiming that Alabama's great tackle T. S. Sims was ineligible to play because he wasn't a student. Pollard proved him wrong and Sims bore a heavy load during the game. Pollard had secretly been practicing a radical new offense, the "Military" (or possibly "Minnesota") Shift, which had been used at his alma mater, Dartmouth, but was unknown in the South. Alabama football historian James S. Edson describes it this way: "The entire line, except the center, would take their position behind the line of scrimmage and join hands. Then, quickly, the men would return to their regular positions or to the right or left side of the line, resulting most of the time in an unbalanced line."

Stars of the game for Alabama were halfback Auxford Burks, who scored the only touchdown and kicked the only field goal, and the team's 120-pound quarterback, Emile "Chick" Hannon. Auburn coach Mike Donahue was so indignant about Pollard's perfidious Military Shift formation he threatened to cancel future games with the University and in fact, after the next season, the series was indeed canceled for the next forty-one years.

In 1907, as waves of political unrest that later erupted into the First World War echoed through Europe and the Balkans, the Thin Red Line compiled a 5-1-2 season, but the lone loss was a humiliating 54-4 drubbing by Sewanee. In the Auburn game, the Tigers came on as a 3-1 favorite but the tricky Pollard bamboozled them with yet another peculiar stunt, the "Varsity Two-Step," a variation on the Military Shift. In this razzle-dazzle formation, the center faces the backfield and the line divides itself right and left, then one side shifts crabwise with the backs following. A sportswriter of the day described it as being "dainty as the minuet." The game ended in a 6-6 tie.

Perhaps of more significance is the fact that after the Auburn game the Alabama team began to lose the moniker "Thin Red Line," and a new description was ushered in—"Crimson Tide." It seems that the field in Birmingham had become a sea of red mud and a Birmingham sportswriter coined the phrase "Crimson Tide" to describe Alabama's surging mudders offense that day. Needless to say, it stuck.

The year 1908 marked the beginning of a four-decade hiatus in the football rivalry with Auburn. It was caused in part by unseemly haggling over money. In those days the host team gave the opponents a per diem allowance

Opposite page, above: *From the* Corolla*—1907.* **Opposite page, below**: *In 1907 Alabama was forced to settle for a disagreeable 6-6 tie with Auburn. Here a squad of cheerleaders are grouped beside their automobile while the team's "sponsors" sit in the car.* **Left**: *From the* Corolla*—1909.* **Above**: *From the* Corolla*—1910.*

for their hotel and restaurant expenses. Auburn wanted $3.50 but Bama only wanted to pay $3.00. In addition, Alabama objected to Auburn's intention to bring twenty players to Birmingham, arguing they did not need that many. There was also a dispute over referees, and by the time the whole thing was sorted out it was too late to schedule the game and nobody bothered to do it again for nearly forty years.

Alabama went 6-1-1 that year, losing only to Georgia Tech which, according to reports, "resorted to trick plays." They weren't the only ones, however. When Alabama dueled the University of Georgia that year to a 6-6 tie, they almost pulled off the game in the last moments with the following chicanery: Bama halfback Thomas Reidy, indicating a field goal attempt, got on his knees and began piling up dirt for the placement try. But when the center snapped the ball, he snapped it instead to fullback Derrill Pratt, who not only faked a kick but heaved his headgear into the air toward the goal to further befuddle the Georgia Bulldogs. Meantime, Pratt "slipped the ball to Reidy who tore out around right end for a twenty-five yard gain." Georgia held, however, and the game ended on the sour note of a tie.

The 1910 varsity at practice. The man in the suit and hat is probably coach Guy S. Lowman, who retired after an unsatisfying 4-4 season.

But according to witnesses, the most spectacular game of 1908 was against the Haskell Indian Institution, captained by a man called Island Eagle, whose players outweighed Bama's by twenty-five pounds per man. According to contemporary football historian James S. Edson the Indians played "with a hotheadedness and savageness that was characteristic of the race and the crowd was amazed at the spectacle of the Thin Red Line holding such giants." Alabama won it 9-8 in the closing seconds.

In 1909 Alabama went 5-1-2 but outscored its opponents by a combined 68-17, the sole loss being a 12-6 defeat at the hands of LSU. The Crimson Tide also drubbed Tennessee 10-0 for the seventh time in eight outings in a Knoxville game marked by bad behavior. With Alabama leading in the second half, the Volunteers drove to the Bama ten but the umpire, a man named Elgin, called back the play and penalized the Vols fifteen yards for holding. The Tennessee fans viewed this with such gravity that Elgin was not only booed but after the game was chased by the crowd to the streetcar, where someone struck him on the head with a stone. Further, the mob hectored him all the way to his hotel "where he was subjected to further abuse." On Tennessee's behalf, it was noted in the Knoxville papers that a twenty-five-dollar reward had been offered for the name of Elgin's assailant.

Thus ended—for reasons clouded by time—Doc Pollard's coaching career at Alabama, not only the lengthiest so far, but the most successful as well.

In 1910—the year in which Mark Twain, Leo Tolstoy, and Florence Nightingale died—Guy Summer Lowman, of Springfield College, took over as head coach of Bama. He produced a dreary 4-4 season, with Alabama losing all its big games—Georgia, Georgia Tech, and Mississippi as well as Bama's eternal nemesis, Sewanee. The lone win players might have taken some comfort in was against Washington & Lee, now coached by none other than their old tormentor, Doc Pollard. Alabama beat W&L 9-0 on Thanksgiving Day in Birmingham. At the end of the season, Guy Lowman was gone and Dorset Vandeventer Graves, from the University of Missouri, was in. He was Alabama's thirteenth coach since the game began there nineteen years earlier. Hardly a tradition.

Graves, like Pollard before him, would remain at Alabama for four years during which he compiled a winning 21-12-3 record. Trouble was, most of the wins were against lesser opponents, the likes of Marion Institute, Howard, and Owington College, while the University frequently lost to big rivals such as Georgia, Georgia Tech, Mississippi State, and, of course, the ever-irritating Sewanee, which Alabama never beat during Graves's tenure.

Nevertheless, the Graves period contained some interesting times for the University and the football program, and one could argue that after nearly a quarter century of Alabama football, an old era was ending and a new, more splendid one was near at hand.

Graves was a tall, young, and startlingly handsome man who basically did things by the book. In 1912 he made the following observation about his team, a motley, ill-knit collection, lacking size and strength: "In September the squad looked light and of poor physical development. Everything was discouraging. I had not yet become familiar with the Alabama Spirit—that indescribable something which made the efforts of a light team bring seemingly impossible results."

Top and center: *Bama's "Thin Red Line" goes up against Washington & Lee in Birmingham on a cold Thanksgiving Day.* **Bottom:** *The players wrap themselves in blankets to keep warm during halftime. Note the chalk marks lining the field into a grid. Hence the name "gridiron."*

If Graves liked to do things by the book, it was not always so with his opponents, and if he thought they would not stoop to cunning, he was wrong. A notorious example was the game with Georgia in 1912. The Crimson Tide kicked off to the Bulldogs to start the contest before a sellout crowd in Columbus. While waiting to receive, a Georgia substitute named Autry took his place at right end, just inside the sideline, dressed in white overalls and carrying a water bucket. A Georgia receiver caught the kickoff and ran to his left—away from Autry in his waterboy disguise—while Autry himself, still carrying the bucket, ran straight down the sideline, keeping away from the action. When they lined up for the first play off-scrimmage, Autry dropped the bucket and ran down the field where he caught a pass from the Georgia quarterback for a forty-five-yard gain.

Alabama vigorously denounced this deceit but the umpire ruled the play legal. News accounts say the Georgia coach himself agreed the play was unfair and offered to start the game anew but was overruled. However, in its winter meeting, the Southern Conference rules committee addressed the subject and forbade such perfidious stratagems in the future.

Other notable games that year included a 6-6 tie with Sewanee, a 6-0 victory over Tennessee, during which it became so dark in the fourth quar-

ter the match had to be finished in the glare of automobile headlights—The University of Alabama's first "night game," and the final contest of the season, a Thanksgiving Day brawl with Mississippi State in which police had to be called onto the field to quell a dispute between the coaches.

But in 1912, the year the Titanic sank, an event overtook the University that marked a decisive stage in the history of Alabama football. This was the arrival of Dr. George Hutcheson "Mike" Denny as president of the school. Not only was Denny a great educator, he loved football and was determined to apply its virtues wherever he could to build the University into a nationally recognized institution. Denny graduated from Virginia's Hampden-Sydney College in 1896 and received his Ph.D. from the University of Virginia. During those years he observed that the immense and ever-growing popularity of football could literally put a school on the national map through press coverage. When Denny arrived in Tuscaloosa on January 1, 1912, there were four hundred students enrolled on campus. When he retired a quarter century later, there were more than five thousand, many from the Northeast who had come, in part, because of the legendary prowess of Alabama's football teams.

Denny combined a mixture of administrative vision and personal charm to raise revenues and establish various schools and colleges within the University, all the while fixing his keen and unrelenting gaze on the progress of Alabama's football program. At the time of his arrival, the squad still practiced and played on the quadrangle in front of what is now Gorgas Library, but Denny perceived a more appropriate field was in order and three years later the Crimson Tide opened its first season at Denny Field, which was then between Barnwell and Parham Halls. Denny also took a personal hand in the selection of coaches.

In 1913 the Panama Canal opened and Congress first passed the income tax, while Alabama went 6-3, outscoring its opponents 188 to 40. Twenty years earlier football legend Walter Camp had begun picking an All-American team and in 1913 tackle W. T. "Bully" Vandegraaff was selected—the University's first All-American. He was one of the three famous Vandegraaff brothers of Tuscaloosa who starred on Crimson Tide teams in those early years. To lend some idea of the Alabama "fighting spirit" Coach Graves had earlier remarked upon, in the 6-0 win against Tennessee, Bully Vandegraaff nearly lost an ear, whether from a bite or some other cause we are not told. But his opposite number in the Tennessee line, tackle Bull Bayer, had this to say about it: "His ear had a real nasty cut and it was dangling from his head, bleeding badly. He grabbed his ear and tried to yank it from his head. His teammates stopped him and the managers bandaged him. Man, was that guy a tough one. He wanted to tear off his own ear so he could keep playing."

In 1914 the storm of World War I finally burst over Europe; Alabama went 5-4 but still somehow outscored its opponents by a combined 211-64. Bama handily won its first four games but then disaster struck. The Crimson Tide's versatile quarterback, Charlie Joplin, was ruled ineligible to compete after refusing to sign a document for the Southern Conference saying he had not played professional baseball. Without Joplin's skillful passing and

A Bully Vandegraaff run against Tulane on the new playing field, now the site of Bryant-Denny Stadium. Sorority houses are in the background. Note the Tulane players wearing a primitive and fearsome-looking device called a "nose-guard," which they strapped around their helmets.

Above: *T. D. "Turkey" Bowman became famous in 1915 as the "All-Southern Cheerleader," when Alabama was in the Southern Conference.* **Top right:** *Thanksgiving Day, 1915—Alabama beat Ole Miss 53-0 in Birmingham. Pictured is a goal after touchdown, probably being kicked by the third—and most famous—of all the Vandegraaff brothers, W. T. "Bully" Vandegraaff, Bama's first All-American. Note that he is "drop-kicking" the ball, a common practice before the regulation ball assumed the current streamlined shape more suitable for passing.* **Right, above and below:** *Early Bama teams played at Birmingham's Rickwood Field, built in 1910, until Legion Field went up in 1926, with games beginning there in 1927.* **Opposite page, below:** *One of Bully Vandegraaff's legendary field goals in 1915. Bama lost only to Georgia Tech and Texas that year.*

The team of 1914. Bully Vandegraaff is fourth from left on back row. The despondent-looking man on the far left, back row, with the "M" on his jersey was either the manager, or possibly an Ole Miss player who jumped ship after Bama whipped his team 53-0 that season. Next to him is the coach, D. V. Graves. At the far right, wearing a hat, is Dr. Eugene Smith, University professor, state geologist, and team benefactor.

ball handling, the season quickly went downhill. In the last game Alabama was beaten by the Carlisle Indian Institute, 20-3, but Bully Vandegraaff was paid a grand compliment by the usually taciturn Indian coach, Wahoo, who declared that Vandegraaff "could play on any team in the country."

When the 1915 season opened, Coach Graves was gone and Thomas Kelley, a gigantic 250-pound cigar-smoking alumnus of the University of Chicago, then a powerhouse under Amos Alonzo Stagg, took the reins. Kelley had been handpicked by President Denny. Alabama won its first four games before calamity struck again. Just before the big match with Sewanee, Kelley came down with typhoid fever and was lost for the remainder of the season.

Lonnie Noojin, the athletics director, and Farley Moody, captain of the 1912 team, took over. The Crimson Tide had not beaten Sewanee since 1894, and it looked like they wouldn't this time when Sewanee tied up the score 10-10 in the final quarter. Worse, Alabama's quarterback Griff Harsh was ejected from the game for cursing, even though the cursing had actually been done by an end, Lovick Stephenson. A contemporary observer remarked, "I cannot understand how anyone could get Griff and Lovick confused but the referee did. They don't look alike and they certainly don't act alike."

Nevertheless, the magnificent Bully Vandegraaff lived up to his All-American reputation again that afternoon. In the few remaining minutes he knocked the ball from the hands of a Sewanee passer, caught it himself, ran sixty-five yards for a touchdown, and then kicked the goal. Not only that, he hit two more field goals in short order. When the game finally ended the score was Alabama 23, Sewanee 10, to the delight of the frenzied crowd in Birmingham.

In 1916 Coach Kelley returned, one hundred pounds lighter from his illness, and, after winning the first six games—including a 7-6 cliffhanger against Sewanee—led Alabama to a 6-3 season. In 1917, as the war in Europe reached its most pitiless intensity and Russia fell to communism, Alabama went 5-2-1, including a disappointing 3-3 tie with Sewanee. The war was already making an impression on collegiate football: consider that Alabama opened its season that year with a game against the Second Ambulance Company of Ohio, then training with the 37th Infantry Division in Montgomery, and closed with a 19-6 defeat at the hands of Camp Gordon, Georgia, whose team featured a number of former college all-stars, including one of the celebrated Vandegraaff brothers.

Because of the war, there was no season in 1918. As America entered the great conflict, numerous Alabama players and former players joined the service, most as officers. Three of the old Thin Red Line fell in combat: Charlie Joplin, quarterback of the 1914 team, who was ruled ineligible mid-season because he had played professional baseball, big E. W. Maynor, center on the team of 1916, and little Farley Moody, red-haired Tuscaloosan and captain and quarterback of the team of 1912, who was killed a month to the day before the armistice. In Evergreen Cemetery, just across the street from the present Bryant-Denny Stadium, forever easily within sound of a Saturday's cheering, lies a tombstone with this inscription:

Farley W. Moody, quarterback and captain of the team of 1912. Five years later, as a first lieutenant in the army, he was killed in France during World War I, only a month before the armistice. He is buried in Evergreen Cemetery within the very shadows of Bryant-Denny Stadium.

FARLEY WILLIAM MOODY
BORN SEPTEMBER 18, 1891 OCTOBER 11, 1918
FIRST LIEUTENANT, COMPANY B
325ᵀᴴ INF. 82ND DIV. U.S.A.
FELL LEADING HIS MEN IN THE BATTLE
OF ARGONNE, FRANCE

HIS LAST WORDS WERE:
"I'M NOT DEAD YET; LIFT MY HEAD A LITTLE;
SPREAD OUT THERE MORE MEN, SERGEANT."
HE REMEMBERED HIS CREATOR IN THE DAYS OF HIS YOUTH.

Chapter Two

DYNASTY

1919 ～ 1930

LOOK AT THE SEPIA PHOTOGRAPHS of the Alabama team of 1919 and you must come away with the extraordinary sense of character and determination in the men's faces. There is a worldliness about them, a certain maturity not evident even in the faces of the team of 1917, just before America entered the war. These men are also noticeably larger and sturdier; compare this picture with the photograph of the debut team of 1892. The latter look almost like schoolboys.

In 1919 Alabama had its best season ever, 8-1, and would have been conference champions except for a heartbreaking 16-12 loss to Vanderbilt. Coach Kelley hadn't returned that year and Dr. Denny's shrewd selection to replace him was, of all things, a horse-racing writer from Cleveland named Xen Scott. Scott had not played big-time football but understood the game brilliantly. Alabama breezed through its first five games, including a 40-0 stomping of Sewanee. That year, fullback Riggs Stephenson and halfback "Mully" Lenoir were named All-Southern Conference, as was tackle Ike Rogers.

The 1920 Bama season was a replay of the previous year, only better. The world at large was on the cusp of a new postwar era. In America Congress passed a law prohibiting the selling of alcoholic beverages, women were given the right to vote, and, in defeated Germany, an army corporal named Adolf Hitler formed a political party based, among other things, on hatred of Jews.

At Alabama, with both Stephenson and Lenoir back in the lineup, the Crimson Tide went 10-1, avenging their loss to Vanderbilt the year before and stumbling only to Georgia in a game that might best be described as a comedy of errors. Georgia returned two blocked kicks and a fumble for touchdowns to account for all its scoring—the last one to break a 14-14 tie late in the fourth quarter. Riggs Stephenson went on to become a baseball star for the Cleveland Indians and the Chicago Cubs and Mully Lenoir set an all-time record of twenty-five touchdowns in a single season.

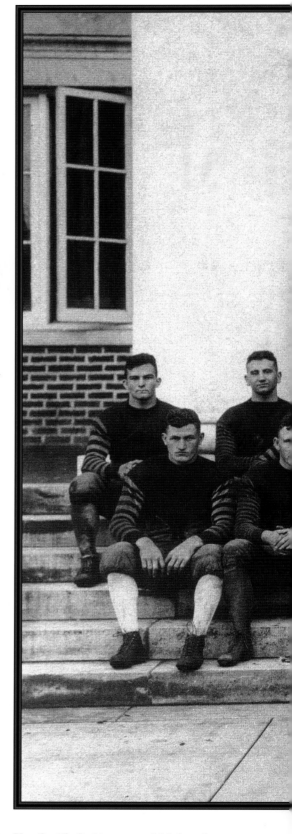

Xen Scott's first team went 10-1 and behind the running of Riggs Stephenson (second row, far left) became Southern Conference champions.

Top: *A new coach, Xen Scott, hired by Dr. Denny in 1919, seemed an unlikely choice. He was a horse-racing writer from Cleveland.* Right: *Meanwhile, up in South Bend, Notre Dame was led by a small, wiry quarterback named Frank Thomas who, ten years later would coach the Crimson Tide to days of glory and Rose Bowl fame.* Above: *A 1920 Alabama-Sewanee game program. The Tide's overall record against the Mountain Tigers now stands at 17-10-3, and probably forever will.*

Next year was rebuilding time for the team. With most of its star players gone, Alabama still squeaked to a meager 5-4-2 season in 1921 but lost most of its important games. The finale against Tulane in New Orleans ended in a riot and according to reports, "police protection for Referee Finlay was required." Here is what happened:

Nobody scored in the first three quarters, but late in the fourth Tulane led Alabama 7-0. Alabama scored twice in quick succession making it 14-7. Then, as the clock ticked off its final second, Tulane, deep in Alabama territory, completed a touchdown pass that would have tied the game. Referee

Finlay, however, ruled that he had blown the game-ending whistle before the ball had been put into play and thus the play was dead. In fact, some of the Alabama players had already taken off their headgear and were walking off the field when the ball was snapped. Incensed Tulane fans rushed onto the gridiron and began threatening and belaboring Referee Finlay until a police cordon hurried him away and back to his hotel.

In 1922 Bama posted a 6-3-1 injury-plagued season with these notable episodes:

~ It beat Marion Institute by the amazing score of 110-0, the largest score ever attained by an Alabama team.

~ It tied Sewanee 7-7 in a game in which the Tide held the Mountain Tigers to a mere six yards rushing and a lone first down from a pass, at the same time fumbling the ball itself an unbelievable twelve times.

~ It gained national prominence for the first time by journeying to Philadelphia to whip one of the best football teams in the country, the University of Pennsylvania, by a score of 9-7. This victory stunned not only the twenty-five thousand fans on hand for the game, but the national sportswriting fraternity as well, who had not given Alabama— or for that matter any southern team— the remotest chance to beat a big eastern powerhouse like Penn. It was as remarkable to some as if today a team from, say, Norway, came to Tuscaloosa and beat Alabama.

The team was greeted at the Tuscaloosa railroad depot by a throng of thousands. Somebody whitewashed the score, Alabama 9, Penn 7, onto the red brick side of Rex's Drugstore on University Boulevard where it could still be faintly seen a quarter century later. John Forney, the legendary Bama radio commentator and Crimson Tide historian whose father, Mack, played for Bama around that time (and whose great-grandfather, by the way, was a

Bama's captain shakes hands with Penn's captain prior to the famous 1922 game in which the Tide went north and whipped the University of Pennsylvania 9-7. The upset victory put Alabama in the national sports spotlight for the first time.

Confederate general), mused that the team was "the biggest group of Southerners to cross the Pennsylvania line to have a contest with Pennsylvanians since Lee's army went to Gettysburg in 1863."

~ It marked the appearance on the field for the first time of the fabulous backfield star A. T. S. "Pooley" Hubert, who in coming seasons would lead the Crimson Tide to never imagined heights of glory. Hubert had joined the navy at age sixteen and served aboard a destroyer in World War I. He finished high school at a military academy and enrolled at then football powerhouse Princeton but departed a few weeks later, disenchanted with harsh

Right: *Denny Field was an early predecessor on the site of Bryant-Denny Stadium that now seats eighty-three-thousand.* **Below and bottom:** *The 1923 Crimson Tide in action against an unidentified opponent. The famous Pooley Hubert (below, with ball) in his first year at Bama, eludes a tackler.*

Opposite page, above: *Coach Hank Crisp was beloved by generations of Crimson Tide players. He joined the Bama coaching staff during the Xen Scott era and remained for thirty-five years, coaching football, baseball, basketball and track, as well as serving as the University's athletics director. He died in 1970, the night he was to be inducted into the Alabama Sports Hall of Fame.*
Opposite page, below: *Bama's Big End, Al Clemens, All-Southern Conference, 1921, 1922, 1923.*

academics and the smug attitudes of his fellow students. Hubert arrived at The University of Alabama as a twenty-year-old freshman. His teammates called him "Papa."

It might be noted that by this time many, but not all, players had taken to wearing leather helmets. (Pooley Hubert declined to wear one most of his career, thus earning him the sobriquet "The Durable Bean.") Alabama's uniforms were now solid crimson with white bands on the jersey sleeves and numbers on the back. But the uniform and even the game itself were still crude. Al Clemens, an end on the 1921 team, remembered their footwear: "We'd get a chunk of leather, punch holes and drive nails into the soles of our shoes." Clemens also recalled his astonishment upon first seeing Franklin Field in Philadelphia before the match with Penn: "What I remember most was that the field had grass. Most of the fields back then were really dusty and dry. You played on the same fields you practiced on, so there weren't any grass fields."

Also, the University's famed Million Dollar Band had been formed—so named, one legend has it, because of a remark by U.S. Army Commanding General John J. Pershing that regimental bands had been "worth a million dollars to the American Expeditionary Forces" during the war. Another story is that a Georgia sportswriter remarked, "The Alabama team didn't look good but the band played like a million dollars." In any case, Alabama as well as other Southern Conference teams were playing to markedly larger crowds as football rapidly gained in popularity—ten thousand was not now an uncommon figure, though even the Tide still must have been amazed at the mob of twenty-five thousand that showed up to witness the Penn upset.

During the 1922 season Coach Scott had already fallen ill from the cancer that would eventually kill him, but the slight, olive-skinned horse-racing writer compiled an admirable 29-9-3 record in his four years as coach of the Crimson Tide. Aside from this, Scott's most enduring legacy to the Alabama football program was most certainly the hiring of assistant coach Henry G. "Hank" Crisp, one of the most valuable and beloved figures in the athletic department for the next thirty-five years, and about whom we will hear much more later. Crisp never got to be *head* coach of football; he was for years the line coach, but he *was* head coach of baseball, basketball, and track as well as athletics director.

In those early days few recognized the difference between winning games and establishing a lasting dynasty. President Mike Denny was an exception. Denny now cannily picked for head football coach a man whose name would be synonymous with the rise to national greatness of the Crimson Tide. He was Wallace Wade, a graduate of Brown, a former cavalry captain in World War I, and at the time an assistant coach at Vanderbilt. Wade was a stern disciplinarian, big on basics and incessant repetition during practice of the few plays he had. He was the exact opposite of the man he had replaced. It was said football was his life; his only other hobby, reportedly, was golf. Wade insisted on absolute precision in the performance of his plays, going so far as to use a musical metronome to ensure perfect timing. He also insisted on perfection in the fundamentals of blocking and tackling, and above all else this is what Alabama became known for during his tenure. Coach Crisp, for his part, had no need of a metronome. As a youth he had lost his right hand to an agricultural accident and wore a leather cap over the stump. But to make sure all players got off the line exactly at the snap, Crisp would squat behind them, one by one, the leather stump between their legs, counting "1-2-3". . . and if the snap was "3," they had best be off and running.

Wade would generate in the 1920s the first of Alabama's great football dynasties. In his tenure from 1923 to 1930 Wade compiled a 61-13-3 record, taking Alabama to three Rose Bowls, three national championships, and three Southern Conference titles. Meanwhile, most national attention was still focused almost exclusively on northern and western teams, such as Notre Dame with its famed "Four Horsemen."

In 1923, after the death of Xen Scott, Alabama got a new coach. Wallace Wade (opposite page) would, over the next eight years, take the Crimson Tide to unimagined heights of glory with three Rose Bowls and a 61-13-3 record. With halfback Johnny Mack Brown (above left), quarterback Pooley Hubert (above right), and end Wu Winslett in the lineup, Wade established the Crimson Tide's first football dynasty.

Wade opened reasonably well in 1923 with a 7-2-1 season. In his backfield he had three of the finest athletes ever to play ball at the University: quarterback Pooley Hubert, from Meridian, Mississippi, and Dothan halfback Johnny Mack Brown who, in future decades, would accelerate to incomparable fame as one of the great cowboy stars of Hollywood movies. Also there was the great end Hoyt "Wu" Winslett who remembered his recruitment by Alabama this way: "Dadeville was War Eagle country in those days. They took it for granted that I was going to Auburn and didn't do much. Later when I decided to go to Alabama, I got a nasty letter from Mike Donahue, the Auburn coach."

〜

IN THE THIRD GAME THAT YEAR, the Crimson Tide got massacred by Syracuse, described this way by someone wishing to put a better face on things: "Alabama did a very creditable job in holding Syracuse to a score of 23-0." Wade himself remarked that he had learned more about football that day than in all the rest of his life. Next week, the Tide was leading old rival Sewanee when, in the last seconds of the final period, a Sewanee end caught a pass that would have tied the game. But he stumbled over a kickoff tee that had been inadvertently left on the field and dropped the ball. Alabama 7, Sewanee 0. The Tide lost to Florida that year in a rain-swept Birmingham game played in what reporters called "a lake." All in all, though, it was a very good season.

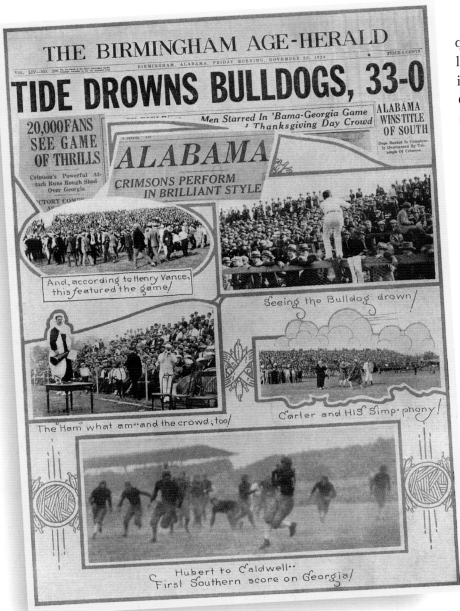

The Birmingham Age-Herald

TIDE DROWNS BULLDOGS, 33-0

VOL. LIV—NO. 296   BIRMINGHAM, ALABAMA, FRIDAY MORNING, NOVEMBER 28, 1924   PRICE 5 CENTS

20,000 FANS SEE GAME OF THRILLS

Men Starred In 'Bama-Georgia Game; Thanksgiving Day Crowd

ALABAMA WINS TITLE OF SOUTH

Dope Bucket Is Complete-ly Overturned By Tri-umph Of Crimson

Crimson's Powerful At-tack Runs Rough Shod Over Georgia

VICTORY COM...

ALABAMA

CRIMSONS PERFORM IN BRILLIANT STYLE

And, according to Henry Vance, this featured the game!

Seeing the Bulldog drown!

The "Ham" what am" and the crowd; too!

Carter and HIS "Simp-phony!

Hubert to Caldwell. First Southern score on Georgia!

Above: *A Corolla page celebrating the 1924 Georgia Game. Bama won it 33-0. Note cheerleader "Ham" standing on a table in order to be seen.* **Opposite page:** *The starting lineup of Bama's 1924 Southern Conference Champion-ship team (center). Most are looking ahead, but Johnny Mack Brown, later a cowboy movie star, is looking straight at the camera. Also seen are Bama's cheerleaders (top) and team sponsors (below left). In the lower right corner, donor Champ Pickens is holding the Southern Conference championship trophy won by Bama in 1924.*

By 1924 Wallace Wade was ready. With quarterback Pooley Hubert, end Wu Wins-lett, and halfback Johnny Mack Brown still in the lineup, Alabama won the Southern Conference championship with an 8-1 sea-son in which the Tide outscored its oppo-nents 290 to 24. The only loss, to Wade's un-deniable chagrin, came at the hands of Kentucky's little Centre College "Colonels," who came to Birmingham and outplayed a surprised Alabama 17-0.

Things only got better. Next year Wade hit his stride with a perfect 10-0 record. This 1925 season became nothing less than a benchmark for the University's football program, and coaches and players ever since have striven to equal or surpass it. When they don't it is always something of a letdown. That year, it began to dawn on some people that the Tide might be invincible. They outscored their oppo-nents by a phenomenal 277 to 7, and the cry of "Defense!" echoed through the sta-diums. Hubert, Brown, and Winslett were elected to the All-Southern Confer-ence team and Hubert and Winslett made All-America as well.

Before the final game against Geor-gia, coach Hank Crisp stole a march from "Win one for the Gipper" Knute Rockne. On the field just before kickoff he buttonholed every player in the starting lineup with motivating language. To Winslett he said, "We've been keeping you around here for four or five years and you haven't done a damn thing yet. We're giving you one last chance!" When he finally got to Hubert he told him: "Pooley, your mama's sick in bed, over there in Meridian, listening to the radio and hoping you'll do something good." Ole "Papa" Hubert started cry-ing and then Crisp shouted, "All right, let's go beat the hell out of Georgia!" They did, 27-0.

The toughest match though was against Georgia Tech in Atlanta before a crowd of twenty thousand. Alabama won 7-0 in what was described as "Pooley Hubert's greatest game." The contest seemed destined for a tie until late in the third quarter when one play made the victory for the Tide. Tech had punted to Johnny Mack Brown, who took it at his own forty-five. Despite the horde of swarming Engineers that converged to stop him, Alabama's offense cut down *each* and *every* Tech player on the field—as well as the referee—and Brown scored! Afterward, an *Atlanta Constitution* sportswriter pronounced Pooley

Sheik • Waldo and Ham

Southdom's greatest

"Match these, if you can"

Champ Pickens • donor of this cup • the Southern Trophy

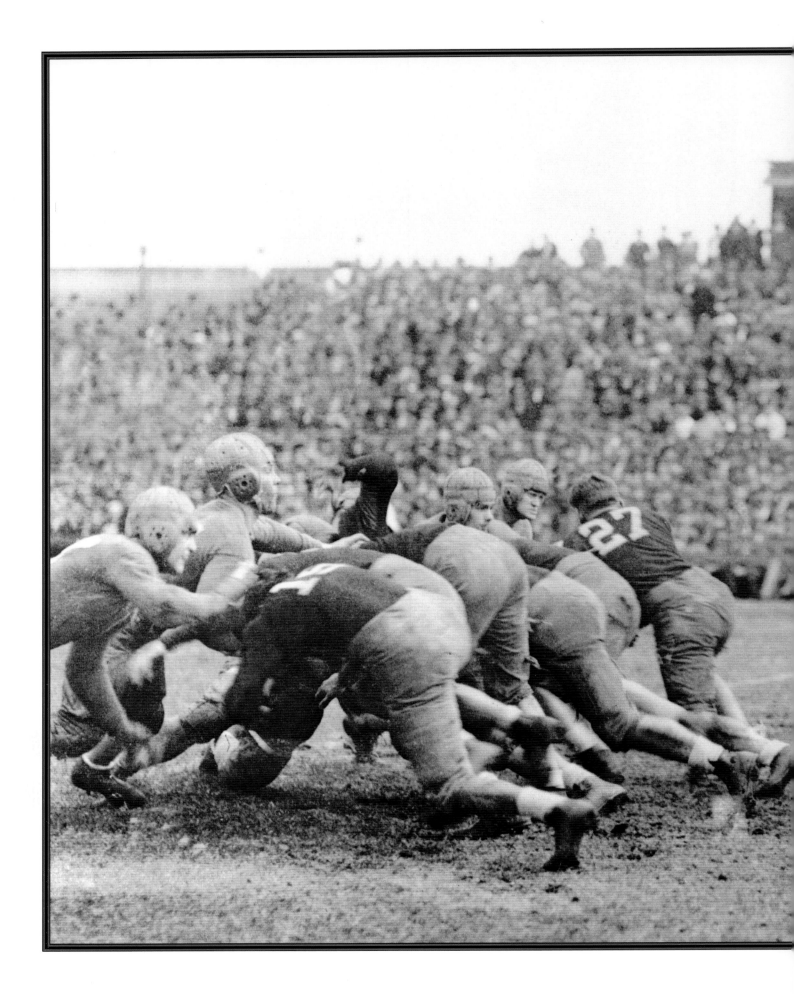

Get Low! The 1925 championship team in action at Rickwood Field in Birmingham in the 27-0 win over Georgia. In backfield, Johnny Mack Brown coming around for a reverse. Pooley Hubert (without helmet—his trademark) is blocking.

Hubert—who had made an amazing twenty-three tackles that afternoon—"the greatest defensive back ever to appear on Grant Field."

Among the eminencies not so impressed with Alabama's prowess that year was the Rose Bowl Committee in Pasadena, California. Even with the Tide's perfect season, so low was the committee's regard for any team from Dixie that their invitation to play in what was then considered the undisputed national championship game went first to Dartmouth, then Yale, then Colgate. But these schools bowed under pressure from the American Association of University Professors, who had recently issued a report stating that football promoted drinking, dishonesty, and poor academics. This silly

Bama hauls it in against the Georgia Bulldogs. Coach Crisp had tried to inspire Pooley Hubert before the game by telling him that his mother was sick at home, listening on the radio, and expecting a strong performance. Next stop: Pasadena.

document also recommended that players be allowed to play only one season. In any case, each of these schools declined the Rose Bowl offers. Alabama, the next evident choice, was disparaged this way by one of the Rose Bowl's agents: "I've never heard of Alabama as a football team and can't take a chance on mixing a lemon with a rose." Nonetheless, the Rose Bowl Committee reluctantly issued an invitation to the Tide. What happened next is now considered not only an athletic phenomenon, but a sociological, cultural, and political one as well.

News of the invitation hit the University early in December when Luny J. Smith, a star member of the track team who moonlighted as a cub sportswriter on the *Tuscaloosa News*, got wind of it over the telegraph wire. He immediately ran to see Coach Crisp. According to Luny Smith, Crisp's first reaction was, "Oh my God, where is Pooley! Go find him. If he's fallen off the 'water wagon' get him back on it. If he hasn't fallen off, be sure to see that he doesn't!" Fortunately, when Hubert was located he was pronounced sober, a condition in which he remained until after the Rose Bowl.

Wade geared up in the face of sniffing predictions by the nation's sportswriters that Alabama would never be able to stay on the field with a team like the University of Washington. One L.A. columnist branded Alabama's players "Swamp Students," and even lovable old cowboy comedian Will Rogers made a remark about "Tusca-losers." Dr. Denny had urged the team to study academics on the four-day trip to Pasadena, but Wade put his men on the train two weeks before the game and at every stop made them get off and run. In Arizona, during a longer layover, Wade made them roll up their trousers and have a dummy scrimmage on a high school field. He even brought along fifty-five-gallon drums of Alabama drinking water to ensure against the players being contaminated by something along the way.

Meanwhile, the publicity engines were working overtime. While the big national press was disparaging Alabama's chances, most of the southern papers were whipping sports fans into a frenzy with hopes of an Alabama win. No southern team had ever been to the Rose Bowl, and in some quarters an Alabama victory would be considered as important as Fredericksburg, Chancellors-ville, and First and Second Manassas rolled into one. In those days the South was still reeling from the effects of Reconstruction and the damage of having an economy still rooted in the soil. Worse, northerners tended to denigrate the South as a dark land of unreconstructed yahoos. For their part, southerners despised what they saw as the superior snootiness of

the North, and in many a household the word "Yankee" had for years always been preceded by the word "damn." The game was shaping up to be the largest intersectional conflict since the Civil War. Historian Wayne Flynt observes that by this time the Crimson Tide was not just the football team of Alabama, "it was the football team of the entire South." The University of Washington, like it or not, was cast into the role of the Yankees, even though during the Late Unpleasantness their ancestors had been fighting not Confederates, but Indians. In fact, some isolated southerners actually believed the Huskies were a team from the detested Washington, D.C.

The Crimson Tide arrived in Pasadena on Christmas Eve and Wade made them practice on Christmas Day. At night players were wined and dined by transplanted southerners and got to meet all sorts of movie stars and Hollywood personalities. A *Birmingham News* columnist remarked: "Johnny Mack Brown will have enough experience posing for the cameramen to enter the movies after his stay at the Rose Bowl." In this he was correct. Brown's easy personality and winning smile were soon to land him starring roles and a long movie career.

At last Wade had enough of these distractions and brought it all to a halt, closeting the team in its hotel and holding closed practices. By then some football writers were predicting Alabama would lose by fifty points or more.

On New Year's Day, 1926, the Crimson Tide stepped into the Rose Bowl, overawed by fifty thousand roaring spectators. The Washington Huskies' star player was one George "Wildcat" Wilson, All-American halfback, so huge that Wu Winslett described him as looking like "a bale of cotton." Back home, not just in Alabama but throughout the South, fans clustered in halls and auditoriums to get the play-by-play by the only means available—the telegraph. To start the game rolling, Wildcat Wilson intercepted a Bama pass, setting up a touchdown. Another Washington touchdown made it Huskies 12, Alabama 0. It was looking bad for southern pride. At one point Pooley Hubert asked for time out, called the team over, put his hands on his hips, and said only this: "All right, what the hell's going on around here!" Then Wildcat Wilson made, in retrospect, an unfortunate mistake. In tackling Johnny Mack Brown he used unnecessary roughness, viciously twisting Brown's leg well after he had him down on the ground. This was clearly shown in the game films. Next play, Wilson was removed from the game for the remainder of the half, courtesy of Brown's incensed teammates.

In the clubhouse at halftime, Wade walked into the locker room, looked around at the expectant faces, and said: "They told me boys from the south would fight." Then he left. But by now Wade had discovered a flaw in his own planning. Most of Washington's gains had been made through Bama's ends, so he replaced his light first-stringers with two heavier substitutes and this stopped the Huskies almost cold. In the third quarter the Tide came alive. Pooley Hubert, who had been held back from running the ball in the first half out of concern that he might be injured, carried the ball five consecutive times, finally for a touchdown. Next, after holding Washington to a punt, Alabama unleashed a pass to Johnny Mack Brown which he caught without

Opposite page, above: *Just before the game, Coach Wade points out the stars on the Washington squad. No southern team had ever played in the Rose Bowl and some sportswriters were predicting the Crimson Tide would lose by 50 points or more.* **Opposite page, below:** *Hoyt "Wu" Winslett, a standout end on the team of '25.* **Below:** *The Huskies All-American George "Wildcat" Wilson on one of his spectacular runs. Bama's Wu Winslett described Wilson as "big as a bale of cotton." Pooley Hubert (10) is closing in. In the first half Wilson made the mistake of brutally twisting Johnny Mack Brown's leg on a tackle and the next play was removed from the game, courtesy of Brown's incensed teammates.*

Touchdown, Alabama! At halftime it was Washington 12, Bama 0 and things were looking grim. But in the third period Pooley Hubert (10), who had been told not to run it himself for fear he might be injured, carried the ball five consecutive times, the last for a touchdown, seen above.

Johnny Mack Brown on the run in the 1926 Rose Bowl, with referee Eckerstall, a famous All-American himself, coming at full tilt.

breaking stride and went in for the goal. A few plays later Alabama recovered a Washington fumble and Pooley Hubert threw to Brown again for another touchdown. Alabama 20, Washington 12.

But in the fourth quarter Washington scored again, led by Wildcat Wilson, now back in the game. Alabama 20, Washington 19. In the final seconds the Huskies were knocking on Alabama's goal line but Bama brazenly repelled them. Brown— often criticized by Wade as a poor tackler—succeeded in smacking down the giant Wilson single-handedly—a feat said to be nearly impossible. Washington lost the ball on downs and Alabama marched into the annals of football fame.

It was deemed "the most significant victory in southern football history" as well as "the most exciting game in Rose Bowl history, then or since." The Washington coach was so mortified he stormed off the field without the courtesy of shaking hands with Wallace Wade, but it didn't matter. Alabama had won.

All the way along the long route home, people gathered at train depots large and small to shout and cheer and pay their respects. The team was almost mobbed in New Orleans. Aging William Little, who had started the whole football business at Bama back in 1892, was by that time a probate judge in Livingston. He arranged for the train to stop there and presented the players with turkeys and cakes. When the cavalcade finally reached Tuscaloosa a city-wide holiday was proclaimed, and the players were paraded triumphantly through the streets and onto the campus in horse drays drawn by freshmen. One writer compared it to the "return of a Roman legion from a war of conquest," all of it led down University Boulevard by the Million Dollar Band. Long afterward, Birmingham newspaper editor John T. Graves summed it up this way:

For all the last stands, all the lost causes and sacrificings in vain, the South had a heart and a tradition. But the South had a new tradition for something else. It was for survival and victory. It had come from the football field. It had come from those mighty afternoons in the Rose Bowl in Pasadena when Alabama's Crimson Tide had rolled to glory. The South had come by way of football to think in terms of causes won, not lost.

And so it was as if the entire southern region—at least in its momentary delirium—was suddenly unburdened of a seventy-year legacy of defeat, poverty, and isolation by a handful of Alabama boys during a single sunny afternoon on a green playing field in southern California.

THE DOTHAN ANTELOPE

~

Philip Beidler

THE STORY OF JOHNNY MACK Brown, the Alabama All-American halfback and hero of the 1926 Rose Bowl game who went on to become a Hollywood cowboy star, reads, itself, like something out of the movies. Descended of the early Alabama settler Lachlan McGillivray and the Creek princess Sehoy, and billed on the basis of high school exploits in track, baseball, and football as "the Dothan Antelope," he arrived at Alabama just in time to become a key performer under the legendary Wallace Wade during a period that saw the Tide win 25, lose 3, and tie 1. Most importantly, he rose to true greatness on that January day in Pasadena, when he not only scored two touchdowns in a come-from-behind victory over heavily favored Washington, but also on defense probably made a game-saving tackle on the last play against the formidable George Wilson, his All-American opposite number.

Meanwhile, Brown carried his exploits with a winning modesty. Fellow hall-of-fame inductee and teammate Wu Winslett, for instance, described him as "one heckuva player, about as good as I have seen," adding also that Brown was "about the most humble individual I have ever been around. There was no arrogance about him, absolutely no egotism."

After graduation and marriage to his college sweetheart, Cornelia Foster, daughter of a local judge, the Hollywood part of the story shortly ensued. On the basis of a screen test, Brown signed a five-year MGM contract, working his way through a series of pretty boy roles until gaining major western stardom in *Billy the Kid*. And from there on, through a career lasting well into the fifties, Brown was a mainstay matinee idol of the sagebrush set, making sixty-six films with Monogram alone and later continuing to be a favorite in comic books and television reruns.

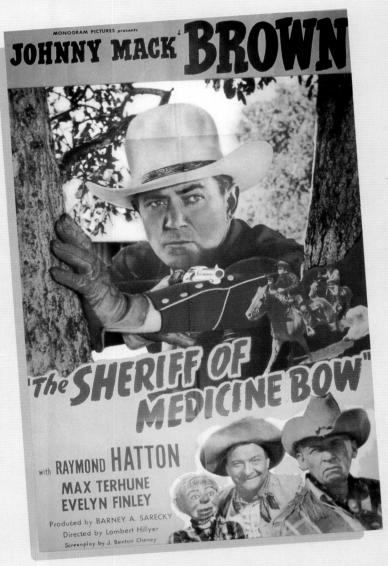

A graceful retirement followed, highlighted by a happy family life and occasional celebrity appearances, including a hometown visit during the 1950 Dothan Peanut Festival and induction into the 1957 National Football Foundation Hall of Fame. Most important, however, was Brown's 1969 induction as a charter member, along with Paul Bryant, Don Hutson, Shug Jordan, Joe Louis,

Above: *Dothan's Johnny Mack Brown relaxes with the crowd at the 1926 Rose Bowl.* **Left:** *Johnny Mack Brown soon became the famous western movie star. Here he is pictured with John Wayne.* **Opposite page:** The Sheriff of Medicine Bow *was one of sixty-six films Brown made for Monogram Pictures.*

and others into the Alabama Sports Hall of Fame. There, as the first of the group to be recognized, he set the tone for the proceedings with what the *Montgomery Advertiser* described as a brief but moving speech, "delivered in the soft, poetical voice of the longtime star of the Hollywood cowboy movies." Again, quiet dignity was in character. He had enjoyed his movie heroics, Brown said, in a lifetime of make-believe shoot-outs having been vanquished only thrice, and thereby posting a record 297 marks in the win column. "But I treasure this more than anything," he concluded of the evening's commemoration of his football exploits, "this coming back to be honored in such a manner." Thus in his valedictory, as on the football field and the screen, Brown remained Alabama's genuine All-American.

Philip Beidler is a professor of English at UA.

Top: *Football champions of the world—1925. (Wallace Wade, Jr., manager, holding the ball).* **Above:** *1925 Rose Bowl pennant.* **Opposite page, above:** *At railroad stops all the way across the south, throngs gathered to congratulate the victorious Crimson Tide. Here the team is mobbed as they finally reach the Tuscaloosa depot.* **Opposite page, below:** *In 1926 the big question was, "Can they do it again?" Here Red Brown, Johnny Mack's younger brother, goes airborne in a 42-0 win over Florida.*

COULD THEY DO IT AGAIN? It was the question that burned in the mind of the South and in the twitching fingers of sportswriters all over the nation as the new season opened in the autumn of 1926. Pooley Hubert and Johnny Mack Brown were gone. Only end Wu Winslett and a handful of others remained from the star-studded Rose Bowl champions of the year before. But Wade had developed that team with depth, and now it began to show. As football historian James S. Edson tells us, "It was a cold, a calculating and relentless outfit. It played smart football in this game, gained confidence as the season progressed." It ended the season, as in the previous year, undefeated and untied, outscoring its opponents 242 to 20. The only real squeak came in the game with Alabama's tenacious old foe Sewanee, which the Tide finally managed to vanquish 2-0 in the final minute on a safety after a blocked punt by Alabama's All-Conference tackle Freddie Pickhard. All-American Wu Winslett did yeoman's duty the entire season, running or passing the ball far more than he received or blocked, which was the way some ends were utilized in those days.

Inevitably the Rose Bowl invitation was issued and accepted—actually it had been issued after Alabama's sixth game of the season. The Tide's opponent would be a strong Stanford team coached by the legendary Pop Warner who, after scouting an early Alabama game and taking note of the speed of Wade's men, ordered specially made super-light red silk pants for his Rose Bowl players. The Stanford Indians outplayed Alabama three to one or better

in all statistics except one: the final score—Alabama 7, Stanford 7. It wasn't a victory but it wasn't a loss either, and in those days ties were not uncommon. Bear Bryant, however, later characterized this kind of disappointment as "about as satisfying as kissing your sister." But for these exhausted boys, it was enough. Enough for one last afternoon in the fading shadows of the Rose Bowl. They had held in there; it was all they could do.

Afterward, the players were deeply saddened to learn that one of their most ardent fans, Judge James J. Mayfield, class of 1885, prominent Tuscaloosa attorney and former Alabama Supreme Court Justice, had died of a heart attack while listening to the game over the radio. According to newspaper reports, Judge Mayfield's final words were, "Why don't they resort to the pass?" Not long afterward a memorial granite boulder was placed on the university campus near the old law school, adjacent to University Boulevard. The monument now rests on the grounds of the new law school.

Minutes before the end of the game, with Stanford leading 7-0, big tackle Babe Pearce blocked a Stanford punt and the Tide took over at the Indians' fourteen. With end Wu Winslett and Alabama back Jimmy Johnson running the ball, the Tide scored and was just one point down, 7-6. As they lined up for the all-important extra point, Stanford dug in, determined to thwart a tie. Bama captain Emile Barnes began calling numbers but suddenly raised up and abruptly shouted "Signals off!" In that instant, as the Indians momentarily relaxed, the ball was snapped and kicked directly through the uprights. It was a trick play Wade had thought up and the only time he used it. Interestingly, one of the stars of the game was halfback Red Brown, Johnny Mack's little brother. Five players on that team were named All-Southern Conference, and Alabama—and the South—had proved to the nation they were no flash in the pan.

Meanwhile the ever-scheming president Mike Denny had grandiose plans to exploit Alabama's new national celebrity. He began to take out newspaper advertisements in the Northeast heralding the Crimson Tide's football fame and touting the state's warm climate and the reasonable cost of attending school at the genteel Tuscaloosa campus. The results were spectacular. Northern students, many of them Jewish, poured into the University.

Alabama English professor Don Noble, in his introduction to *Mud on the Stars*, William Bradford Huie's semi-fictional account of the University during that era, describes the exodus thusly:

The administration decided to capitalize on this fame [of the Rose Bowl victory] *and advertised the school in the metropolitan New York City newspapers. The University could boast of the championship football team, low out-of-state tuition rates, mild winters, and no "quotas," and it was quotas that were keeping many Jewish students in the Northeast out of some of the more prestigious schools. Jewish students came, four hundred in 1926 and eight hundred in 1927. By 1930, spurred on by the stock-market crash of 1929 and the subsequent depression, one-third of the student body of The University of Alabama was Jewish. . . . Sixty years later it is not unusual for a professor to ask a Jewish student from Newark how he came to choose The University of Alabama and hear in response: "My family has always gone to school here."*

Top: *Like the team of '25, the Crimson Tide of '26 went undefeated and untied and returned to the Rose Bowl against Stanford. Before the game the team was allowed to clown around on movie sets. Here they pose with the famous cowboy actor Tom Mix.* **Above:** *1927 Rose Bowl program.* **Opposite page:** *Big Freddie Pickhard, All-Southern Conference tackle for the Tide was a standout in the Rose Bowl.*

Left: *Stanford quarterback Hoffman passing as Wu Winslett (58) closes in during the '27 Rose Bowl.* **Below:** *In 1929 the new Denny Stadium is filled to capacity at homecoming while the Million Dollar Band plays the Alma Mater.*

Opposite page, above: *In 1930 the Crimson Tide rejuvenated itself. Coach Wade had announced his resignation the previous year, but agreed to finish out his contract for the following season. As one sportswriter put it, "It was the greatest swan song in the history of football." Bama went 9-0 in the regular season and the Rose Bowl came knocking again.* **Opposite page, below:** *At the same time Bama was playing in the 1931 Rose Bowl, down in Moro Bottom, Arkansas, a high school player was developing who would later have his name added to Denny Stadium—Paul "Bear" Bryant.*

This trend continued for many years, and to some extent does today. The University's enrollment now includes students from every state in the Union, as well as many foreign nations. Much of this was a direct result of all the attention garnered by the football teams of the Crimson Tide.

GOOD THINGS CAN'T LAST FOREVER AND FOR ALABAMA THEY DIDN'T. During the next three seasons Wade established a creditable record of 17-10-1, but mere winning seasons weren't enough anymore for fans and alumni accustomed to Rose Bowl grandeur and national championship fame. A most painful impression was created that Wade had lost his touch and the press was often critical. These teams were plagued by physical injuries, fumblitis, and passdrop-syndrome. Among the stars of the period were the splendid All-American tackle Fred Sington, who later starred for the Washington Senators and the Brooklyn Dodgers, guard Frank Howard, who would go on to coach renowned Clemson football teams, and J. B. "Ears" Whitworth who, a quarter century later, would return to Alabama to coach several not-so-memo-

rable seasons. The Tide's uniforms now contained vertical red and white stripes, much more padding, and improved leather headgear that resembled, more or less, a stockpot. Meantime, Mike Denny had concluded that the team needed more suitable accommodations for their home games, which were then played where they practiced, at what is now Thomas Field. In 1929 Denny Stadium was completed, with a seating capacity of twelve thousand.

Wade remained ever the fierce disciplinarian during this period. Players remember his wrath if they were caught even talking to a girl. Halfback John Henry Suther, later sheriff of Tuscaloosa County, who played from 1927 to 1931, remembered the time Coach Crisp caught tackle Troy Barker holding hands with a girl on the way to class. At practice that afternoon Crisp called Barker over, took hold of his hand, and walked him around the practice field several times, much to the delight of his bemused teammates. "He never did tell Troy why he was holding his hand," Suther said, "but Troy got the message."

But Crisp was also notorious for taking care of his players—football, baseball, basketball, or track. He was always lending them money, mostly out of

his own pocket. Most were poor and didn't have cash even for the essentials. Here is just one of dozens of similar stories:

Before a Rose Bowl game, tackle Max Jackson examined the one suit his daddy had bought him several years earlier when he came to Alabama. It had become threadbare and he was ashamed of it. "The more I thought about boarding that big train and going on that long trip to California and seeing all those movie stars and celebrities, the more I knew I had to have a new suit of clothes, because the seat of my pants were as shiny as a new silver dollar." One day after practice, Jackson made a particularly good tackle and figured, "it was now or never, cause time was getting short." He sidled up to Crisp and asked if there was any way he might be able to get a suit of clothes. Crisp said to meet him next morning in the Club Room. "I was up bright and early," Jackson remembered, "cause I never wanted anything as bad in my life as I wanted that suit of clothes." Crisp arrived, reached in his pocket, handed Jackson forty dollars, and told him to go downtown to Black, Friedman and Winston and get fitted.

Above: *Program cover for the 1931 Rose Bowl game.* **Right:** *In Pasadena on New Year's Day, 1931, Bama captain "Foots" Clement and the Washington State captain meet on the field. The woman in the middle is described on the back of this photograph as "...an unidentified lady, thought to be a movie star."*

Left: *Crimson Tide All-American tackle Fred Sington, who starred in the '31 Rose Bowl. The story goes that a few weeks earlier the singer Rudy Vallee had written a song about him that became popular nationwide. Each time they lined up, Sington's opposite number in the Bama line, Frank Howard, would tease him by singing the song: "Football Freddie, rugged and tan/Football Freddie, collegiate man. . . ."* **Below:** *A 1931 Rose Bowl ticket. Some seventy thousand fans had them.*

Meanwhile, Wade was becoming more and more irritated by the negative gossip that continued to swirl around the topic of his coaching ability. He was nearing the end of a five-year contract with the University that expired after the 1930 season, and Duke had offered him a big salary to come to North Carolina. Also, Wade was having his problems with president Mike Denny, whom he thought was meddling too much in the affairs of the team. Wade was clearly unhappy and after a disappointing 6-3 season in 1929 he handed in his resignation. It was accepted, but Wade did agree to fulfill the remainder of his contract by coaching the team of 1930. As Clyde Bolton of the *Birmingham News* put it, "It was the greatest swan song in the history of football."

Alabama went on to a 10-0 season, outscoring its opponents 271-13. That was also the year Alabama picked up the elephant emblem. During the game against Ole Miss, which Bama won 64-0, one of the spectators shouted that Alabama had "the horses." Another fan hollered back, "Those aren't horses, they're elephants!" An Atlanta sportswriter picked this up and the University had a new mascot.

Below: *Bama guard John Miller (left) and center Joe Sharpe (right) in Rose Bowl action against Washington State in 1931.* **Opposite page above:** *Monk Campbell kicks the extra point after scoring a touchdown in Bama's 24-0 stomping of Washington State in the '31 Rose Bowl.* **Opposite page below:** *A spectacular catch by Bama's Ray Hansen against the Cougars of Washington State in the '31 Rose Bowl. In a particularly interesting piece of gamesmanship, Coach Wade threw the westerners off guard from the outset by starting his second string against them.*

Alabama was offered and accepted yet another invitation to the Rose Bowl, and the team boarded the train for Pasadena to play the 9-0 Washington State Cougars. En route they made stops in Meridian, Mississippi, where Pooley Hubert came to the depot to greet them; in Picayune, Mississippi, so that Frank Howard's mother could ride to New Orleans with her son; and in Arizona, where they laid over for a scrimmage. There an Alabama alum presented the team with a baby burro, about two feet tall. Coach Crisp's wife nursed it with a baby bottle in the baggage car all the way to California and back. Fred Sington declared wryly, "He might be a burro in Texas or California, but back in Alabama he's a jackass."

In his final game coaching Alabama, Wade was relentless as ever. After a very brief day of sightseeing in which they saw Johnny Mack Brown making a motion picture with Wallace Beery, Wade closeted the players again. Of Brown's accomplishments as a movie star, Wade remarked, "He has to make a living doing something." Wade wouldn't even let the players watch the Rose Bowl parade, though it was only a few blocks from their hotel. At one point he invigorated the team by announcing they were all going for an "outing." The initial excitement turned to disappointment when they discovered that Wade's idea of an outing was to take them on a visit to an orange grove. "We picked two oranges each and came back. That was his big outing," Fred Sington grumbled decades later.

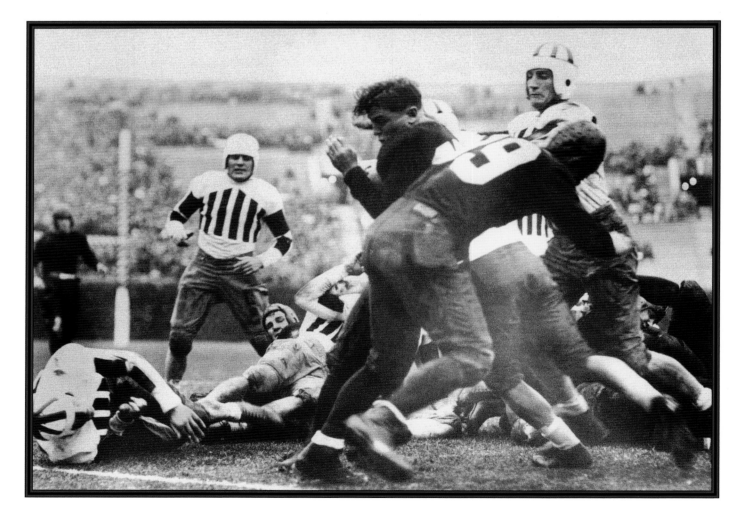

But Wade had a tender side too. Alabama had a scrub player named Bell who was from California but didn't make the traveling squad. Bell hitchhiked to the West Coast to watch the game but when he got there couldn't find a ticket. Wade compassionately gave him a uniform and let him sit on the bench.

The stakes in this game were no less than the national championship and on Rose Bowl day Wade shocked not only his team but everyone else, especially sportswriters, when he started his second string against Washington State. This gamesmanship had two objectives: to confuse and frighten the opposition and, when the first team did get into the game, to send them in fresh and ferocious.

In a drizzling rain before a crowd of seventy thousand, Washington State held its own against Bama's second string, but the Cougars were clearly outclassed when the starting team finally came on the field in the second quarter. As the story goes, famed singer and movie star Rudy Vallee had recently written a hit song, "Football Freddie," and dedicated it to All-American Fred Sington. Each time they lined up, Frank Howard, Sington's opposite number on the left side of Bama's line, would tease him by singing: "Football Freddie, rugged and tan; Football Freddie, collegiate man. . . ." Alabama manhandled Washington State 24-0 that afternoon, and every Crimson Tide player got a chance to get into the game including, courtesy of Coach Wade, the scrub, Bell, who had thumbed all the way out to California. Sington recalled of him nostalgically: "He played three minutes and got a gold football with an American Beauty rose carved on it." Wade was carried off on the shoulders of his men and with that, a magnificent era ended for The University of Alabama.

Chapter Three

GLORY

1931 〜 1946

Above: *A montage of Rose Bowl tickets from 1935, 1938, and 1946, on display at the Bryant Museum.* **Opposite page:** *Bama is the only football team that has the Rose Bowl as a fixture in its fight song, but after the Crimson Tide's 34-14 destruction of USC in 1946, the Rose Bowl Committee elected not to play any more teams from the SEC.*

VEN BEFORE THE 1930 SEASON BEGAN, president Mike Denny knew he had a momentous decision on his hands. The legendary Wallace Wade was leaving: who could replace him? As it turned out, Coach Wade himself already had someone in mind. That man was Frank W. Thomas, son of ironworking Welsh immigrants, who had starred as quarterback on Knute Rockne's Notre Dame teams and whose roommate had been the famed George "The Gipper" Gipp. At present, Thomas was backfield coach at Georgia.

"I don't believe you could pick a better man," Wade told Denny. Borden Burr, founder of the vast Birmingham law firm Burr-Foreman and a backfield player on the teams of 1892-93, arranged a meeting. At the end of it, Thomas was hired. As they left the room, Denny issued Thomas what almost amounted to a warning. "It is my conviction that material is 90 percent, coaching ability ten percent. I desire further to say that you will be provided with the ninety percent and that you will be held to strict accounting for delivering the remaining ten percent." Thomas left thinking, "Those were the hardest, coldest words I ever heard."

What impact they had on Thomas's coaching program is uncertain but it is undisputed that he became, up to then, Alabama's greatest coach of all time. In his decade and a half at the University Frank Thomas would amass a 115-24-7 record, going three times to the Rose Bowl, as well as to the Sugar, Cotton, and Orange Bowls. Only Bryant would surpass this. Thomas's teams would produce seventeen All-Americans, including Joe Domnanovich, Harry Gilmer, "Dixie" Howell, Don Hutson, Bill Lee, Vaughn Mancha, and Riley Smith. There were twenty-six Alabama All-SEC selections during the Thomas era. It might also be mentioned that among Thomas's stalwart players in the 1933-35 seasons was a tough young end from Moro Bottom, Arkansas, named Paul "Bear" Bryant.

Thomas's problems were apparent to him even before the '31 football year opened; the team had lost to graduation ten of the eleven starters in

Pigskin Review

Southern California vs. Alabama

TOURNAMENT OF ROSES

ROSE BOWL
JANUARY 1, 1946

PRICE 25¢

Right: *During a stopover on the Rose Bowl trip of 1931, a Bama alumnus presented the Tide with a baby burro. Coach Crisp's wife nursed the beast with a baby bottle in the baggage car all the way to California and back, and it became a sort of team mascot for a while, named "Tom Heflin."*

Above: *After the 1931 Rose Bowl, the now-famous Crimson Tide journeyed to Washington, D.C., to play a series of charity exhibition games. They played one quarter each against such schools as Georgetown, George Washington, and Catholic University. Here the team is pictured at the White House with President Herbert Hoover, standing in center.*

Wade's famed perfect season. But Thomas, stubby and dark-eyed, was a man who understood the game with an almost uncanny ability to turn glaring liabilities into stunning assets. Knute Rockne was once quoted as having observed during Thomas's last year at Notre Dame, "It's amazing how much football sense that Thomas kid has. He can't miss becoming a great coach someday." Thomas was undoubtedly saddened that year by news that his old mentor Rockne had been killed in a plane crash.

Coach Thomas had one ace in the hole despite the loss of practically all his starters. This was the return of fullback and punter Johnny Cain, who still had two more years' eligibility. Thomas chucked Wade's single wing and put in the Notre Dame Box formation he knew so well. This opened up the offensive game for passing and provided more versatility for running plays to either side of the line. Alabama beat all of its opponents that season except one, but it was becoming an important one—the University of Tennessee. Nonetheless, Thomas's new offense was working splendidly. The Tide outscored its opponents that year by a then amazing 360-57.

Thomas had gotten rid of the gaudy striped uniforms and the Tide now played in either solid crimson or white jerseys. Bama teams had grown immensely in numbers, with sixty or more players—triple the size of teams only six or seven years before. Coaching staffs had grown, too, with Thomas adding, in addition to Hank Crisp, former Tide players Clyde Propst and two others: Harold "Red" Drew and J. B. "Ears" Whitworth, who in the l950s would both become Alabama head coaches themselves. Also, by now the players had a rudimentary athletic dorm, known around campus as "B.O. House." It was located in an old two-story house, since demolished, and the players took their meals there, some serving as waiters to earn a little money.

~

In 1932, with All-Southern Conference Johnny Cain back in the lineup, Thomas went 8-2, losing only to Tennessee and Georgia Tech. Tennessee only won 7-3 but the loss was rankling. It looked like it was becoming a habit. It was a spectacular game, though, and simple in its character: *defense.* Tennessee had a player called Beattie Feathers who was a sensational punter, and the match, played in a cold downpour, quickly developed into a kicking duel between Feathers and Alabama's equally sensational Johnny Cain. In those days the quick kick was a prime weapon in most offensive arrays. It stunned opponents by suddenly putting them far back in their own territory when they least expected it. Later the quick

kick fell out of fashion before being revived by Bear Bryant in the late '50s. Feathers punted twenty-one times that afternoon averaging forty-three yards per kick, and Cain replied nineteen times for a forty-eight-yard average. Both teams frequently kicked on first or second down. One of Cain's kicks went nearly seventy yards. In the closing minutes of the third quarter Alabama was ahead 3-0 but then Feathers booted a breathtaking punt that settled on the Bama one-yard line. Far back in his own end zone Cain desperately tried to kick away to safety but the pass from center was low and struck him in the

Top: *Bama's new coach Frank Thomas in 1931 with his future All-American halfback Millard "Dixie" Howell. Under his reign, the Crimson Tide would amass a 115-24-7 record.* **Above:** *This home, dubbed "B.O. House," served as the athletic dorm until the 1950s.*

Right: *Bama's secret weapon for the new season of 1931 was future All-American fullback Johnny Cain, a punter of lethal abilities. In the game as it was played then, the quick kick was a potent offensive weapon. In 1932 Cain got into a spectacular punting contest against Tennessee's Beattie Feathers. Cain kicked 19 times, averaging 48 yards, and Feathers punted 21 times for an average of 43 yards.*

Above: *Two players on the team of '32: "The Right End," future All-American Don Hutson (right) and "The Other End," Paul "Bear" Bryant (left).*
Opposite page: *The spectacular Don Hutson went on to immortalize himself as a Green Bay Packer, leading the league in scoring five times.*

knee. He only managed a wobbly twelve-yard punt, and three plays later Feathers carried the ball across Alabama's goal for the Tennessee win.

The following season loomed large on Coach Thomas's horizon. As usual a lot of starters had been lost to graduation, including the seemingly irreplaceable Johnny Cain. But Thomas was soon to discover that this 1933 team would be one of the most star-studded in Crimson Tide history: fabulous halfback Dixie Howell, a pair of ends from Arkansas, Bear Bryant and Don Hutson, tackle Bill Lee, quarterback Riley Smith, and a big fullback from Bayonne, New Jersey, named Joe Demyanovich.

The Great Depression was now in full dark bloom. Franklin Roosevelt, now in the White House, ended Prohibition, the Nazi party had a stranglehold on Germany, and Japan was under the sway of militarists. Meantime, the old Southern Conference had divided up and Alabama found itself in something new called the Southeastern Conference—the SEC. After an annoying 0-0 tie with Ole Miss, the Tide went to Knoxville and finally whipped Tennessee 12-6, the first time the Vols had lost on their home field in nearly

a decade. It was said Coach Thomas was so nervous during the game that at one point he stuck the lighted end of his cigar in his mouth. But Dixie Howell had stepped neatly into Johnny Cain's punting shoes, airing out one boomer for eighty-five yards. This time, Feathers was effectively bottled up by Bama's defense. In the fourth period Tennessee—with Alabama leading by only a touchdown—found itself on Bama's six-yard line, first and goal with three minutes left in the game. In one of the Tide's greatest goal line stands, Feathers was thrown for losses time and again and Alabama took over on downs as the game-ending whistle blew.

Next, Alabama journeyed to New York's Polo Grounds where a throng of sixty thousand watched them lose to a powerful Fordham team, 2-0. It was the only loss of the season, though, and Frank Thomas would be awarded his first Southeastern Conference championship with the outstanding guard Thomas Hupke receiving All-America honors. Both Howell and Hupke were elected All-SEC as well.

Hank Crisp remained the stalwart of Alabama's tough line-playing, cursing and praising players all at the same time. Crisp reportedly could use profanity in sublime proportions. It was said that one time he cursed a player for at least five minutes without using the same curse word twice. But his affection and generosity for "Hank's Boys" remained legendary. Bear Bryant remembered the time when a bunch of football players had gathered, as they often did, in "Hoochman's room," down in the cellar of the old gym. Hoochman was the longtime janitor of the building and enjoyed the occasional drink, which had earned him his nickname. That night one of the players, Sandy Sanford, showed the other boys his shoes, which were in a very dilapidated condition. Crisp was there too, wearing a brand-new pair of shoes, Bryant recalled, and when Crisp saw Sanford's old shoes he took off one of his own and shoved it over to Sanford, telling him to try it on. "It fit perfectly, so he gave him the other shoe," Bryant remembered, "then he put on the old shoes of Sandy's and walked out."

THEY ALL CAME BACK FOR THE SPLENDID SEASON OF 1934 and fate lay heavily upon them. Thomas guided the Tide to a perfect 10-0 record and another national championship, outscoring the opposition 316-45 and avenging the 1926 Rose Bowl tie with Stanford by stomping the Indians 29-13. After coasting through the first three games of that season, Alabama met General Neyland's Tennessee Volunteers at Legion Field on the annual Third Saturday in October. It was a collision more than a football game and few breathed comfortably until the final whistle blew. It was Bama 13, Tennessee 6 late in the fourth

Opposite page, above: *In the old days, Crimson Tiders sometimes amused themselves with what today might be considered strange diversions for football players. In 1932, clockwise from left: end Ralph Gandy and center Joe Demyanovich play chess while Don Hutson and Ray White look on.* **Opposite page, below:** *"Hoochman" Collins, long-time janitor at the athletic department, lived in the basement with the furnace. Players and sometimes coaches would come down to take a drink with him. Bryant visited his room often in the 1930s and when he returned as head coach in 1958 set up the Hoochman with his own house.* **Below:** *In October 1933 Bama played Fordham at New York's Polo Grounds. They lost the contest 2-0 before sixty thousand people.*

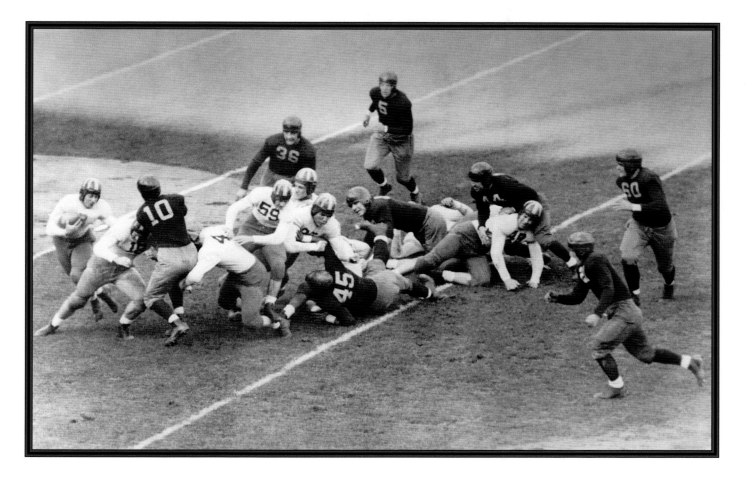

Top: *Denny Field grasscutters—summer, 1934 (left to right): Zeke Kimbrough (basketball), Bear Bryant, Chesty Moseley, Jim Whatley, Rayford Ellis and Joe Dildy.* **Above:** *Dixie Howell scores a touchdown in the 1935 Rose Bowl. West Coast sportswriters later accused Howell of thumbing his nose at Stanford's Buck Van Dellen while scampering for a sixty-seven-yard touchdown. Howell denied any unsportsmanlike conduct, saying he had merely "waved" at Van Dellen as he ran past him.*

period when Dixie Howell punted and the Vols' receiver made a dash straight through Alabama's converging defense until Howell himself—the last man on the field who could have done so—brought him down. General Neyland declared after the game that Dixie Howell was the greatest back in the South and later paid the entire Crimson Tide perhaps its grandest compliment then or since: "You never know what a football player is made of until he plays against Alabama," he said.

The Rose Bowl came knocking again and the Bama players dutifully boarded the train for California, many of them wearing new suits with a little spending money in their pockets, all of it courtesy of coach Hank Crisp. Tackle Jim Whatley remembered: "Some of us had our clothes in bags, some in paper bags. I had one suit, and I think coach Hank had to help me buy it."

When the train arrived in New Mexico, who should turn up but ex-halfback Johnny Mack Brown, who got on board with a satchel of charts. All season, between movie shoots, he had been scouting 9-0-1 Stanford, Alabama's opponent on New Year's Day.

Thomas's pre-game policies were not as strict as Wade's. Worried about injuries, he canceled contact scrimmages a few days after they arrived in Pasadena and let the players make the requisite visits to movie studios and restaurants.

A week before the game, the Rose Bowl declared a sellout at 84,484 tickets. One sportswriter said this was the best Stanford team in history and other papers—especially back east—lamented that Minnesota had not been selected to play them. All of this combined to get Bama's dander up, to the immense delight of Thomas and Crisp. In the week before the game famous sports journalists like Grantland Rice and Braven Dyer clustered around the players and coaches. Among their number was a young sportscaster who especially liked to curry favor with Frank Thomas. His name was Ronald Reagan.

The game itself was almost no contest, thanks to the passing combination of Dixie Howell to Don Hutson, which accounted for twenty-four of the points the Crimson Tide scored in beating Stanford 29-13. Early in the first period Stanford scored after recovering an Alabama fumble. Humorist Will Rogers called this a mistake: "It just made Alabama mad. That first score was just like holding up a picture of Sherman's March to the Sea." But it might not have gone so well. Howell had been feeling ill all morning and in the second quarter came out of the game with stomach cramps. Fortunately, during halftime doctors managed to relieve the condition and Howell returned for a brilliant second half. Minutes before the end of the first period, Thomas decided they'd better quit passing and hold onto their lead, so he sent Hutson in to tell this to the quarterback. In those days, however, there was a rule that a substitute entering a game could not speak to anyone for one play, so Hutson presented himself in the huddle without comment. Joe Riley, who had replaced Howell, assumed that if Hutson was there it was because Thomas wanted a pass and he called one—much to the astonishment of the coach—throwing a fifty-yarder that Hutson hauled in on Stanford's fourteen and ran in for the score.

Game program cover from the 1935 Rose Bowl, on display at the Bryant Museum.

Losing badly toward the end of the third quarter, Stanford was apparently not above some tacky artifice. Bear Bryant remembered that when he looked down upon coming to the line, he found a bunch of money lying on the ground in front of him. "There was a silver dollar, two or three half dollars and some quarters." This being a great deal of money to Bryant, he "picked it up real fast," but naturally, since there were no pockets in his uniform pants, had to hold the coins in his hand, thinking he could carry them to the sidelines after the play was over. Suddenly Stanford snapped the ball and Bryant found the play was, of course, being run smack at him, since he was now effectively one-handed. "I had to make a decision. It was the only tackle I made the entire game, but I lost my money in the process," he said.

One other incident stirred up a row after the game. It was reported in the West Coast papers that while scampering for a sixty-seven-yard touchdown, Dixie Howell had thumbed his nose at Stanford defensive back Buck Van Dellen, the last man who might have caught him. Howell, however, de-

Above: *National champions: the 1934 team went 10-0 and beat Stanford 29-13 in the Rose Bowl. Coach Thomas had ditched the gaudy uniforms of the Wallace Wade era and the Tide played in plain crimson or white. The old game jerseys were then used for practices.* Right: *Riley Smith, All-American quarterback and a hero of the 1935 Rose Bowl.* Opposite page, above: *Football players could be snappy dressers in the old days. Seen here is Bill Lee, captain of the '34 national championship team, leaving class.* Opposite page, below: *All-American end Don Hutson for yardage in the College All-Star Game in Chicago, 1935.*

nied such unsportsmanlike conduct, stating that he had merely "waved" at Van Dellen as he ran past him.

Afterward, Thomas compared Dixie Howell to his old roommate at Notre Dame, the late great George Gipp. Howell, Don Hutson, and Bill Lee were elected All-Americans that year.

~

WITH HUTSON AND HOWELL NOW GONE, prospects for the season of 1935 looked bleak. Pleasant surprises did not overtake Thomas as in the past and Alabama went 6-2-1 that year. The season opener concluded with a 7-7 tie against rinky-dink Howard (now Samford University). Worse, Denny became embroiled in a controversy with the state legislature as well as his own faculty that led to his resignation after nearly a quarter century as president. The feud with the legislature was mostly technical, but the faculty was vocally complaining about about poor pay and academic facilities as well as Denny's "over-emphasis on athletics." Before long, the great friend of Alabama football would be gone.

Nevertheless, the Crimson Tide went to Knoxville and stunned Tennessee with a 25-0 win. It was Bear Bryant's greatest game as a player and, incredibly, he played it on a broken leg. Ever since the Mississippi State game the week before, Bryant had been hobbling around in a cast and on crutches. But as Tennessee time drew near he discarded these things and managed to catch a touchdown pass as well as lateral to Riley Smith for another score. Next week Alabama was playing Georgia, and *Atlanta Constitution* reporter Ralph McGill was suspicious about the broken-leg story. Before the game he showed up in Tuscaloosa, asked to see Bryant's X-rays and, to his chagrin, was forced to concede in print there was indeed a fractured fibula. For his part, Bryant commented, "It was just one little bone."

In 1936, as the fascist states of Germany, Italy, and Japan formed the ominous Axis alliance, Frank Thomas's fortunes improved. Denny Stadium was enlarged to seat eighteen thousand and Bama went 8-0-1 in a season marred only by a 0-0 tie with Tennessee which, unfortunately, cost the Tide the SEC championship. They went to no bowl game that year but Phi Beta Kappa guard Arthur "Tarzan" White made the All-America team. Still, Thomas was livid: "Can you imagine going unbeaten with one tie and not getting a bowl bid?"

In 1937 while *Snow White*, *Captains Courageous*, and *Lost Horizon* were delighting mov-

Top: *Alabama's Million Dollar Band in 1935, directed for nearly forty years by Colonel Carleton Butler.* **Above:** *Game program cover from the 1938 Rose Bowl, on display at the Bryant Museum.*

iegoers, Bama roared along through a 9-0 perfect season. Guard Leroy Monsky, tackle Jim Ryba, and halfback Joe Kilgrow were unanimously voted All-Americans. Alabama was invited first to the fledgling Sugar Bowl but held out for a few days until, as anticipated, the Tide got an invitation to go to Pasadena yet again. On the way to California a grotesque incident occurred on a practice field in Arizona where they had a layover. Thomas had the team run a dummy scrimmage, and at one point the pulling guard on the other end of the line from All-American Monsky pulled the wrong way and the two collided. Monsky wound up with twenty-five stitches in his forehead. Though he managed to play in the Rose Bowl, no one can say what effect this damage had. Alabama played the University of California and the Bears simply overwhelmed them 13-0. It was a disappointing end to an otherwise perfect season.

William Faulkner once described the mule as one of the earth's smartest animals since "he will wait patiently for ten years for the chance to kick you once." Faulkner might as well have been describing Frank Thomas. By a scheduling coincidence, Alabama's first game of the next season, 1938, was to be against the University of Southern California in the Los Angeles Coliseum. If Thomas couldn't wreak vengeance on the California Bears, he would at least wreak it on another California team, the USC Trojans. Thomas began laying out his game plan in the spring and then, in mid-August, ordered the team to report to the campus—ostensibly to help conduct a clinic for high school coaches, but in reality to get them a couple of extra weeks' practice time.

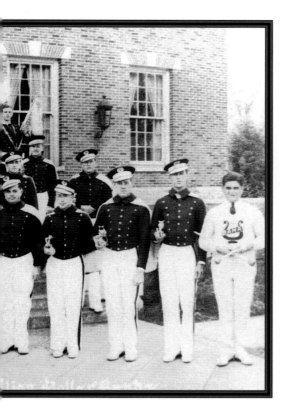

Left: *One of the press people covering the Rose Bowl was a young sportscaster named Ronald Reagan.* **Below:** *Before the '38 Rose Bowl the team visited the movie set of* The Adventures of Robin Hood. *They are pictured here with Errol Flynn and Basil Rathbone and Michael Curtiz, the director (holding ball). In the center is All-American guard Leroy Monsky with a bandage over his eye. At no-pads practice during the ritual stopover in Arizona the opposite guard pulled the wrong way and collided with Monsky, who needed twenty-five stitches in his head. He played in the Rose Bowl anyway.*

Out in Los Angeles, it all paid off. Before a crowd of sixty-five thousand in the Coliseum, Bama dusted USC 19-7 behind the running and passing of Herschel Mosley and the blocking and tackling of big Fred Davis, Walter Merrill, and Bobby Wood. The rest of the season was good but not spectacular, with the Tide losing to Tennessee and tying Georgia Tech for a 7-1-1 year. Fullback Charlie Holm was selected All-SEC.

As the world blundered haplessly toward a second world war, Bama finished its 1939 season with a so-so 5-3-1 but managed to upset eastern powerhouse Fordham 7-6 at New York's Polo Grounds. In one galling loss, rival Tennessee was too powerful for the Tide, and, for the first time in seventeen years, Alabama failed to beat Kentucky, though they managed to tie them. Center Carey Cox was selected All-American. Thus the '30s ended.

In 1940 Alabama recorded a respectable 7-2 season but lost again to Tennessee, as well as to Mississippi State. It also played its first night game—if you don't count the time with Tennessee way back in 1911, when they had to turn on the headlights to finish the contest—against Spring Hill College at Mobile's Murphy High stadium. Louisville tackle Fred Davis was All-SEC and received honorable mention for All-American. Halfback Jimmy Nelson and end Holt Rast also were All-SEC. Davis later had a great career with the Washington Redskins and the Chicago Bears and his son, Fred, Jr., returned to play tackle for the Tide in 1964.

Next year, with Davis graduated but Holt Rast and Jimmy Nelson back in the lineup, the Crimson Tide of 1941 compiled a 9-2 record, including a long-needed win over Tennessee. Three weeks after the Japanese attack on Pearl Harbor, the team went to the Cotton Bowl on a gloomy New Year's Day, 1942, to play Southwest Conference champions Texas A&M. The weather seemed to match the mood of the country. Bama only made one first down that afternoon but intercepted seven A&M passes and recovered five fumbles to win the game 29-21 and secure a small piece of the national title. Holt Rast was a unanimous All-America selection.

Stunned by America's sudden entry into World War II, many of the players were nonetheless able to return for the '42 season, but as the draft cranked up glaring holes began to appear in the depth charts. Still, Alabama posted an 8-3 season. In a terrifically exciting and hard-won game the Tide subdued a determined Tennessee team 8-0 at Legion Field. It was another punting duel reminiscent of the famous contests a decade earlier between Tennessee's Feathers and Bama's Johnny Cain. The Tide opened the second half with a

Above: *Running back Herschel "Herky" Mosley sprinting past a pile of California Golden Bears in the 1938 Rose Bowl. SEC champion Alabama lost it 13-0.* **Opposite page, above:** *Coach Frank Thomas with his staff in 1939: Campbell, Crisp, Thomas, Drew, Burnum, and Bryant.* **Opposite page, below left:** *Halfback Charlie Boswell tears through the Georgia Tech line in '38. The game ended in a 14-14 tie.* **Opposite page, below right:** *When America entered the war in 1941, Coach Bryant received his commission as a navy officer and served in the Mediterranean Theatre.*

kickoff safety against the Vols but it was only minutes before the end of the game that Alabama iced it with a spectacular thirty-eight-yard touchdown by fullback Bobby Jenkins.

As during the World War I years, Bama had on its playing schedule in 1942 teams composed of former college all-stars now stationed at nearby military bases. The Tide beat the Flyers of the Pensacola Naval Air Station but lost badly in its final game with the Georgia Pre-Flight Skycrackers, whose squad not only included numerous former All-Americans but also, standing on its sidelines as a coach, none other than Hank Crisp, now stationed at the Athens army base.

Alabama went to the Orange Bowl that year and came from behind to whip Boston College 37-21. Mid-season, stalwart tackle Jack McKewen and end Sam Sharpe had been called to Officer's Candidate School at Columbus, Georgia, but faithful old alumnus and former player Borden Burr managed through connections to spring them for the game. After just a few plays Bama fell behind BC 14-0 but center Joe Domnanovich was having none of it. Exhorting them during a time-out, he said: "Don't give up. We haven't had a chance to go with the ball yet. We're going to receive and we're going to run them into the ground." At the end of the season Domnanovich and tackle Don Whitmire were selected All-Americans. Also, since there was no team the next year, Whitmire and fullback Bobby Jenkins entered the Naval Academy where both became All-Americans and Whitmire eventually rose to the rank of admiral.

In 1943 Thomas tried to have a season, but between enlistments and the draft few schools, including Alabama, could field a team, let alone find opponents who could, and so football in '43 was called on account of war.

By 1944 some men had returned, the draft had eased a bit—or at least had become more predictable—and Thomas was able to cobble together a squad of sorts consisting of seventeen-year-olds, students medically disqualified from military service, and a few early returning veterans. The War Babies, as they became known, were to become one of the most fabulous

teams in the annals of Alabama football. By this time the service academies were chock full of former all-stars from other colleges, as were schools like Duke and Georgia Tech that had been selected by the military to conduct its advance training programs.

During the lull in seasons of '43, somebody pointed out to Thomas that there was a little tailback playing for Woodlawn High School in Birmingham he ought to keep his eye on. Thomas did and the boy's name turned out to be Harry Gilmer. Thomas's main hope going into the season of 1944 was that his team would not "disgrace the University." Bama could only scrape up twenty players that year—compared with fifty they fielded in the pre-war '42 season.

Given the thin and ragtag material Thomas had to work with, it is remarkable he even managed a 5-2-2 season. But Alabama knew it had a winner on opening day when—even though the game ended in a 27-27 tie—little 157-pound Harry Gilmer took a kickoff and ran it back ninety-five yards through the whole LSU team for a touchdown. With freshmen Gilmer and Vaughn Mancha, at center, the Tide managed a bid to the Sugar Bowl where Gilmer dazzled a crowd of seventy-two thousand. It was a seesaw contest all that sunny afternoon in New Orleans with Gilmer putting on a breathtaking exhibition of running, passing, punting, and tackling rarely seen on football fields, ever. He could do it all. Though the Tide lost to Duke in the last moments, 29-26,

Opposite page, above: *In 1942 Alabama went to the Cotton Bowl, where they beat Texas A&M 29-21. Here, the starting linemen celebrate New Year's Eve in Dallas.* **Opposite page, below:** *Bama won it, 37-21.* **Top:** *The homecoming parade in 1941.* **Above:** *Marching to Legion Field: pre-game parade in Birmingham.*

Gilmer had made an impression. Afterward, sportswriter Grantland Rice declared him "the greatest college passer I ever saw."

Gilmer was a virtual one-man flea circus. Next year, with the war over, he led Bama to a perfect 10-0 season. The Tide was back at full strength now, sixty players on the squad, and outscored its opponents an amazing 430-80. Alabama whipped its first big opponent, LSU, 26-7 in a night game at Tiger Stadium. Vaughn Mancha and a Louisiana State player named Kellum were ejected from the game for fighting. Afterward, Coach Thomas told Mancha: "Vaughn, I never want a thing like that to happen again. No matter what the other fellow does, I don't want my boys to get in fights. We must uphold the dignity of the University of Alabama."

Bama also vanquished Georgia 28-14, Kentucky 60-19, Vanderbilt 70-0, and, at homecoming, stomped Mississippi State 55-13. The expected Rose Bowl bid arrived and Alabama headed once again to Pasadena. Out on the coast, sportswriters were having a field day predicting how badly Southern Cal would beat the Tide. "Alabama has won the Rose Bowl before but, Alabama, you have never met the likes of Southern Cal before. It will be a different story for you," one of them crowed threateningly.

On game day, January 1, 1946, the Crimson Tide simply swamped Southern Cal. Before a dismayed crowd of ninety-five thousand, Bama shunned the passing game everyone anticipated and launched a running attack that left the vaunted Trojans trailing 34-0 in the fourth period. That was when Thomas put his subs in the game, prompting Southern Cal coach Jeff Cravath to issue this opinion of Thomas: "There goes a great man. I'll never forget what he did today. If he had wanted, he could have named the score." The final tally was Alabama 34, Southern Cal 14.

It was a great ending to a great season, saddened only by the toll the

Top: *During the war years the young man pictured did his duty as a Boy Scout. A few years later, Harry Gilmer would become one of the most fabulous quarterbacks in Bama history.* **Above:** *Harry Gilmer in his first game made a spectacular ninety-five-yard kickoff return for a touchdown against LSU.*

war had taken on the Crimson Tide. Of its number, Tom "Hog" Borders, tackle, 1939; Cliff "Swede" Hansen, tackle, 1940-41; James "Babs" Roberts, end, 1940-42; Johnny Roberts, fullback, 1937; and Jimmy Walker, end, 1935, died serving their country.

∼

VAST CHANGES LOOMED ON ALABAMA'S HORIZON as the season of 1946 drew near.

First, there were to be no more Rose Bowl trips. After the final thrashing the Tide gave Southern Cal, the Rose Bowl Committee made a permanent arrangement to play their Pacific Coast schools only against teams from the Big Ten. There also arose the thorny question of whether or not Alabama should resume playing Auburn. Coach Thomas was dead set against it on the

theory that Alabama had much to lose while Auburn had nothing to lose. But the discussion dragged on until the state legislature finally got mixed up in it. Representatives threatened not to pass funding bills for the schools unless an amendment was tacked on requiring them to play each other. This got the attention of the university administrations and they met to work things out. The first game was scheduled for 1948. The student body presidents of both

One of Harry Gilmer's famous leaping passes against Tennessee in 1945. Bama won it 25-7 at Legion Field. Gilmer developed the technique in sandlot ball because he was so short he couldn't see over the line.

schools met in Birmingham and buried a symbolic hatchet in a city park. Meantime, Denny Stadium was enlarged again to seat twenty-five thousand.

Finally, this would be Coach Thomas's last season. For years he had been suffering from high blood pressure and the condition was steadily worsening. By 1946 he was reduced to coaching while seated in a little covered wooden wagon. His voice was so weak he had to use loudspeakers to direct activities on the practice field.

The 1946 season would not be Thomas's finest, but it was certainly nothing to be ashamed of. The Tide went 7-4. The most disagreeable loss was a 31-21 drop to LSU, whose athletic department had soaked the grass at Tiger Stadium the morning of the game in order to slow down the irrepressible Harry Gilmer. Apparently it worked, but it was an ungracious thing to do. Bama also lost that year to Tennessee, Georgia, and Boston College, but the War Babies

Above: *A stack of cheerleaders in 1945.* **Right:** *Coach Thomas with his All-American quarterback Harry Gilmer. Gilmer starred all four years at the University and led the team to the 1946 Rose Bowl where the Crimson Tide beat Southern Cal 34-14. That team was known as the "War Babies" because many were 4-Fs or came of age too late to be drafted. Thomas said they were his favorite of all his teams.* **Opposite page, above:** *As his coaching career wound down, Thomas fell ill with heart disease. Here he greets the team of 1946 seated in a little wagon, equipped with loudspeakers because even his voice was weak. People have remarked that it was the first "coaching tower" at the University.* **Opposite page, below:** *In the locker room with the "War Babies:" fullback Lowell Tew, All-SEC center Vaughn Mancha, and Harry Gilmer.*

gave Thomas an appreciative send-off with a final-game 24-7 whipping of Mississippi State in Denny Stadium. Later, Thomas was to say:

"That 1934 team was my greatest. It had what it took. But my favorite team of all was that green 1944 eleven. Oh, how I loved those War Babies! Those boys were just kids but they worked with all their strength and heart to win."

Thomas stayed on as athletics director for a few more years. In 1951 he was elected to the College Football Hall of Fame and on May 10, 1954, he died in Tuscaloosa. Of Thomas, Harry Gilmer said, "He was more than a coach to me. He was more like a father. I never made a move without asking and receiving his advice. It was always the right advice, too." Frank Thomas had coached Alabama through fifteen seasons with a winning percentage record of .812 in which Bama outscored her opponents 3,408 to 921. But a new and unsettling era was about to descend on the Crimson Tide.

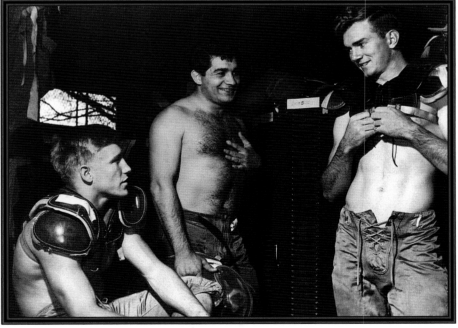

Chapter Four

TRIBULATION

1947 ~ 1957

TENNESSEE vs ALABAMA

OFFICIAL PROGRAM • THIRTY-FIVE CENTS

SHIELDS-WATKINS FIELD • OCTOBER 15 • 1948

Above: *Bama lost it, 21-6.* **Opposite page:** *Quarterback Bart Starr, one of the bright lights of the Red Drew era, went on to an exceptional professional career as quarterback and later head coach of the Green Bay Packers. He was the MVP of the first two Super Bowls.*

 O MANY, THOMAS SEEMED almost irreplaceable, but the game had to go on. Thomas was still athletics director and had a major say in who would succeed him. The man he chose was Harold "Red" Drew, who had served as his assistant coach for fourteen years before becoming head coach at Ole Miss. Drew was a big, florid, affable native of Maine. Though he produced some good teams in those years and his overall record of 54-28-7 was a winning one, it was still considered mediocre by Bama fans accustomed not just to winning games but winning championships. One of Drew's teams in fact did present an SEC championship to Alabama in 1953, but they somehow did it with a 6-3-3 season. Worse, in 1951 the Tide concluded its first losing year in nearly half a century.

When Drew took over for the season of '47 his team was filled with war veterans—plus the beloved returning War Babies such as Harry Gilmer and Vaughn Mancha, who were now in their senior year. Alabama started off slow. After beating Mississippi Southern it was upset by both Tulane and Vanderbilt. But in the fourth game the Tide came alive. First it beat Duquesne 26-0 in a newly enlarged Denny Stadium designed to seat thirty-one thousand. After that, Bama rolled over all her regular season opponents including Tennessee, Georgia, Georgia Tech, LSU, Kentucky, and Miami. The Sugar Bowl beckoned and on New Year's Day, 1948, Alabama met Texas in New Orleans.

It was billed to be a sensational aerial contest between Harry Gilmer, then the best passer in the nation, and the fabulous Bobby Layne of Texas. As it turned out this assessment was only half correct. Layne dominated play while Gilmer had his worst game ever, completing only three of eleven passes and rushing for a total of five yards on nine carries. Texas won 27-7.

With Gilmer gone, Drew junked Thomas's Notre Dame Box, installed a split-T formation and built his game in 1948 around Ed Salem, a sophomore quarterback from Birmingham. Salem had gotten a taste of what it meant to play for Bama as a scrub freshman in the locker room at halftime of the

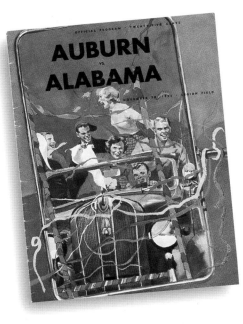

Georgia game, when first-string tackle Charley Compton ordered him to go find some pliers. Salem figured Compton wanted to use them to fix his cleats, but when he gave Compton the pliers the big lineman used them instead to pull out a tooth he'd broken in the second quarter.

It was a so-so season for Drew. The Tide got upset by Tulane in the opening game, then tied with Vandy, but, as in the previous year, in the third contest it whipped Duquesne 48-6. People thought this would signal a replay of '47 but they were wrong. Bama proceeded to lose to Tennessee, Georgia, and LSU, though managing to beat Florida, Mississippi Southern, and Georgia Tech.

But something new was impending that year which could now make or break an Alabama season no matter how it had played the rest of the time.

Auburn.

Finally, after more than forty years, the rivalry was resumed and on a crisp December afternoon in Birmingham the Crimson Tide met the Auburn Tigers on Legion Field. Ed Salem was the star of the game. Before a frantic

Above: *Bama won it, 10-7. In 1948, the Alabama-Auburn series was resumed and the cross-state arch rivals met for the first time since their 1907 game.* **Right:** *With Coach Thomas gone the duties now fell to Harold "Red" Drew, who had been his assistant. Drew coached the Tide for eight years with mostly winning seasons, but just barely. Even though in 1952 he took the team to the Orange Bowl and beat Syracuse 61-6, when Bama failed to rise beyond a 4-5-2 season in 1954, Drew was gone. Always jovial, his parting words were: "They said my teams were too slow, so they made me the track coach."*

Above: *Coach Drew getting a victory ride early in his tenure.* **Left:** *Legion Field on a cold wet afternoon in 1948.*

Bama crowd and a mob of horrified Auburnites he passed for three touchdowns, ran another in himself, and kicked seven extra points, leading the Tide to a 55-0 victory. It wasn't a perfect season, but that made it good enough.

The year 1949 found Alabama gnashing its teeth. The Tide lost the first two games to Tulane and Vanderbilt before its ritual bashing of unfortunate Duquesne. Bama then went on to tie Tennessee and beat in succession Mississippi State, Georgia, Georgia Tech, Mississippi Southern, and Florida. The team was 6-2-1 going into the contest with Auburn and a win would have made the season tolerable. It wasn't to be. The Tigers had won only a single game that year, but on December third they roared into Legion Field looking for revenge and got it. An intercepted Ed Salem pass became an Auburn touchdown. When Alabama evened it up Auburn answered with another touchdown. Late in the final quarter Bama scored again but Salem missed the vital extra point. Delirious Auburn fans watched in legitimate and unconcealed satisfaction as the clock ran out with Auburn ahead 14-13.

The new decade of 1950 began with Alabama losing but two games—Vanderbilt and the University of Tennessee. The Tide backfield was huge for those times, averaging well over two hundred pounds. Center Pat O'Sullivan remembered the team practiced eleven months a year back then, before the NCAA rules changed. In one-hundred-degree heat, they went at it twice a day; the team would turn over a couple of hundred freshmen each year, O'Sullivan recalled, "who just couldn't handle that."

Bama outscored its opponents 328 to 107 that season with Ed Salem accounting for more than twelve hundred yards of total offense and being selected All-American. In addition, Salem, guard Mike Mizerany, and O'Sullivan made All-SEC. But the 9-2 Tide received no bowl bid that year, a bitter and unfair pill to swallow. A 34-0 victory over Auburn made it bearable, and there was another bright light on the horizon too: a sophomore halfback named Bobby Marlow broke all previous rushing records for a single season with 882 yards. In the 54-19 drubbing of Georgia Tech, Marlow had scored three touchdowns in the first four minutes of the game.

~

RED DREW, O'SULLIVAN RECOLLECTED, WAS A GREAT coach, but not a great motivator. "He'd tell us some stories about his past football career and other teams he had coached, but he never fired us up like you think of a football coach firing up his team." In the following year, 1951, Drew's stock began to sink as he recorded Alabama's first losing season since 1903. Still outscoring her opponents 263-188, Bama went an unsatisfactory 5-6, brightened only by Marlow's continued domination of the rushing game and a 25-7 thrashing of Auburn on December 2.

The 1952 season was shaping up to be a good one. With Bobby Marlow and Bobby Luna in the backfield, Bama won the first four games but then lost miserably to Tennessee in Knoxville, 20-0. Alabama then proceeded to win its next three games before losing a heartbreaker to unbeaten Georgia Tech 7-3, costing Bama the SEC championship. The Tide rebounded to whip powerful Maryland with a stunning 27-7 victory, as well as Auburn, for a 9-2 regular season. This time it was the Orange Bowl that came calling.

On New Year's Day, 1953, the Crimson Tide took on the University of Syracuse, eastern champions, before sixty thousand fans in Miami. It was the most lopsided game in post-season bowl history. The team was excited

Top: *Homecoming queen Sue Donegan riding "Alamite," a predecessor of Big Al. The live elephants were popular until 1950 when it was decided they were too expensive.* **Above:** *Sometimes the elephants were painted crimson and white.*

SPORTS GAY-ZING AT THE CRIMSON WHITE

~

Gay Talese

T WAS MY GOOD FORTUNE IN THE fall of 1951, in my junior year at The University of Alabama, to have been elected the sports editor of the campus weekly newspaper, the *Crimson White,* which allowed me to elect myself as its columnist—a column I called "Sports Gay-zing." My column, which was inspired almost to the point of plagiarism by the bittersweet romanticism of Irwin Shaw's short stories in the *New Yorker* and by Red Smith's lyrical musings on athleticism in the *New York Herald-Tribune,* was nonetheless hailed for its originality by my readers and encouraged me to maintain an attitude of tolerance and munificence in all that I wrote about Alabama's athletic program, and most particularly its 1951 football team—which was perhaps the least successful squad that the University had assembled in nearly a half century.

It had opened the season with a rout of Delta State, but the latter's sports editor pointed out that Alabama had more football scholarship students than Delta State had students. Furthermore, it dropped the next four games in a row and the Alabama alumni and most of its younger fans called for the dismissal of Bama's head coach Harold "Red" Drew and his line coach, Henry "Hank" Crisp.

But in my column I advocated patience and forbearance, not failing to mention that Coach Drew had fallen far enough already in the national interest: he had jumped two thousand feet out of blimps into the Caribbean Sea on many occasions as a naval parachutist stationed in the Panama Canal Zone during the war. I further hinted that throughout the 1951 season Drew's team had been destabilized by such non-football factors as the faculty's decision to fail out of school the talented and indispens-

able Ken MacAfee just because he regularly cut classes and never made passing grades! In the glorious days of the permissive past, I reminded my readers, a star tackle had been able to boast upon graduating from Alabama that he "never went to the library once in my four years of school, and I never even knew where the library was!"

Perhaps as much dignity as could be salvaged by a team with a 5-6 losing season *had* been salvaged when Alabama defeated its despised interstate rival, Auburn, in the final game, 25-7, highlighted by a three-touchdown effort by a Troy, Alabama, native named Bobby Marlow. With Marlow due to return the following season, and with Coach Drew promising drastic reforms in the sexual as well as athletic inclinations of his entire squad (all players would hereafter be banned from dating and/or marrying and participating in panty raids), it was expected that the more erotically deprived 1952 football team would vent its frustrations upon its opponents by hitting them harder, by thoroughly overwhelming them with Spartan resolve, and would ultimately produce the desired result—a winning record.

I myself had doubts that Coach Drew's policies against hedonism would succeed, but in any case, as I planned my sports coverage and resumed my "Sports Gay-zing" column the next season, I tried *not* to allow the fate of the football team to totally dominate the purpose of my sports pages. I thus began publishing several items about golf, tennis, wrestling, sorority volleyball, and various human interest features that revealed athletes in most unfamiliar circumstances: such as when a senior end named Harold Manley attended summer school and made the Dean's List.

But the fact that Coach Drew's 1952 team crushed its first four opponents quickly altered my attitude and

Gay Talese, lower right, pictured in the early 1950s with fellow Crimson White *editors.*

expanded the coverage I gave to football; and even though the footballers would lose to Tennessee and Georgia Tech, they nonetheless beat everyone else to finish with a 9-2 mark that culminated in a 61-6 destruction of Syracuse in the Orange Bowl.

After my graduation a decade passed before I returned to the University campus and so I missed Joe Namath's heyday as the great quarterback. But I did have a chance meeting with him in the lobby of the old Stafford Hotel in Tuscaloosa in May of 1965 when—as a *New York Times* reporter—I had been assigned to visit the campus to interview Alabama's first black graduate, Ms. Vivian Malone. After I had filed my story I headed toward the hotel bar and was greeted along the way by an old friend, Mike Bite, who during my student days had been the manager of the football team. Now he was an attorney and standing next to him was his client, the new $400,000 rookie prospect with the professional New York Jets, Joe Namath, together with the team's head coach, Weeb Ewbank.

Mike Bite boasted that I was a wise and worldly figure from the Big Apple who might later serve as a useful avuncular figure to his star client when the latter made his permanent residence there.

"Well, I might be able to help Joe find a nice apartment in Manhattan," I began, but Coach Ewbank immediately interrupted: "No, no, it would be better if he lived in Queens, right near the stadium."

Namath lowered his blue eyes, and began to shake his head slowly as if one of his perfectly thrown passes had been dropped by a teammate.

"Joe might get a little lonely out there at night after football practice," I said, as Namath's expression brightened.

"No, no," insisted Ewbank, "he'll have plenty to do. He can watch films. Every player is entitled to a projector, and at night they can watch films."

"Aw, coach," Namath said, "suppose some night I have a date."

"She can watch films too," Ewbank said. "That's what our guys do with the girlfriends and wives—they watch films. I don't care where they put the projector."

Namath lowered his head again, but his lawyer Mike Bite rested his hand on his client's leg in a reassuring gesture, and then turning to Ewbank he said, "Oh, don't worry, coach, Joe wants to win. Isn't that right, Joe, you want to win?"

"Right," said Joe. "And I'm going to win, but I don't know about living in Queens."

There was an awkward moment of silence. Then I changed the subject and asked Mike Bite if he were married.

"No," he said. "Maybe when I come up to Manhattan to see Joe you'll get me a date?"

"Sure," I said, "I'll get you a date."

"What about me?" Joe Namath asked.

"I'll fix you up, too," I said.

"Hell you will," said Coach Ewbank of the man who in the future would gain great fame on the football field and also a nighttime notoriety as Broadway Joe, "He'll always be too busy in Queens watching films."

Best-selling author Gay Talese was the first recipient of UA's annual Clarence Cason Writing Award.

to be in south Florida in the mid-winter and looking forward to spending time on the beach. Drew was not amenable to this, however, and according to former player and later Alabama athletics director Hootie Ingram, he practiced them all day long.

Drew's strategy paid off. Syracuse scored once, but after that it was all Alabama. The Tide led 21-6 at the half and as the fourth quarter wore down was ahead an astonishing 54-6. Bobby Marlow had broken his toe and was not supposed to play but begged Drew to put him in. Drew agreed—but for one play only, and he further gave instructions to the quarterback, a freshman named Bart Starr, not to involve Marlow in any action. Marlow, however, had other designs. He collared the young Starr in the huddle and told him to give him the ball. Starr did and Marlow raced for fourteen yards. In the last few seconds of the game Hootie Ingram took a punt on his own twenty

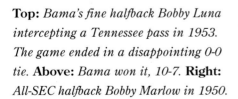

Top: *Bama's fine halfback Bobby Luna intercepting a Tennessee pass in 1953. The game ended in a disappointing 0-0 tie.* **Above:** *Bama won it, 10-7.* **Right:** *All-SEC halfback Bobby Marlow in 1950.*

Above: *End Jerry Lambert forcing a Virginia Tech fumble at homecoming, 1952—the season Drew took his team to the Orange Bowl. At right is Harry Lee, about to pounce on the ball.* **Left:** *Cecil "Hootie" Ingram, Bama's athletics director in the Stallings era, returning a Syracuse punt for a touchdown in the final moments of the 1953 Orange Bowl. When he came back to the sideline a coach congratulated him not only for the score but also, "because you are so slow, you ran out the clock!"*

and ran it back for a touchdown. When he came to the sidelines one coach congratulated him not only for the score but also for his speed—or lack thereof, saying, "Because you are so slow, you ran out the clock!" Alabama 61, Syracuse 6. Marlow, Ingram, and Jerry Watford made All-SEC that year.

The next year, 1953, looked even better for Coach Drew and the Crimson Tide but about the best that can be said for that season is that it was peculiar. First, Bama won the SEC championship despite losing to Mississippi Southern and Maryland and tying LSU, Tennessee, and Mississippi State. In the Auburn game the Tide narrowly averted another tie by kicking a late field goal to win 10-7. With this mediocre 6-2-3 season behind them, Bama received a bid to play in the Cotton Bowl, a game which became the most peculiar of that year—and maybe of all time.

Whatever else happened, and not much did on Alabama's part—Rice beat them 28-6—the Tide gained immediate national attention of an unwanted sort. In the second period, with Rice leading 7-6, Owls halfback Dickie Moegle broke straight through the Bama defense from his own five and raced down the sideline for an almost certain ninety-five-yard touchdown. As Moegle ran toward the Alabama bench, he looked back to see who was following him when suddenly he was flattened by a man who was not supposed to have been there at all. This man was Tide fullback Tommy Lewis, one of Bama's team captains, who had momentarily taken leave of his sanity. Standing bareheaded on the sideline in front of the bench, and watching Moegle approach, Lewis turned to halfback Corky Tharp and said, "He's going all the way!" to which Tharp replied, "He sure is, Lew." And then, as if seized by some Pavlovian reflex, Lewis suddenly dashed onto the field and unloaded on the unsuspecting Owl as he sped past.

Everybody in the stadium was dumbfounded. So were the millions in the television audience. Bart Starr, who had been one of those chasing Moegle, pulled up short and thought, "What is this?" Lewis quickly realized what he had done, went back to the bench, sat down, and hid his head under a towel. The crowd began to boo. The officials gathered to assess this unprecedented turn of events and awarded Rice a touchdown. It was one of the strangest things ever to happen in big-time football. At the half a mortified Lewis went to the Rice dressing room and apologized to Moegle and his whole team. He went back after the game and did it again. The Owls coach, Jess Neely, had this to say: "Son, you might as well get ready to live with it because it's going to be with you for the rest of your life."

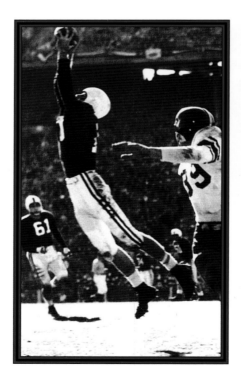

Left: *In 1954 the Tide went to the Cotton Bowl. Here, Bart Starr intercepts a pass by the Rice Owls, but Bama lost the game, 28-6.*

Drew didn't know what to think, but he let Lewis play out the rest of the game. Next day the *Dallas Morning News* ran a sympathetic editorial praising Lewis's competitive spirit, even suggesting that Rice fans "Drop him a line and let him know he hasn't lost his last friend." Not only that but the *Ed Sullivan Show* invited him on a couple of days later. Lewis reluctantly appeared, hoping he could demonstrate to the rest of the country "that I was not a total, absolute fool." He needn't have worried. People understood.

Bama's Tommy Lewis (42), in a purely instinctive reaction, comes off the sidelines to tackle Rice's Dickie Moegle, who was headed for a touchdown in the 1954 Cotton Bowl. Mortified, Lewis said later: "If I'd had time to think or plan this thing, I'd at least have had my headgear."

Not that it had anything to do with Tommy Lewis and his quaint notion of defense, but after that something seemed to deflate in the Crimson Tide. In 1954 Bama lost to Mississippi Southern, beat LSU, Vanderbilt, Tulsa, and Tennessee, and then didn't win any more games at all. With this miserable 4-5-2 season, including a 28-0 drubbing by Auburn, Red Drew resigned. A lot of it was beyond Drew's control. His team had been hit hard by injuries and recruiting had become more difficult with the arrival at Auburn of Shug Jordan. In any case, Drew was gone. Despite his misfortune in the football arena, Drew remained so popular on campus that he was persuaded to stay on in the athletic department. Drew wryly assessed it this way: "They said my football teams were too slow, so they made me the track coach."

~

THERE WERE ANY NUMBER OF CHOICES TO replace Red Drew. John Forney, then an unofficial fixture around the athletic department, recommended the young Mississippi State coach Darrell Royal. He was ignored. Bear Bryant's name came up. After serving as a naval officer in World War II, Bryant had coached at Maryland and Kentucky and was presently head coach at

Top: *Even though the Drew years did not produce teams of exceptional greatness, Bama fans were always enthusiastic, as seen here at Legion Field in 1948.* **Above:** *Cheerleaders entertaining the crowd.*

Texas A&M, where in his first year he went 1-9—his first and only losing season. These things might have accounted for Bryant's not being tapped for the job at Alabama, but there are other versions. Bryant said he was approached but since Drew had coached him back in the thirties he didn't want to become the one to replace him. Others thought that Bryant was reluctant to take the job because he worried about friction with the indomitable Hank Crisp, currently the athletics director. In any case, Bryant stayed at Texas A&M and the Board of Trustees athletic committee settled on former Tide player J. B. "Ears" Whitworth to lead the Crimson Tide out of its morass. Whitworth was a chunky, good-humored man, currently head coach at Oklahoma A&M. He had played guard alongside Fred Sington in the great Rose Bowl victory of 1931. Little did

Bama supporters suspect that their troubles had just begun.

Whitworth assumed control in a time of bitter confusion in the athletic department. Director Crisp allowed him to hire only two coaches, the rest being leftovers from Drew's and even Thomas's old staffs. Also, he was not the stern disciplinarian that his predecessors were. Players of the era remember that Whitworth's coaching methods ranged from lax to nonexistent. Practices were often chaotic. Whitworth had a fine quarterback in senior Bart Starr, who would go on to greatness with the Green Bay Packers, but Starr was benched much of the season with back injuries.

Worse, discipline problems were festering among the athletes. By this time the old "B.O. House" was gone, and Alabama players had a fine new facility named Friedman Hall after Hugo Friedman, an Alabama alumnus, former *Corolla* editor, and longtime benefactor of the University and the team. Unfortunately, Friedman Hall soon became known as the "Ape Dorm," inside which activities were being conducted that make the movie *Animal House* seem like a tea party. Players roamed around drinking, smoking, fighting, hazing, breaking windows, and ripping off doors and bathroom fixtures. Often fires were deliberately set. Some say gunshots could be heard. Most people gave the place a wide berth. Even outside the dorm, players occasionally attacked and intimidated fellow members of the student body. It had gotten out of control.

All of this, of course, showed up on Saturday afternoons. To the dismay of everyone, Whitworth's first season at Alabama was an unmitigated catastrophe. He ended 1955 without winning a single game—a relentless, tortured, 0-10 nightmare in which the vaunted Crimson Tide was outscored by her opponents 256-48. The only good thing that could be said of it was that there was no place else to go but up. If this was Whitworth's vision of "rebuilding," it did not bode well.

By the early 1950s, Alabama's football players were living in Friedman Hall, named after a longtime benefactor of the team, Hugo Friedman, pictured above.

Next year wasn't much better, though the Tide did manage to win two games. After losing the first four Bama squeaked a one-point victory over Mississippi State—the first win in twenty games. It also beat Tulane and tied Mississippi Southern before a humiliating 34-7 blowout by Auburn. Whitworth was clearly out of touch. Players remember him saying at practices, "This is the way we did it in Oklahoma."

Perhaps the lowest point was reached that year when the players literally revolted against authority. Whitworth and the athletic department had endeavored to impose some sort of discipline over the boorish behavior at

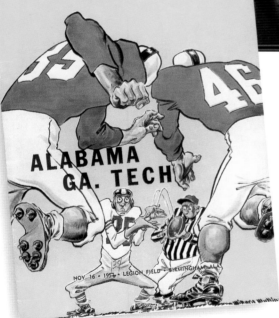

Top: *J. B. "Ears" Whitworth, whose record as Alabama coach was a miserable 4-24-2, is shown here in one of his few "victory rides."* **Above:** *Bama lost it, 10-7.*

Friedman Hall—mandatory curfews, study halls, sign-out rules, and so forth. In the spring 199 athletes—football, basketball, and track—moved out, saying they would live somewhere else unless their demands for a relaxation of the rules were met. Astonishingly, many demands were, the players moved back in, and the rude behavior continued into the 1960s.

Nineteen-fifty-seven was the final year of Whitworth's three-year contract. Any notion of a magical turnaround was quickly dispelled. The Tide was stomped by LSU, tied Vandy, then went on to lose to TCU, Tennessee, and Mississippi State at homecoming. During half-time of that game Johnny Mack Brown, now an aging movie star, returned to receive honors from his old school. Bama next managed a one-point win over Georgia before losing to Tulane and Georgia Tech. A happier note to the miserable season came in a 29-2 win over Mississippi Southern and, as an indication of just how pathetic things had become, Whitworth was triumphantly carried off the field by his players after this less than remarkable victory.

There was never a question of whether Whitworth must go—his overall record had sunk to 4-24-2—but of who would replace him. People had been talking about it openly since midway through the previous season, and most had their eyes on one man out in College Station, Texas: Paul "Bear" Bryant.

Bryant had indeed turned around the lowly Aggies of Texas A&M. Fans and players alike still remark on the legendary story of how he took his first team to his own special hellhole as fall practice began. This was an old army base in barren scrubland called Junction, Texas, 250 miles from A&M. And there he put them through the meat grinder. More than one hundred made the trip. At the end of ten days, twenty-nine remained, but Bryant had his team. After the lousy 1-9 season in 1954, A&M went 7-2-1 in 1955 and in 1956 was undefeated with a Southwestern Conference championship. By now he was looming huge in the eyes of Alabama supporters.

In 1957 Bryant's A&M, now the top-ranked team in the nation, was undefeated in eight games coming into the contest with Rice on November 17. Several days earlier a delegation from Alabama—including its incoming president Dr. Frank Rose, as well as Fred Sington, then president of the Alumni Association—had met in secret with Bryant in Houston and offered him the job of head coach and athletics director at the University. Bryant had reservations about what would become of his old friend Crisp but the veteran curmudgeon readily indicated he was willing to step aside. At the end of the afternoon Bryant had agreed to a ten-year contract at an annual salary of $17,000 plus a house. The way he later expressed his decision to leave the number-one team in the nation and return to Alabama was pure Bryant. "Mama called," was what he said. When they left the room, the "secret," naturally, had leaked out and the men were mobbed by the press. The day before the Rice game newspapers reported Bryant was leaving A&M to go to Bama, and Bryant blamed his 7-6 loss to the Owls, which cost him the national title, on the furor and consternation created by this revelation.

Nevertheless, even before his Texas Aggies played Tennessee in the Gator Bowl, Bryant flew to Tuscaloosa and addressed the expectant faces of what would be his team of 1958. In his now famous speech Bryant told them straight out what to expect: previous seasons were now behind them forever. Total commitment was required. They had to make their grades, make their beds, write their mamas, and say their prayers. He would provide them with everything else first class—from room and board to uniforms and modes of travel to coaching. But they had to *perform* first class or they were out.

"I don't know any of you and I don't want to know you," he told them. "I'll know who I want to know after spring training." Then he turned and walked out.

Thus, a new sun rose upon the most exhilarating chapter so far in the history of Alabama football. People had expected a Moses to lead the Crimson Tide out of the wilderness. What they got instead was God.

Quarterback Bobby Jackson shows his disappointment in the final moments of Alabama's 14-8 loss to Auburn in 1958. But a bright new era of Crimson Tide football had begun, and Bama would not lose to the Tigers again until 1963.

RESURRECTION

1958 ~ 1969

A NYBODY WITH A BRAIN COULD FIGURE what was coming next and for those who couldn't, spring training set them straight. Fans rejoiced to be rid of Whitworth, but the older players had adored him and were skeptical of Bryant's fierce reputation. Later though, one of them summed it up this way: "I thought we had a good organization at the time, but after seeing coach Bryant's, I realized we didn't have a very good organization."

Bryant inherited some good players from the Whitworth years: quarterback Bobby Jackson, fullback Gary O'Steen, halfback Marlin "Scooter" Dyess, fullback Red Stickney, guard Don Cochran, tackle Fred Sington, Jr., halfback Duff Morrison, and end Norbie Ronsonet. Bryant also had a freshman class that would soon become legendary—Bill Battle, Tommy Brooker, Billy Neighbors, Charlie Pell, Jimmy Sharpe, Pat Trammell, and Richard Williamson among others.

Bryant's spring practice was a replay of his notorious training ordeal at Junction, Texas. Twenty-two veteran players quit the squad that spring, and during the fall pre-season another sixteen bit the dust. "My plan was to bleed 'em and gut 'em because I didn't want any well-wishers hanging around," was the way Bryant put it later. (It was during this time he put up the first of his famous coaching towers at Thomas Field. It was a simple wooden affair, nothing like the Eiffel Towerish thing he would erect some years later.) Toward the end of an especially grueling scrimmage somebody remembered a guard on the team saying he was going to quit. Everybody in the huddle told him not to, but on the next play instead of running his assignment he ran straight for the gate at the big chain link fence, which Bryant kept locked. Desperate, the guard scrambled up and over and was gone. Shaking his head at the spectacle, Bryant announced that if there was anyone else who wanted to leave, just come tell him and he'd unlock the gate.

The Tide opened the 1958 season against LSU in Mobile. The Bengal Tigers that year were a powerhouse led by Heisman Trophy winner Billy

Above: *A Bama cheerleader jumps for joy in 1958.* **Opposite page:** *Victory ride for Coach Paul W. "Bear" Bryant after the Tide beat Auburn in 1960. It was the second win in a row, after five consecutive losses.*

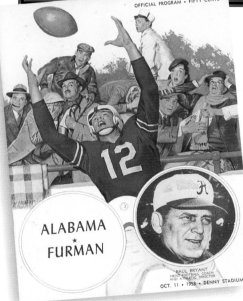

Top: *Bama's first offensive play for Coach Bryant. Halfback Mack Wise picks up five yards against LSU in a night game in Mobile. The Tide lost it 13-3 against one of LSU's championship teams, but Bryant told them afterward he was proud of them.* **Above:** *Bama won it, 29-6. This was the first time Coach Bryant appeared on a program cover.*

Cannon and would go on to win the national championship. Nobody gave Bama much of a chance but at halftime it was Alabama 3, LSU 0. The Tigers went on to take it 13-3 but something mystical had happened in that game. Bryant had instilled in his team the key ingredient of his magic potion, pride, and the players found an inner confidence they had not known before. By now everyone on the team was certain Bryant was going to deliver them from their ignominy.

He also pulled other tricks out of his bag. One was reintroducing the quick kick to the modern game. The offensive unit was the weakest point in Bryant's array, and he relished the notion of setting an opponent far back in his own territory when he least expected it, then pressuring him to make a mistake. Doubtless he divined this tactic from his own playing days under Thomas twenty years earlier. Also Bryant had a knack for taking small, strong, backfield players and making linemen out of them—such as 179-pound Charlie Pell, who became an outstanding tackle. This gave the team the speed, quickness, and agility to throw the opposition off balance.

Bryant in his first season wound up 5-4-1, losing to LSU, Tennessee, Tulane, and Auburn, but those losses were all close games and the Tide now outscored her opponents 106-75—the fewest points allowed by an Alabama team since 1939. It wasn't great but at least they were winning again. This was what Bryant and everyone else wanted to see.

Next year, 1959, Bryant's turnabout shifted into higher gear. With a 7-2-2 season the Tide held its opponents to a measly fifty-nine points, reminiscent of Coach Thomas's great defensive teams of the 1930s. Sophomores such as Trammell, Neighbors, and Brooker were now bearing the brunt of the action. Bama tied Tennessee that fall—breaking, at least temporarily, the disgusting habit of getting beat by the Vols—and to cap it off the Tide also whipped Auburn 10-0.

Now for the first time in seven years the bowls were again interested. On December 19 Alabama met Penn State in a bitterly cold Liberty Bowl in Philadelphia. Defense, as Bryant had planned, was the order of the day but the Nittany Lions scored a touchdown in the first half on a fake field goal and that was all the scoring there was. Bryant was livid and so to begin the second half he benched all the first-stringers and replaced them with subs. Later he reinstated the starters but it didn't do any good. The Nittany Lions' defense was as good as Alabama's, led by Chuck Jenarette, the first black player Alabama had ever faced. It wound up Penn State 7, Bama 0.

As the decade turned, the 1960 Crimson Tide seemed poised to go all the way but a shocking 6-6 tie with Tulane and an appalling 20-7 drubbing by Tennessee foreclosed that possibility. Nonetheless, this was a team that had found itself. People still talk about the comeback Bama made against Georgia Tech that year. Playing on Grant Field in Atlanta, Alabama found itself behind 15-0 to the Yellow Jackets at halftime. When Bryant came into

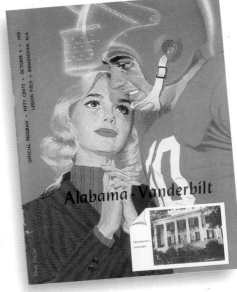

the locker room, all uneagerly anticipated one of his scathing tirades. Instead the coach was all smiles, slapping players on the back and telling them it was great. "Now we have them right where we want them!" he would say. "They'll see what we've got in us!"

It worked. In the fourth period Trammell connected on a pass deep in Tech's territory and fullback Leon Fuller carried in for the score. Then Trammell hurt his knee and was replaced by Bobby Skelton who marched them down the field—despite having to face four fourth downs—finally tossing to end Ronsonet for a touchdown. With just minutes to go Bama was still behind two points when Skelton marched them downfield again, completing a pass to Butch Wilson at the Tech six-yard line. There was just time for a field goal, and Richard "Digger" O'Dell stepped in for an injured Tommy Brooker to boot a cliffhanging wobbler that hit the crossbar and tumbled over for the goal. They had won it in the last three seconds with an amazing display of courage and fortitude. Coach Bryant was greatly pleased.

Unfortunately for Digger O'Dell, when the team returned to Tuscaloosa that night an enthusiastic crowd was waiting, but not for him. It seems the radio broadcaster had announced it was Brooker who had kicked the winning goal and O'Dell was all but ignored.

Top: *A 0-0 tie.* **Above:** *Big grins after a big win. Left to right: Darwin Holt, Pat Trammell, Billy Rice, and Billy Neighbors.*

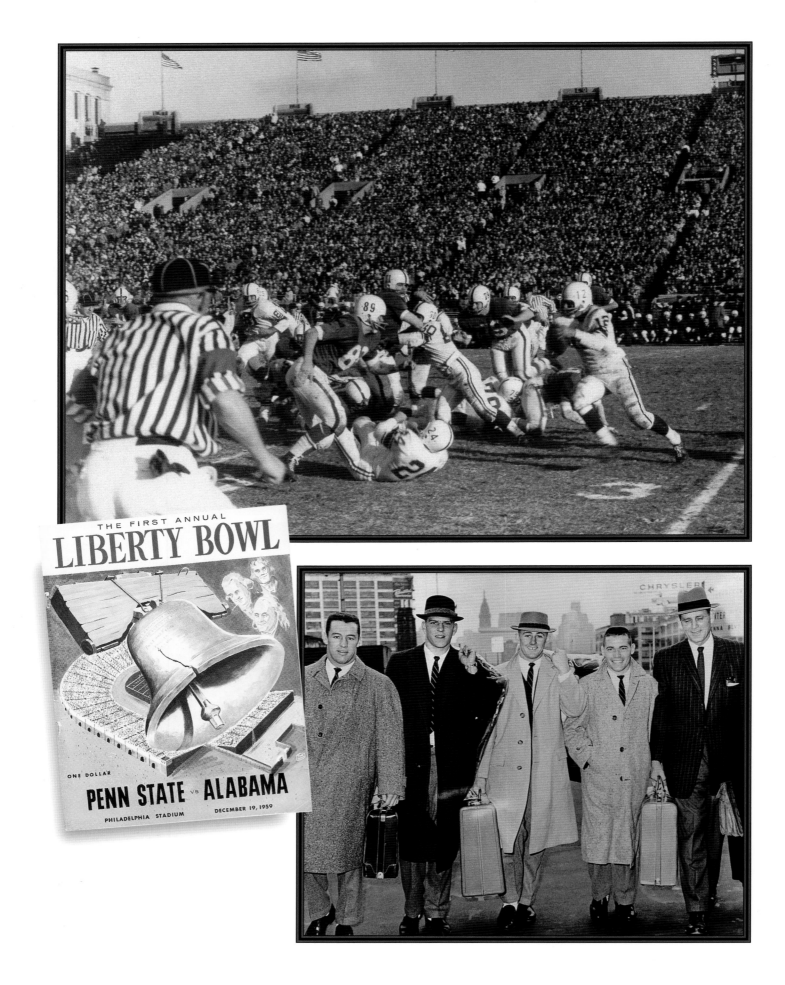

The Bluebonnet Bowl came calling that year and Bama went out to meet the University of Texas. In a game marked by questionable officiating, the score ended in an unsatisfying 3-3 tie.

But now Bryant was prepared to fulfill the pledge he had made to the team three years earlier—that if they did as he counseled, they would win the national championship. And this they did spectacularly in 1961 with a perfect 11-0 season. Alabama fell on its opponents one by one like a pack of beasts, but they were the sort of beasts Bear Bryant had trained them to be: strong, fast, sleek, agile, cunning, and most of all audacious. Almost everybody was back: Bill Battle, Tommy Brooker, Cotton Clark, Mike Fracchia, Lee Roy Jordan, Billy Neighbors, and Pat Trammell. Nobody even came near to beating them and the Tide held the opposition to a mere twenty-five points during the whole season.

Opposite page, above and below left: *The 1959 Liberty Bowl against Penn State was Bear Bryant's first bowl game as head coach for Bama. The Tide lost it, 7-0, but better times lay ahead.* **Opposite page, below right:** *In Philadelphia for the Liberty Bowl, left to right: Gary Phillips, Pat Trammell, Bobby Skelton, Marlin Dyess, and Bryant.* **Below:** *Bama's national championship team of 1961 in huddle against Mississippi State at Denny Stadium. Bama won it, 24-0.*

The only blemish stemmed from an incident late in the season during the Georgia Tech game when Bama linebacker Darwin Holt hit Tech quarterback Emile "Chick" Granning with an elbow that fractured his jaw. Some thought it was a late hit and a cheap shot but Holt wasn't penalized—even though a referee was standing right there watching the whole thing. Next day the Atlanta papers screamed bloody murder about dirty football being sanctioned at Alabama. The uproar festered until it erupted into a full-fledged scandal a year later.

Meantime all sorts of awards and honors were heaped upon Alabama, including the national and SEC championships. Bryant was named National Coach of the Year. Lee Roy Jordan, Billy Neighbors, and Pat Trammell were All-Americans and All-SEC, and Mike Fracchia made All-SEC as well. Bama received a bid from the Sugar Bowl to play Arkansas, which the Tide beat 10-3. Mike Fracchia won the Outstanding Player award. Soon afterward, Denny Stadium was again enlarged to seat forty-three thousand. It didn't get any better than this.

Above: *Coach Bryant with quarterback Pat Trammell at homecoming 1961; Bama beat Mississippi State 24-0.* **Right:** *The Tide nails a Tennessee receiver in 1961 in a 34-3 victory over the Vols.*

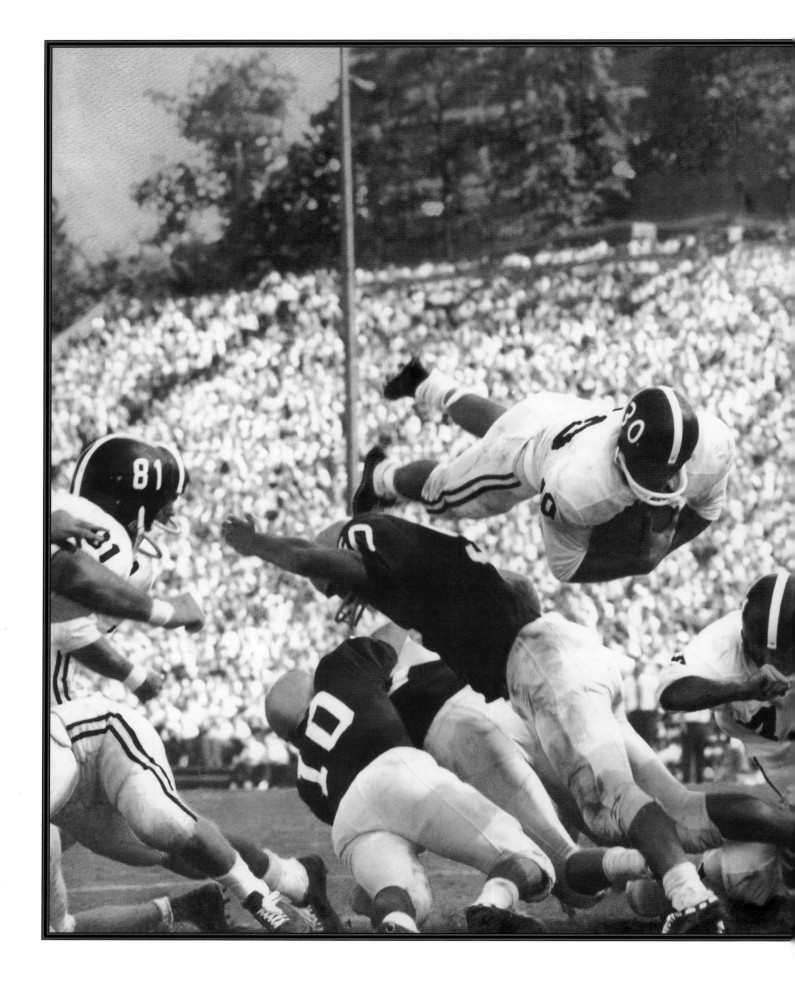

Left: *Mike Fracchia employing his special airborne tactics to score against Georgia in a 32-6 Bama victory.*
Above: *All-American quarterback Pat Trammell, who captained the '61 championship team. When he died of cancer seven years later, Bryant said, "This is the saddest day of my life."*

Above: *Bama halfback Butch Wilson eluding a flying Razorback in the 1962 Sugar Bowl. Bama won it, 10-3.* **Right:** *Royalty at the '62 Sugar Bowl. Left, Miss Arkansas; center, Delores Howard, Miss Alabama; right, the Sugar Bowl Queen.* **Opposite page, above:** *Bama's great placekicker Tim Davis puts one through in the '62 Sugar Bowl (right), while in the stands a high school band member tries to make the catch (left).* **Opposite page, below:** *On December 6, 1961, President John F. Kennedy attended the Hall of Fame dinner in New York City to honor Alabama's national championship team.*

BAMA WON ALL ITS GAMES IN 1962 EXCEPT FOR a bitter 7-6 loss to the Georgia Tech Yellow Jackets, who were still smarting from the Holt-Granning incident the previous year. A month before the game the *Saturday Evening Post* published an article by *Atlanta Constitution* sportswriter Furman Bisher claiming that "College Football Is Going Berserk." Of course the Holt-Granning affair was the centerpiece of the story and the magazine went on to imply that Bryant was responsible for foul and dirty play by The University of Alabama. Stung by these imputations on his integrity, Bryant sued for libel but the real storm was yet to burst.

Meantime, the fabulous Pat Trammell was graduated, but Bryant had another actor waiting in the wings. He was a shy sophomore from Beaver Falls, Pennsylvania, named Joe Namath. Also gone were such stalwarts as Billy Neighbors, Tommy Brooker, and a host of others, including workhorse fullback Mike Fracchia, who was out with injuries. Nevertheless, behind Namath's staggering aerial performances, backed by the play of halfbacks Cotton Clark and Benny Nelson, center Gaylon McCollough, and linebacker Lee Roy Jordan, Bama continued to rack up victories. The Tide finished a 10-1 season by demolishing Oklahoma 17-0 in the Orange Bowl. Lee Roy Jordan, of Excel, Alabama, chalked up thirty-one tackles that day, was a unanimous All-American and All-SEC, and went on to become one of the most dazzling linebackers in pro football history. Before the game, Bryant had remarked of his team, "They play like it is a sin to give up a point."

Top and Above: *Bama fans are loyal come rain . . . or come shine.* **Opposite page, above:** *All-American linebacker Lee Roy Jordan. Bryant said of him: "If they stay inside the sidelines, Lee Roy will get them."* **Opposite page, below:** *Joe Namath could throw . . . Orange Bowl, 1963: Bama 17, Oklahoma 0.*

President Kennedy was in the stands that day but visited only Oklahoma's dressing room, not Alabama's, which many took as a snub associated with the strained relations between the state and the Kennedy administration over integration. It is possible that Kennedy was merely paying his respects to Oklahoma coach Bud Wilkinson, who was on his Physical Fitness Council, but nevertheless it rankled.

That spring the *Saturday Evening Post* went after Bama again, big time. In a story that stunned the nation, the *Post* accused Bear Bryant and Georgia athletics director Wally Butts of conspiring to fix the Alabama-Georgia game (which Bama had won 35-0!), presumably so they could bet on it. The story was based on a report by a crackpot who claimed his phone line had somehow got plugged into a long-distance conversation between Bryant and Butts and that he had overheard the two planning the alleged conspiracy. The piece also intimated Bryant had thrown the controversial 7-6 loss to Georgia Tech in 1961. Bryant and Butts were furious and each sued the *Saturday Evening Post*'s parent company, Curtis Publishing. Five months later a court awarded Butts $460,000 in libel damages and a few months later Curtis Publishing settled with Bryant for $300,000. Though publicly vindicated by the settlement and a retraction from the publisher, Bryant never quite got over this shabby treatment in the national media.

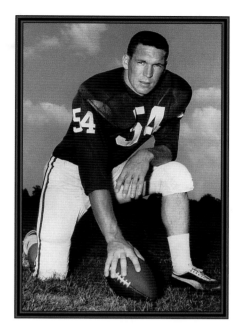

In 1963 Alabama lost only two games: Florida by four points and Auburn by two. Lee Roy Jordan and many other starters were gone now, but Namath was back, as well as Mike Fracchia, Benny Nelson, and kicker Tim Davis. Losing to Auburn was bad enough, but Alabama had two more games to play that year and they were to play them without the services of Namath.

After Auburn, Bama played a makeup game against Miami that had been postponed for national television because of the assassination of President Kennedy. Also, the Tide was invited to meet Ole Miss in the Sugar Bowl. But Namath got caught drinking beer and Bryant kicked him out of the athletic dorm and suspended him "for as long as it takes." Some moaned that this was a stupid thing to do, but it wasn't. Discipline had gotten Bryant's teams where they were and he wasn't about to play favorites. Here, as much as anyplace else, he displayed the qualities of courage and determination that won him his name and fame. In any case, with his star player on the sidelines, Bryant started second-string Jack Hurlbut against Miami's celebrated quarterback George Mira, known as the "Matador." Bama went into the second half with a comfortable 17-0 lead but Mira hustled the Hurricanes back to within five points. Then the Tide dug in—or, in Bryant's lingo, "sucked it up"—and won 17-12.

Bama's esteemed placekicker Tim Davis remembers someone telling him Bryant had remarked just before the Sugar Bowl, "We've got about as much

Above: *"Shorty" Price, a perennial candidate for governor, was a fixture at Bama football games for decades in the 1950s, '60s, and '70s. He was often ejected before halftime for violating the school's prohibition against alcohol in the stadium.* **Right:** *Cheerleaders in front of Denny Chimes, ca. 1962.*

chance of winning down here as it has of snowing." Next day, three inches of snow fell on New Orleans, coating the palm, citrus, and banana trees all over town. The astonished Crimson Tiders arrived at Tulane Stadium to find a big snowman grinning at them from the lawn. Namath was still in the doghouse and Bryant started sophomore Steve Sloan against Ole Miss. There was still snow piled on the sidelines and end zones, and fans pelted each other with snowballs waiting for the game to begin. During halftime, fans in the upper deck collected a huge mound of snow, fashioned it into a boulder-size snowball, and rolled it off onto the stands below. The writer of this book can testify about that because much of it landed on him and his date.

It was an extraordinary contest. Mississippi scored one touchdown and Bama scored none. But a spectacular performance by Tim Davis saved the day; he booted goals of 31, 46, 22, and 48 yards—the last a bowl record—to win it for the Tide 12-7. After the game Namath was observed buttonholing fans at the exit and leading them in shouts of "Roll Tide!" Tim Davis, now a doctor in Birmingham, had kicked the most field goals in Sugar Bowl history and was named Outstanding Player of the game. Flashy running back Benny Nelson made All-SEC.

In the 1964 Sugar Bowl, played with snow piled in the end zones, kicker Tim Davis scored all the points in a 12-7 Bama victory over Ole Miss.

Next year, 1964, the Tide won the national championship again with a perfect 10-0 season and accomplished much of this on the now shaky knees of Joe Namath. Until this season Namath had been a spectacular running quarterback as well as a passing one. But in the fourth game against North Carolina State, after completing seven of eight passes, Namath rolled out and suddenly went down on the grass. He was helped off the field and returned to sit on the bench with his knee heavily bandaged. Steve Sloan came in to replace him and the Tide won 21-0, but Namath was enduring a player's worst nightmare.

Though Namath played when he was able, Sloan bore the brunt of the quarterbacking the rest of the season. But Namath was still dangerous as

Joe Namath levitates himself in 1964 before a worshipful North Carolina State player (right) as Bama won it, 21-0. But Namath sustained a knee injury in the game (above) that limited his playing time and style from then on.

Above: *Drum major Bill Fuqua and Miss Alabama Carol Self marching in the 1964 homecoming parade.* **Right:** *Bryant had his troubles with Georgia Tech in the early '60s. At the 1964 game in Atlanta, he wore a protective helmet onto the field.*

Above: *Homecoming bonfire in the 1960s.* **Left:** *Joe Namath shook hands with a lot of his receivers. Shown here, Ray Perkins during the '64 Auburn game.*

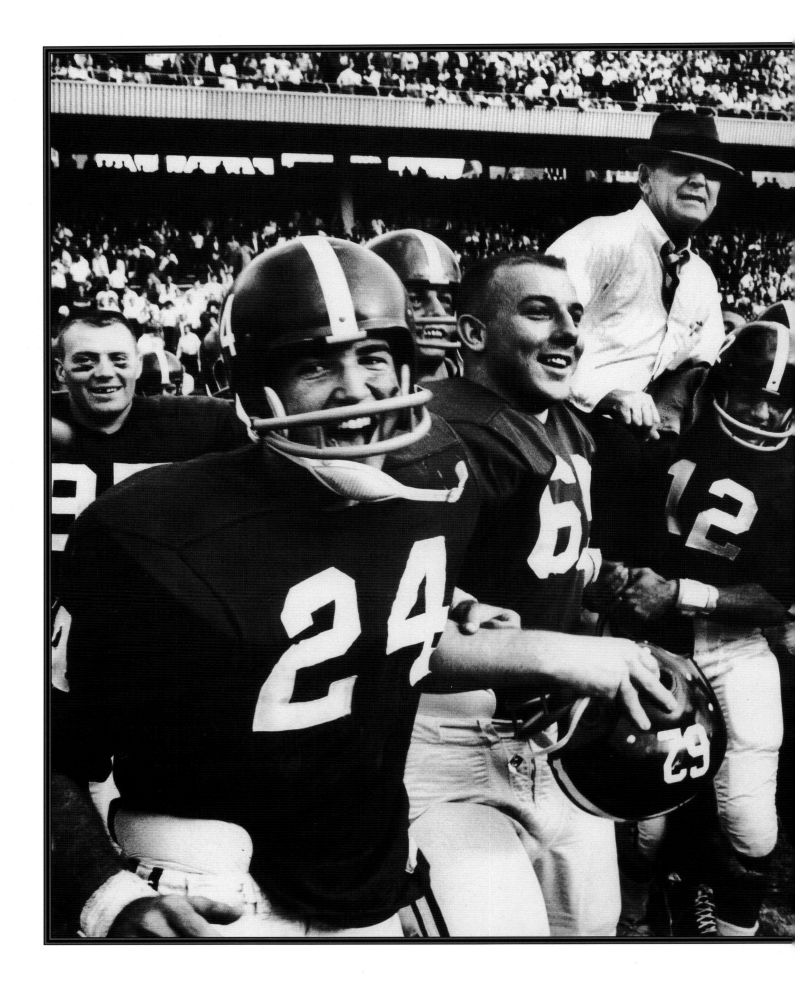

OFFICIAL PROGRAM
Fifty Cents

NCAA Member

MISSISSIPPI STATE / ALABAMA
MEMORIAL STADIUM — OCTOBER 31, 1964

Left: *Yet another Bryant victory ride in 1964—this one coming after the 24-7 win against Georgia Tech. The Tide won the national championship that year but lost to Texas 21-17 in the Orange Bowl.* **Above:** *Bama won it, 23-6.*

Thirty First Annual

orange bowl classic

ALABAMA vs. TEXAS
JANUARY 1, 1965

$1.00
Tax Included
ONE DOLLAR

In a game marked by questionable officiating, Bama lost to Texas 21-17 in the 1965 Orange Bowl. With the clock running out the Tide had the ball fourth and inches from the Texas goal when Joe Namath tried a sneak. It was ruled he had not crossed the goal, but afterward Namath said: "I'll go to my grave knowing I scored."

ever when he got into a game. In the next-to-last contest Alabama and Georgia Tech were locked in an acerbic 0-0 tie late in the second quarter. The stadium erupted when Namath shuffled onto the field and set up back in a pro pocket formation. When the period ended less than two minutes later, the Tide was ahead 14-0. Namath did the same in the 21-14 win over Auburn, throwing to Ray Perkins for a touchdown that cinched it for Bama. That game also saw the thrilling 108-yard touchdown run by Ray Ogden at the second-half opening kickoff.

Bama got a bid from the Orange Bowl to play Texas on New Year's in a night game marred by questionable officiating. By this time Sloan also was semi-hobbled by a knee injury and he and Namath saw duty when they could. Just before the half with Bama trailing 14-7, Texas called for a pass. As it developed, cornerback Mickey Andrews bumped into a Texas receiver and an official called interference. But when they looked back upfield the Texas passer was flat on his back with the ball still in his hands. Andrews protested that interference can't be called unless the ball is thrown, so the official (a Southwest Conference field judge) changed his mind and called holding instead. It gave Texas a first down deep in Bama territory. They scored and went into the half 21-7.

In the second half Namath came off the bench with some spectacular aerial fireworks that brought the Tide within four points of Texas. Then, as the closing seconds ticked off, Namath drove Bama to the Texas six, where fullback Steve Bowman bucked it down to the four, the two, and finally to the six-inch line, fourth down. Namath called a sneak and hit the line. Center Gaylon McCollough remembers, "Joe happened to be lying right on top of me. I was in the end zone and Joe was in the end zone too. We all jumped up and started celebrating." An official had already raised his hands indicating a touchdown. But to Alabama's dismay he was suddenly overruled by yet another referee from the Southwest Conference, who turned the ball over to Texas for the win.

Fullback Steve Bowman later said: "I didn't think I'd scored, but I'll always think Joe did." Namath put it even more strongly: "I'll go to my grave knowing I scored. I have a sick, infuriating feeling [about it]." Bryant, for his part, was more laconic. He was standing on the sidelines, arms folded, scowling, when a player passed by and said sourly, "We scored." Gaylon McCollough was there to overhear Bryant's reply: "If he'd walked into the end zone with the football, then there'd be no question about it, would there?" McCollough, now a physician in Birmingham, would never forget the remark. "I think the lesson taught by Coach Bryant was this: If you want to accomplish something in life, don't do just enough to get the job done, because the world's referees might not make the right call either."

In any case they could still take magnificent satisfaction in being national champions once again. Joe Willie Namath was selected Outstanding Player of the game and went on to become one of the greatest NFL players of all time. In addition to Namath, guard Wayne Freeman, tackle Dan Kearley, and halfback David Ray were accorded All-America honors. Each received All-SEC status too, as did fullback Steve Bowman.

～

IF THE '64 SEASON ENDED ON THE SOUR NOTE of dubious officiating, the bright and expectant year of 1965 began on one. Alabama lost only a single game that season, the first, to underdog Georgia, in one they're still talking about. In a nationally televised match, Bryant arrived in Athens with an impressive array of talent: Joe Namath was gone but Steve Sloan was back, as well as a young sophomore quarterback from Foley, Alabama, Kenny Stabler. The team also included such all-stars as Steve Bowman, Paul Crane, Jerry Duncan, Dennis Homan, Ray Perkins, and Jackie Sherrill.

The Georgia game was closer than most people thought it would be, but the Tide was leading 17-10 late in the fourth period. Then, with two minutes left to play, the unimaginable happened. Deep in their own territory the Bulldogs threw a pass to end Pat Hodgson who had to stretch for it, but then fell with his knees on the grass with the ball in his hands. At that point the whistle should have blown. But it didn't. Hodgson pitched a lateral to a Georgia halfback, who scampered sixty-four yards for a touchdown. Georgia converted for a two-pointer and won the game 18-17. The official ruling was that somehow Hodgson had "batted" the ball, not lateraled it.

The shouting had barely died down next day when stop-action film clearly showed that not only were Hodgson's knees firmly down on the turf but that *both* his hands were holding the ball—not "batting" it. But then, as now, there was no such thing as the instant replay in the college game. As usual, Bryant was taciturn about the whole business, growling to reporters, "You don't win games in the movies on Monday."

Bama cruised through Tulane, Mississippi, and Vanderbilt before encountering a tough Tennessee squad at Legion Field. In the Ole Miss game Bryant pulled a stunt that caused another uproar. With Bama behind he told Steve Sloan to call a trick tackle-eligible play in which Jerry Duncan set up

Lineman Jerry Duncan hauls in a "tackle-eligible" pass in Bama's '66 win over Mississippi State. Bryant employed the little-used rule to flummox many opponents until an incensed Johnny Vaught, coach at Ole Miss, managed to get the SEC Rules Committee to ban it.

Action in the 1966 Orange Bowl: Steve Sloan to Ray Perkins for the opening touchdown. Bama beat Nebraska, 39-28.

the Alabama go-ahead. It was the perfect ruse: an offensive lineman could become a ball carrier or receiver by lining up just behind the line of scrimmage. Though the play was perfectly legal at the time, the fuming Mississippi coach Johnny Vaught managed to get the SEC to outlaw the practice in future seasons.

Tennessee dueled Bama to a distressing 7-7 tie after Kenny Stabler, operating inside the Vols' twenty as time ran out, scrambled for an eternity on third down before racing to within feet of the Tennessee goal. The scoreboard was still showing third down. Stabler thought he had made enough yardage for the first, but in the excitement and confusion apparently failed to check the linesman's marker, which indicated it was now fourth down, and on the next play he immediately threw the ball out of bounds to stop the clock and get a kicker in. Thus, to the understandable shock and consternation of Alabama fans, the ball was turned over to the Volunteers who jubilantly ran out the clock.

They made no more mistakes that year, rolling over Florida State, Mississippi State, LSU, South Carolina, and Auburn for the SEC championship, and giving up only thirty-one points while scoring more than a hundred. Now it was bowl time, with the Crimson Tide ranked number four nationwide.

Some of the seniors wanted to go to the Cotton Bowl because they'd already been to the Sugar and the Orange but Bryant persuaded them otherwise. According to Bryant historian Keith Dunnavant, the coach proceeded to forecast for them a fantastic chain of outcomes in other bowls which, if all came true, would place Alabama number one in the country—if only they could whip Nebraska in the Orange Bowl.

And so it was.

Bama went to Miami 8-1-1, outweighed umpteen pounds per man, to meet the undefeated Cornhuskers of Nebraska. Here Bryant seemed to invoke the ghostly arts. By nature a conservative coach, he tossed away all his playbooks that night and eighty thousand fans watched The University of Alabama simply demolish the bewildered Huskers. Bryant opened up straight off with the soon-to-be-banned tackle-eligible play to Jerry Duncan. Sloan proceeded to throw everything but the kitchen sink. To everyone's amazement the Tide utilized a successful onside kick just before the half—and scored a field goal off it—to trot into the dressing room leading 24-7. The Huskers were completely flummoxed, reduced to foot-stamping and teethgnashing at the unorthodox razzle-dazzle Bryant was coming at them with. Second half, Nebraska opened with some offensive fireworks of its own, but there was no way they could catch up. Bama 39, Huskers 28—and another national championship. Steve Sloan shattered all Orange Bowl passing records and was the Outstanding Player of the game. Sloan and Paul Crane were selected All-Americans and Crane, Steve Bowman, Creed Gilmer, Bobby Johns, and Tommy Tolleson made All-SEC.

Players who had been under Bryant all four years agree Nebraska was his grandest strategic triumph and still marvel at his willingness to abandon so abruptly his own consecrated ball-playing theorems. Fact was, Bryant was becoming imbued with an almost divine aura. Not long after the game,

on a trip to Mobile, a woman at a dinner party poured a glass of water on the floor and asked Bryant if he would walk on it. Embarrassed, but wishing as a gentleman to accommodate, he did.

⁓

AS THE VIETNAM WAR BEGAN TO CRANK UP IN EARNEST, Bryant in 1966 assembled a team of remarkable perfection. Its backbone consisted of quarterback Kenny Stabler, receivers Ray Perkins and Dennis Homan, defensive back Bobby Johns, tackle Cecil Dowdy, guard John Calvert, halfback Dickey Thompson, and placekicker Steve Davis, who was Tim Davis's younger brother. According to many observers, it might have been Bama's best team ever and it was quartered now in yet another athletic dormitory. Bryant Hall off University Boulevard had been completed a few years earlier and was a splendid brick facility, with study halls and all the accoutrements to keep Alabama athletes comfortable. Architecturally it resembled one of the large houses that were presently being constructed on the new Fraternity Row, and Bryant, having his name on the place, took measures to ensure it did not fall into dilapidation the way Friedman Hall had.

From the beginning the players found a hard confederacy among themselves and did not lose a single game the entire season. As usual, the players were Bryant-style lean and mean. When they whipped LSU, Tigers coach Charlie McClendon remarked, "Those little guys are like lightning. It's the damndest thing I've ever seen." One of his assistants even refused to believe what he read on the Bama roster: "They'd *have* to weigh more than that!" he groused. The closest they came to a scare was an 11-10 edging out of Tennessee up in Knoxville that became one of the all-time classics. More miserable playing conditions would be hard to envision. Huge rainstorms swept the Vols field all afternoon so a passing game was virtually impossible. At halftime Tennessee was ahead 10-0 owing to a couple of Bama fumbles, and the players in the dressing room braced themselves for a chewing out. But now the great persuading personality stood at the summit of his mountain. As in the Georgia Tech game half a decade earlier, Bryant entered the locker room smiling, clapping players on the back, and singing "What a friend we have in Jesus." It was still 10-0 in the last quarter when Kenny Stabler not only managed to score but completed a two-point conversion to bring Bama within two points.

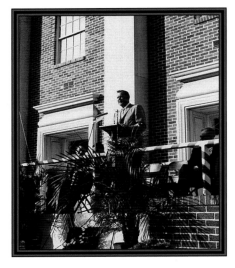

Top: *Right here's his footprint! Bryant argues with an official who called back a Bama touchdown in the '66 Clemson game. Bama won it anyway, 26-0.* **Above:** *Coach Bryant dedicates the athletic hall named in his honor in 1965.* **Opposite page:** *Kenny Stabler hunts a receiver in the 1966 Tennessee game. The Tide slipped by 11-10.* ·

Suddenly, as though by an act of providence, the rain stopped and Stabler marched the Crimson Tide downfield again with a brilliant series of passes. But with Bama inside their ten, the Vols stubbornly dug in. The contest reached critical mass with Alabama on the Tennessee one-foot line, fourth down. And it had begun raining again. Reliable Steve Davis was summoned for duty and Stabler told him, "If you've ever kicked one, kick it now." But the

pass from center was low. Davis remembers it this way: "The center snap came bounding back through the mud, almost with a wake behind it. Only a truly great athlete like Kenny Stabler could have fielded that ball and set it up for kicking." Davis's boot barely cleared the upright, but it did. Bama 11, Vols 10. However, Tennessee wasn't through yet, setting up a last-minute drive that put them on the Tide ten with seconds to go. Now it was the Vols' turn to retort with a game-winning field goal. A hush descended over the Tennessee stadium followed by a collective groan as Gary Wright's kick went wide. Afterward, an ecstatic Bryant crowed, "If he'd kicked it straight, we would have blocked it."

After this exhilaratingly close call, Bama breezed through its next six opponents, allowing a total of only 20 points while racking up 179 of its own, clinching the SEC championship as the only undefeated-untied team in the nation.

They went to the Sugar Bowl to meet up again with Nebraska and it was almost no contest. First play, Stabler unleashed a forty-five-yard pass to Perkins that set the stage for a 34-7 blistering of the Cornhuskers and left Alabama with a perfect 11-0 season. Richard Cole, Cecil Dowdy, Bobby Johns, and Ray Perkins made the All-America list. They also made All-SEC, along with John Calvert and Dickey Thompson. Denny Stadium was reconfigured to seat fifty-nine thousand fans.

The Tide should also have had a third straight national championship, but it was not to be. Before the bowl games Bama was ranked third behind Notre Dame and Michigan State, which had already played each other to a 10-10 tie. But the Associated Press and United Press International decided that year to make their number-one picks *before* the post-season games and so the undefeated, untied ranking champions for the past two years lost out to an arbitrary policy decision by wire service people. Bama fans didn't like it, but they knew who the real champions were.

Above: *All-American quarterback Kenny Stabler went on to a spectacular career in the NFL. Here he consults with Jerry Duncan in the '67 Sugar Bowl.* **Opposite page, above:** *Kenny Stabler eludes Cornhuskers in the Sugar Bowl.* **Opposite page, below:** *In 1967 Bama drubbed Nebraska 34-7 in the Sugar Bowl. In New Orleans Bryant has an animated conversation with three of his stars: Dennis Homan, Kenny Stabler, and Ray Perkins.*

∽

SOME IN ALABAMA SUSPECTED THE NATIONAL CHAMPIONSHIP POLLS that year might have been tilted against the Tide by unfavorable publicity earlier in the decade such as Governor George Wallace's infamous "Stand in the Schoolhouse Door," the fire hoses and biting police dogs of Birmingham police commissioner Eugene "Bull" Connor, the Rosa Parks bus incident in Montgomery, the Selma civil rights march, and other unfortunate symbols of the state that had been displayed in the national media.

There may have been some slight truth in this. First, there was the perceived snub by President Kennedy at the Orange Bowl. And earlier, before post-season bids went out to Bryant's great undefeated team of 1961, the Rose Bowl Committee let it be known they might reverse the policy of hosting only Pac-8—Big-10 schools. If so Bama was the natural and logical choice. But as Bryant historian Keith Dunnavant reports, news columns immediately began to appear in the West Coast press suggesting that an invitation to the Crimson Tide would be equivalent to inviting the Ku Klux Klan to play in the Rose Bowl. No invitation was ever issued.

For his part Bryant itched to get his hands on some of the black athletes presently leaving the state to star at schools in the East and Midwest. Again according to Dunnavant, Bryant would sometimes attend football games between black high schools in Birmingham and shake his head that these talented young men would not be playing for him. After the University was integrated in 1963 there were a handful of black walk-ons but they did not survive to play in the regular season. Neither did most white walk-ons, but while other southern colleges began actively recruiting black athletes, Bryant, for the time being, dutifully bowed to current policy and offered no scholarships to African-Americans. At the same time he quietly fretted at the notion that one day Alabama would be overtaken on the football field because of its discriminatory practices.

The '66 team went 11-0 and should have had the national championship after beating Nebraska in the Sugar Bowl. But that year the wire services decided to pick the champion before the bowl games and so the Tide went wanting. The cartoon here depicts Bama outrage.

AT ANY RATE THE TEAM LOOKED FORWARD TO THE 1967 season with every reason to think they could win another national championship. Kenny Stabler was back and so was Dennis Homan, the splendid receiver, All-American Bobby Johns, linebacker Mike Hall, and end Mike Ford. On paper it might have been one of the best defensive teams in Bama history but this turned out to be a mirage.

In the opener against Florida State the Seminoles mired the Tide in a 37-37 tie whereas the previous year Bama had only given up forty-four points for the entire season! Alabama went on to beat Southern Mississippi, Ole Miss, and Vanderbilt before falling to Tennessee 24-13. But the Tide ripped through the rest of its scheduled games, including a true nail-biter against Auburn on a miserable Legion Field that was churned into a sea of six-inch-deep mud. Players could barely stand up, let alone pass, and Bama was trailing 3-0 late in the fourth quarter when Kenny Stabler made what most acclaim as the most dramatic run of his college career. On a routine option, the "Snake" spotted an opportunity and literally slip-slided through the Tigers' defense for a forty-seven-yard touchdown that won the game.

The Cotton Bowl extended an invitation and on New Year's Day the Tide found itself facing Texas A&M in Dallas. Bryant knew he had a formidable adversary in Aggies coach Gene Stallings, who had played for him at A&M way back in the arduous old days of the Junction, Texas, summer camp— and who had also coached for him at Alabama. The question on everybody's mind was whether the old coach would teach his pupil a lesson or vice versa. At a press conference before the game Stallings came off the practice field in his work clothes while Bryant showed up dressed to the nines and announced to the photographers, "I refuse to have my picture taken with anybody who looks like that!" Not to be outdone at the press conference next day, Stallings left practice early and put on a tuxedo. When he arrived at the press room Bryant was already there, wearing an open western shirt with a bandana, a cowboy hat, and boots.

In the end whatever gamesmanship there was didn't matter. Stallings's team beat Bama 20-16, fair and square, though there was one fluke toward the end that might have cost the Tide the game. Bryant had decided to go for a two-point conversion after a touchdown and told Stabler to run it up the middle instead of outside. He knew from Stallings's days under him at Alabama that he would almost always be looking for the wide run. It didn't work, and the Aggies stopped Bama at the goal. Bryant hated to lose more than anyone but if he had to be beat, at least he could console himself it was Stallings's team who did it. When the siren blew, Bryant met Stallings midfield and lifted him into the air with a giant bear-hug. Afterward he said, referring to the Aggies' goal line stand, "Gene, what's wrong with you? As long as you coached for me you'd always be in some kind of goal line out."

"Coach," Stallings said, "I'm fixin' to tell you something that's gonna hurt you. We only had ten men on the field. My middle linebacker noticed that we didn't have a defensive guard so he just jumped down in that slot. When the ball was snapped he didn't know what to do so he just ran straight ahead. He ran into your ball carrier!"

Stabler, Homan, and Bobby Johns were All-America and All-SEC selections. Mike Hall and Bruce Stephens made All-SEC as well. Stabler went on to a fantastic career in the NFL.

In January 1968 Alabama went to the Cotton Bowl and got beat fair and square by Gene Stallings's Texas Aggies. After the game, Bryant graciously gives his old comrade from A&M days a lift in the air.

The 1968 season opened with a sophomore named Scott Hunter as Bama's quarterback. Hunter was a passer of almost incomparable ability but the running game that year was lacking. So was the defense. Early on the Tide dropped the Ole Miss game 10-8 and lost to Tennessee 10-9 but after that smashed the rest of its opponents, including a 24-16 win over Auburn, a contest which ended on a note of poignancy. Some months earlier a terrible blow had fallen on the Crimson Tide family: legendary quarterback Pat Trammell, then a physician in Birmingham and always one of Bryant's favorites, had become very ill with cancer. It was one game he would not win. When the Auburn game was over the team presented him with the game ball, but the next week Dr. Pat Trammell died. "Coach, don't feel sorry for me," Trammell had told him, "I've had a wonderful 29 years." Bryant wept when he got the news and said, "This is the saddest day of my life."

Alabama lost badly to Missouri in the Gator Bowl that year, 35-10. Linebacker Mike Hall and guard Sammy Gellerstedt were All-Americans and All-SEC. End Mike Ford and tackle Alvin Samples were All-SEC, too. But by now, an 8-3 year was considered sub-par by Bama supporters, who foolishly believed that championship seasons could go on forever. Little did they know.

In 1969 Wilbur Jackson, a young halfback from Ozark, Alabama, became the first black player to sign a grant-in-aid at The University of Alabama. Nobody seems to know how Bryant pulled it off politically, but it was long overdue and of course foreshadowed the great impact on Alabama's teams to come. Bama already had a black basketball star and other SEC football teams were actively recruiting black players. It has

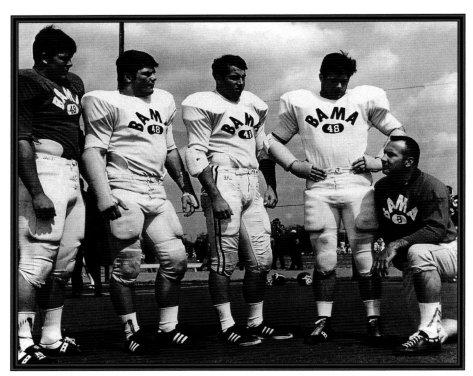

Top: *In 1969 Wilbur Jackson signed a football scholarship with Alabama, becoming the first on a long and illustrious list of great African-American players for Alabama. In 1971 John Mitchell became the first African-American to actually play for the Tide.* **Above:** *A thousand-plus pounds of tough beef. Bama assistant Pat Dye—who went on to a great career coaching Auburn—gives pointers to (left to right) Hannah, Krapf, Faust, and Rouzie.*

been supposed that there was dramatic behind-the-scenes political maneuvering by Bryant to enlist black players for Alabama, but this appears not to be the case. In fact there was an anti-discrimination lawsuit pending against the University for not having black players on the football team, but in pre-trial depositions it was testified that Bryant had for some time been actively trying to recruit minority players only to find no takers. Bryant had decided that to make the transition work smoothly he was going only after the best—but they all had turned him down, preferring to sign with big schools on the West Coast or in the Midwest where they felt they would be more welcome. David Mathews, president of the University then, recently remembered that it was "no big deal."

"At that time," he said, "there were hundreds of black students on campus, black cheerleaders, black student organizations. It logically followed that there would be black football players." In any event even a cursory look at the list of great black athletes who subsequently emerged from the Crimson Tide makes one shudder at the thought of where the team would have been without them.

Unfortunately that year, 1969, the Tide produced its worst season since Bryant arrived a decade earlier. Bama lost to Vanderbilt, Tennessee, and LSU and was humiliated by Auburn 49-26. The one bright light was Scott Hunter's still famous aerial shoot-out with Archie Manning and Ole Miss at Legion Field. Alabama went into the locker room with a relatively safe 14-7 lead but in the second half all hell broke loose. The game became a seesaw contest of pass-generated touchdowns that almost resembled a down-to-the-wire basketball game. Between trying to light his cigarettes and directing the game, Bryant was about to jump out of his skin, time and again firing his assistant coaches—one of them at least three times. At one point when Ole Miss was knocking on Bama's goal line he shouted to put big tackle Frankie McClendon in the game. Someone had to remind Bryant that McClendon had graduated five years earlier. In the closing minutes a huge national television audience watched Bama trailing by five points, fourth and eighteen at the Ole Miss twenty-yard line. Bryant had no suggestions, telling Scott Hunter to just, "Run the best thing you've got." From his pro-style dropback Hunter hurled straight into the hands of George Ranager, who scrambled across the end zone to put the Tide ahead for a spectacular 33-32 win. The fans erupted and mobbed the field. ABC sports commentator Chris Schenkel summed it up when he said: "It was the greatest duel two quarterbacks ever had. You had to be there to believe it." Archie Manning had completed 62 percent of his fifty-two passes for 436 yards and was selected SEC Back of the Week. Hunter had completed *76 percent* of his twenty-nine throws for 300 yards and a week later received a class-act letter from Manning saying he (Hunter) should have gotten MVP since Bama had won the game.

Bama went to the Liberty Bowl and got beat woefully by Colorado. But guard Alvin Samples—who had played the game as a linebacker because of injuries to other players—was selected All-American. He and Danny Ford were also All-SEC.

~

SO THE 1960S DREW TO AN END, a decade of wrenching turmoil in America: mindless assassinations, race riots, violent protests over the Vietnam War, sexual revolution, women's liberation, the end of segregation, and a man on the moon. Against this backdrop The University of Alabama had fielded what has been acclaimed by the *NCAA Record Book* as the "winningest team" of the decade. This might have seemed trivial but it wasn't. Everyday life went on despite the social upheavals, and the miracle of Bear Bryant's Alabama Crimson Tide gave pleasure and satisfaction to countless millions thrilled by young men competing on Saturday afternoons for the sheer joy of sport and a chance for glory most knew would quickly fade.

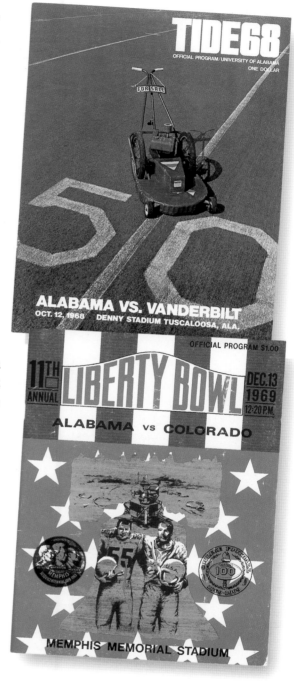

Top: *A forlorn "For Sale" lawnmower anticipates Denny Stadium's switch from grass to turf after the 1968 season. In 1991, the field went back to grass.*
Above: *Bama lost it, 47-33.*

SHOOTOUT WITH ARCHIE MANNING

~

Scott Hunter

ARCHIE MANNING WAS LEAVING THE Legion Field grass and I couldn't locate him. Ole Miss and Alabama players were all over the place hugging and shaking hands. I had to find Archie and congratulate him, then suddenly he was right in front of me. What could I say...?

There was nothing special in the first half about this Ole Miss-Alabama backyard battle on national television. It really started in the third quarter when Archie got hot and brought the Rebels from a 21-14 deficit to take a 26-21 lead early in the fourth. A missed extra point would be the margin but no one knew it or thought about it. But it was obvious in the last quarter watching Archie operate that we would probably have to score every time we had the ball.

Up by a score later in the quarter, I was standing next to Coach Bryant as Ole Miss faced a third and impossible. He was growling some what-to-do-next plans at me between puffs on a spittle-soaked cigarette when Archie fired a twenty-five-yard completion for a first down. Coach Bryant (pardon the redundancy but he will always be "Coach Bryant" to me) quickly forgot the plans and stormed down the sideline yelling at defensive coach Ken Donahue. "Ken, what coverage were we in?" he roared. Archie's perfor-

mance had paralyzed Donahue. He tried to mumble something. Coach Bryant fired him that very moment. Assistant Coach Jimmy Sharpe was standing next to me talking strategy so I whispered to him, "Coach Bryant just fired Coach Donahue." Sharpe nonchalantly looked up at me and said, "Don't worry about it, he's already fired him twice this half."

The score went back and forth until late in the final period. Down 32-27, facing a fourth and long near the Ole Miss twenty, I called time-out and went to the sideline. The bench was pandemonium. Coach Bryant, trying for the umpteenth time to light a well-soaked cigarette, yelled at Coach Sharpe for a play. Sharpe yelled through his headset mike at coach Steve Sloan in the press box for a play; everybody was yelling but nobody was coming up with anything (maybe they were all scared to!). Finally the referee came over and said, "Time's up Alabama captain... the TV commercial is over... let's play ball."

As I ran back toward the huddle I heard Coach Bryant yell, "Run the best thing you got." Red right, 56 comeback in was the best play I knew. Calling it in the huddle I stared directly into wide receiver George Ranager's eyes. He didn't blink.

Ole Miss blitzed seven but Johnny Musso cut down a growing-large-in-my-face defensive tackle who had gotten loose. Set-

Quarterback Scott Hunter (opposite page and above) had his great passing struggle with Ole Miss's Archie Manning in 1969. Hunter threw 29 times for 300 yards and Manning threw 52 times for 436 yards but the Tide won it, 33-32, in what ABC sportscaster Chris Schenkel called, "the greatest duel two quarterbacks ever had!"

ting my back foot just before getting hit I let it fly toward the anticipated spot. Ranager and I had completed this one in practice so often we could do it in the dark. Running a perfect route, Ranager planted, cut back toward me, pulled in a low but on-line throw, wiggled out of the corner man's grasp and dove into the checkered Legion Field end zone, scoring the game-winner for the Tide.

Amazingly, Archie had Ole Miss in field goal range as the clock ran out on the nationally televised 33-32 thriller. As I headed across the field to find Archie, I was thinking what I could say to him and when we finally met I realized there was nothing to say. How do you console a quarterback who just had one of the best games in college football's history and lost? We looked each other in the eyes and shook hands and both knew we had shared something so special that nothing needs to be said . . . it's all in a handshake.

Scott Hunter is the second leading passer in Alabama history. He went on to a career in professional football and sportscasting in Mobile.

Chapter Six

DOMINATION

1970 ~ 1982

Above: *Coach Bryant in his office. Players remember that the sofa he told them to sit on was quite low, making a visit there even more intimidating.*
Opposite page: *With the game plan rolled in his hand, Bryant leans against the Penn State goalpost, November 14, 1981, before his team thrashed the Nittany Lions 31-16. This gave Bryant his 314th career victory, tying the record with the legendary Amos Alonzo Stagg.*

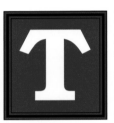

THE 1970S OPENED ON A SAD NOTE. After nearly fifty years at The University of Alabama, Coach Hank Crisp was about to be honored with the state's highest athletic award: his induction into the Alabama Sports Hall of Fame. On a January night an hour before the ceremonies, Crisp and his family attended a cocktail party at the Birmingham Museum of Art along with other legendary sports figures such as Mickey Mantle, Joe Garagiola, Bear Bryant, and Johnny Mack Brown. Moments after he entered, the seventy-five-year-old Crisp collapsed with heart failure. He died almost immediately. Everybody was stunned and horrified. Johnny Mack Brown slumped in a chair, crying—Crisp had coached him in the glorious 1926 Rose Bowl victory. Long recognized for his stern demeanor, Coach Hank was also universally beloved as the players' best friend. He started at the Crimson Tide under Coach Xen Scott in 1921 and remained under Wallace Wade, Frank Thomas, Red Drew, Ears Whitworth, and Bear Bryant.

Those gathered for the event pressed on with the Hall of Fame ceremony later that evening, with Hank Crisp, Jr., accepting the award for his father. After a huge standing ovation, the younger Crisp tearfully told the crowd, "This was the happiest day I've ever seen him have." In 1991 the University dedicated the Hank Crisp Indoor Football Facility in his memory.

~

FOR THE CRIMSON TIDE, the 1970s began with a disagreeable performance: a virtual mirror of the middling 6-5 season of 1969—and in some ways worse. The Tide was humiliated in its opening game at Legion Field by Southern Cal, 42-21, in the first meeting between the schools in a quarter century. The next week, however, Bama demolished Virginia Tech 51-18, proving true a saying originated in the Bryant era: "Woe betide the team that plays Alabama after a loss." But then the Tide got pounded by Ole Miss, Tennessee, LSU, and Auburn and finished up in a repugnant 24-24 tie with Oklahoma in the Bluebonnet Bowl. There were some fine players in 1970: Scott Hunter, in

his last year, as well as All-American tailback Johnny Musso and guard John Hannah. But the team hadn't really clicked for two seasons in a row and from some quarters—as in the brief 1930s slump under Frank Thomas and that under Wallace Wade in 1928—there was grumbling that Bryant had lost his touch. Thus opened the third and final stage of his career.

Fortunately, nobody of consequence said much against Bryant in public because during the eleven years remaining to Bryant at Alabama his teams graced the University with nine SEC championships and three national championships and went to a bowl game every single season. During this period the Crimson Tide won 135 of the 155 games it played, with one tie. In short, during the 1970s Bryant and The University of Alabama simply dominated the sport of college football.

Above: *In the locker room after a game, the team kneels in prayer.* **Opposite page:** *All-American halfback Johnny Musso tore up the opposition in the late '60s and early '70s.*

What then, had happened to Bryant's teams of the past few years? Perhaps nobody assessed it better than Keith Dunnavant in his book *Coach: The Life of Paul "Bear" Bryant:* "The seeds of Alabama's late-1960's nosedive were sown during the championship days of Joe Namath and the quick little boys. Recruiting . . . suffered for a number of reasons. Rivals succeeded in convincing many of the best prospects that they would never play with all those great athletes on the 'Bama roster. Bryant, flush with ambition, erred by going after more boys from outside Alabama and the South, and many quit when the going got tough because the Crimson Tide didn't mean as much to them. The coaching staff proved to be slow adjusting to the evolution of the specialist in the early years of the two-platoon game. The Boss, flush with fame, spent an increasing amount of time off-campus."

This was all too true. Scott Hunter was an incredibly gifted passer and Bryant had built a pro-set drop back game around him. Yet somebody had neglected the vaunted defense that had always been Bryant's trademark. Even though Hunter and Musso shattered many offensive records there was also a downside to so much passing: interceptions and incompletions. As Bryant himself observed later, "Three things can happen to you when you throw the ball, and two of them are bad." Further, no episode opened a wider window on the spectacle than the drubbing by Southern Cal. Two Trojan backs, Sam Cunningham and Clarence Davis, simply tore up the Alabama defense—Cunningham scored three touchdowns and Davis two. Both play

Big John Hannah, guard and two-time All-American, shown here in 1972.

ers were black. More embarrassing, had it not been for the lingering vestiges of segregation, Davis, who was from right around the corner in Birmingham, might just as easily have been dressing out for Bama that night.

And there was the two-platoon system to consider as well. NCAA rules had seesawed since the 1940s on the substitutions rule, until in 1953 the two-platoon system was abolished and players once more went back to playing both ways. It wasn't for another decade that this was reversed. Recruiting for a two-platoon system is markedly different than for a system that allows only limited substitutions. In the latter case, you have to find players who can go all out for sixty minutes of football and these do not generally include 290-pound linemen. Bryant did not like 290-pound linemen anyway, preferring lighter, quicker players for his type of game. But when in the 1970s rules changed to allow offensive linemen limited use of their hands and arms in blocking, the whole concept changed. Immense linemen using arms and hands offset the advantage of light, quick defensive guys. Bryant and his staff were somewhat slow to appreciate this.

In any case, when the 1971 season opened Scott Hunter was graduated to the pros and Bryant knew he had to make adjustments. The previous few years had been a severe strain on the great coach and those trials had stamped themselves into his character. For a while he had been eyeing a radical new offense—radical at least for Bear Bryant. This was the "wishbone," concocted out in Texas by his old pal, Darrell Royal. The principal feature of the wishbone is that it allows a quarterback the option of either handing off as he sees fit, throwing, running the ball himself, or pitching out to a trailing back. Back-to-back national champion Texas used it to flummox many opponents, and the University of Oklahoma had employed it to stymie Bama with the unsavory tie in the Bluebonnet Bowl that year. Bryant saw great possibilities in undertaking the wishbone, mainly because his present depth chart featured no quarterback with the passing ability of a Hunter, Stabler, Sloan, or Namath. So during the summer he flew out to see Darrell Royal in Austin and view his game films. Bryant returned a convert.

Dense fog enshrouded installation of the wishbone at Thomas Field when the Tide arrived for practice in August. Players and staff were sworn to guard it like a military secret. Huge tarps were erected around the entire practice area and if the press or other outsiders appeared the team switched to other stratagems. Bryant orchestrated the thing as if it were the Manhattan Project, for he had a particular atonement in mind: the opening game was against the same Southern Cal that had annihilated Alabama a year before. "We will sink or swim with the wishbone," Bryant told his team. Not only that, but in reviewing past seasons Bryant quickly understood neglecting the defense had been an awful mistake. He therefore took special pains to reestablish this vital element in his arsenal.

The day before the team flew out to California, Bryant ordered a night practice because the USC game was also to be played under the lights. At the same time a huge pep rally was scheduled on the quadrangle, and when the throng of students realized the team was still at practice they marched over to Thomas Field, pulled down the tarps, and watched their boys in action. Bryant let them. He knew the psychological value of such excitement.

Southern Cal stumbled blindly into the trap Bryant had laid. With only last year's films of Bama to go on, they had no inkling the Tide would appear before them in the wishbone with little quarterback Terry Davis at the helm. Davis was ideally suited to the formation. He was small but he was quick and from the opening kickoff marched Bama straight down field until the "Italian Stallion" Johnny Musso drove in for a touchdown. The stunned Trojans gave up another ten points before the half was up. USC came back to score ten of their own but Alabama clearly manhandled their West Coast foe. When the final 17-10 score was posted Bryant rubbed his hands in glee. He had lifted the Crimson Tide from temporary mediocrity back to the top of the game and everybody knew it.

Wilbur Jackson was captain of his 1973 National Championship team.

If there still was anyone who didn't, they would soon find out. That year Bama crushed all its remaining opponents by a combined score of 362-84 for the SEC championship and a shot at the national title against Nebraska in the Orange Bowl. This included a 31-7 pasting of Auburn following which Bryant crowed to reporters, "I know one thing. I'd rather die now than to have died this morning and missed this game."

To call the Nebraska contest disappointing would be a vast understatement. A huge television audience watched the Crimson Tide get swamped by the Cornhuskers 38-6, but even in this fans could take a measure of consolation. Nebraska was peopled by what Bryant derided as "big ole cornfed boys," and if in the past his small teams had been able to deal with them by speed, cunning, and agility, this year's Nebraska hulks were not only big but exceptionally fast and agile themselves. Recognizing this, Bryant divined the wave of the future and stepped up efforts to recruit some "big ole" fast, agile fellows of his own to follow in the tracks of giant linemen Doug Faust, John Hannah, Jim Krapf, and Jeff Rouzie, among others. So this was not, as naysayers had carped, a fifty-eight-year-old man stuck in his ways; Bryant understood the necessity of change and was able to make almost superhuman refinements to his game.

Not surprisingly, John Hannah and Johnny Musso made All-America that year. David Bailey, Johnny Grammer, Steve Higginbotham, Jim Krapf, Robin Parkhouse, and Tom Surlas were All-SEC.

⁓

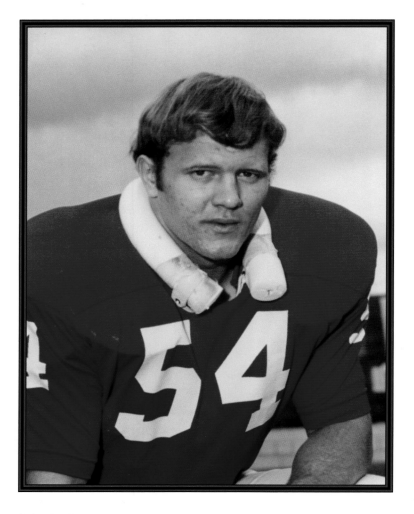

Mike DuBose, Bama defensive end, in 1974.

NINETEEN-SEVENTY-TWO APPEARED TO BE a glorious repeat of the previous year. All through the season Bama fans marveled while their team took apart each and every opponent with a combined point record of 377-116. That is, until the last game. Auburn.

Meanwhile, the mid-season hump Bama had to get over was, as usual, Tennessee. This became a titanic struggle in Knoxville, measured in minutes, until at the very end it seemed certain the Crimson Tide had lost. Bama was behind 10-3 with a little more than two minutes on the clock as Vols fans basked in radiant jubilation. Then with the suddenness of a lightning strike Terry Davis connected on a spectacular pass to end Wayne Wheeler; a slashing run by fullback Steve Bisceglia brought the ball to the Tennessee two, and who else but halfback Wilbur Jackson, the first black player to sign with Bama, carried it in for the touchdown. Bryant decided to kick for one instead of going for the two that might have put the Tide ahead. It was a gutsy call. Sophomore end Mike DuBose remembered it this way: "He knew the wind was at our back and he knew Tennessee would have to throw. I think he felt confident we would get the football back and have the opportunity to win the game."

If what happened next is not a miracle it ought to be. After the kickoff Tennessee had first-and-ten on its own twelve and the Vols quarterback was rolling to pass when Mike DuBose lashed out and slapped the ball from his hands. John Mitchell (another new defensive end who happened to be black) recovered it for the Tide. Then, as the final seconds ticked off before the agitated and deflated army of Tennessee fans, Terry Davis optioned himself from the wishbone and scampered in for the Bama win. Mike DuBose later recalled what Bryant had always preached: "That if you keep playing good defense and hang tough in the fourth quarter, something good is going to happen to you."

⁓

AMONG THE UNSUNG HEROES OF THE GAME are the team's student managers who often put in upwards of seventy hours a week making sure things are running smoothly for the players. They burn the midnight oil checking and rechecking equipment, packing it for road trips, driving the vans, unloading them, and then loading them all up again. They make sure there are water and cold drinks and ice and towels and a zillion other little things to ensure that the players are as comfortable as possible and everything works smoothly.

One such manager was Kirk Wood, who remembered the Tennessee struggle that year as a swirl of perplexed anxiety. It was his job to leave the field three or four minutes before the end of the fourth quarter to do all the myriad stuff managers do: make sure the locker room door was unlocked, the showers were on and the water hot, and provide ice, drinks, and towels. Naturally, that afternoon, with Bama losing 10-3 in the waning minutes, Wood trudged through the dank tunnel into the bowels of Neyland Stadium with a heavy heart and set at his tasks. "There wouldn't be a lot of happy guys coming through the door and I wanted it to be as pleasant an experience as possible," he remembered. One of Coach Bryant's little private traditions was to hand out cigars to the players if the Tide beat Tennessee. It was the only game in which he did this. Wood had packed the cigars low in the bottom of one of the trunks and from what he saw as he left the field, they would not be needed today. "I could hear the roaring from the stadium but I didn't know what was going on," he recalled. "All of a sudden the guys were coming in and they were screaming and whooping and hollering and jumping up and down. One of the managers came in trying to make me understand I needed to get the cigars and get them quickly. I finally got somebody to tell me we had won but it wasn't until the next day when I watched Coach Bryant's TV show that I could figure out *how* we won," Wood said.

In any case, flushed with ten straight victories, the Crimson Tide stormed into Legion Field on a crisp December afternoon to meet the 9-1 Auburn Tigers. It was an excruciating performance. With Alabama comfortably ahead 16-3 and just six minutes left to play, an Auburn man blocked a Bama punt that was snatched up by one of his teammates and the Tigers scored. Minutes later the unthinkable happened: the same Auburn Tiger blocked another Bama punt which also fell into the hands of the same teammate who again scored. Auburn won the game 17-16, and Tide fans spent many an agonizing moment in the years to come with Auburn's taunt, "Punt Bama! Punt!" ringing in their ears.

Poor manager Kirk Wood, who as usual had left early to prepare the locker room, bore the brunt of this experience as he had in the Tennessee locker room, only now from the other side of the coin. "I was standing there with a big smile on my face when the players came in. People were throwing stuff and not saying pleasant things and there were a lot of unhappy faces. Again, I had to ask somebody what happened." After that season the managers began putting a radio in the locker room to listen to the play-by-play, Wood said, "and at least have some indication of how to receive the team when they came in."

Despite this calamity against Auburn, Alabama was awarded the SEC championship that year and went to the Cotton Bowl to meet the University of Texas. Perhaps the loss to Auburn had taken some wind from the sails of the vaunted Tide, for in the battle of the wishbones in Dallas, they lost a

Top: *Majorettes lead the Million Dollar Band onto the field.* **Above:** *In the 1972 Auburn game, with Alabama ahead 16-3 in the final minutes, the Tigers, to the horror of all Crimson Tide fans, blocked two Bama punts and ran them in for touchdowns. Here a Tider howls in agony at the spectacle.*

disheartening game to the Longhorns, 17-13. Still, John Hannah, Jim Krapf, and John Mitchell deservedly were named All-Americans and Hannah went on to become one of the greatest NFL linemen of all time.

Nineteen-seventy-three held much promise and Bama fulfilled it to perfection with an 11-0 regular season. Using two sterling quarterbacks, Gary Rutledge and Richard Todd, Alabama piled up 477 points, the most in Crimson Tide history for a single season, then or now. For the past several years Alabama had been playing an eleven-game schedule and this year they kicked it off with a 66-0 extermination of the University of California and ended with a 35-0 blowout of Auburn. In the Sugar Bowl they lost a distressing nip-and-tuck 24-23 battle with Notre Dame but still claimed a share of the divided

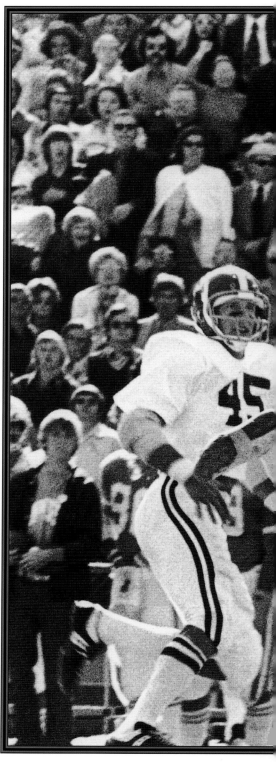

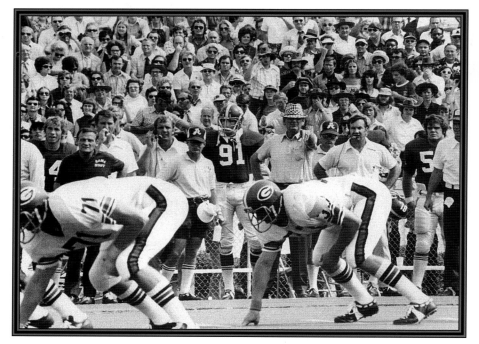

Above left: *The 1973 Georgia line gets a feel of what the Crimson Tide looks like, close up and in your face.* **Left:** *Coach Bryant does not like something he sees in the Georgia backfield.*

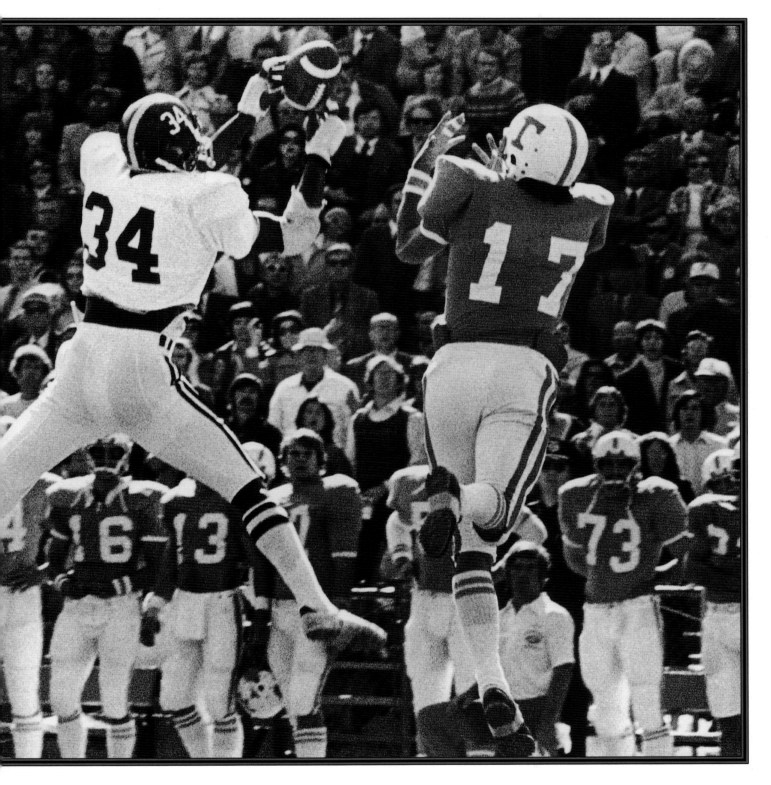

national championship. Buddy Brown, Woodrow Lowe, and Wayne Wheeler became All-Americans.

Nineteen-seventy-four was a repeat performance of '73: an 11-0 regular season despite injuries to both Rutledge and Todd. The Tide this year accepted an invitation to the Orange Bowl, where they would face last year's opponent, Notre Dame. Meanwhile, Bryant had become severely aggravated by his team's failure to win a post-season bowl game for seven years in a row. This time he

Mike Washington, All-SEC defensive back, grabs one from the hands of a hopeful Tennessee receiver in 1974 while Wayne Rhoads, another All-SEC defender (45), closes in to help.

SMACK DAB IN THE MIDDLE OF IT ALL

~

Sela Ward

I WAS A CHEERLEADER at The University of Alabama in the 1970s and my memories are so rich from this chapter of my life. I can still smell the freshly cut grass of the practice field which we shared with the Million Dollar Band and feel the adrenaline rush that shot through my body as the band played and we practiced the double stunts that we were known for. And with coach Paul "Bear" Bryant at the helm, you felt as if you were participating in something larger than life. Tens of thousands of fans in a sea of red and white would weave their way into the stadium. In those days everyone got dressed up—the guys wore a coat and tie and the gals often wore dresses. Bama football was as serious as religion, and to be a cheerleader, down on the field, smack dab in the middle of it all, was a privilege of the highest order!

Memories of my brief encounters with Coach Bryant always make me smile. I once went to his office to get his permission to arrange a pep rally. When I walked in scared to death, he looked up and said, "Well, if I had known you were coming I would have ordered us up some fried chicken!" He had the appearance of being a gruff old bear, but in reality he was warm, charming, and approachable.

He once said to Debbie Purifoy, one of the other cheerleaders, and me, as we said hello to him before a game and reporters snapped photo-ops of the three of us: "The only reason you all ever come talk to me is to get your picture taken." Nothing could have been further from the truth. We were just too intimidated to walk up and start a conversation!

When I think of the cheerleaders, I am left with two big impressions, the first being Patti Rawlinson. When I first arrived at Bama she was already a cheerleading icon, the epitome of the all-American, apple-pie beauty, and the TV cameras loved her! She was the one I so looked up to as a freshman. And joining the team after I got there were the Troxell twins, Harriet and Beth. They were the first young women I knew to be extremely health- and body-conscious, eating apples for snacks and spending long hours working out in the gym. The results were

Crimson Tide cheerleaders of 1976: Debbie Purifoy, Carol Wheeler, Sela Ward, Sandra Whitehead, and Beth Troxell.

these very petite, beautifully sculpted athletic wonders—way ahead of their time! Chip Cornelius was my partner and together with Brian Morgan, whose enthusiasm made him the leader of the cheers, there was never a dull moment. Always lots of fun and laughter.

I have to admit that most of my sideline focus was not on the fans in the stands but on #91 defensive tackle Bob Baumhower, my college sweetheart and later a great all-pro player for the Miami Dolphins! It was an enchanted, storybook time. My best friend and sorority sister dated quarterback Richard Todd; the four of us were inseparable for several of our college years. We were often found practicing "the hustle" (the "line dance" of our day) in the living room of the Chi O house or cruising around in Richard's red Cadillac convertible listening to Lou Rawls sing "Groovy People."

I am often asked how a southern gal from Mississippi ended up an actress in Hollywood. The truth is that it is a direct result of having been a cheerleader for Alabama.

Because our games were so often on national television, cheerleaders actually got fan mail, and one letter never left my impressionable young head. A guy wrote, "you are the next Mary Tyler Moore!" I had no idea what that meant—did I project comedy on the field? However, to me, of course, it meant that I could be in movies: the hubris of youth! And so when the cheerleaders were taken to New York City for the National Invitation Basketball Tournament, I was ready. I fell immediately in love with New York and moved there shortly after I left college. Through a series of connect-the-dots I landed a TV commercial and went off into the land of entertainment. But I'll never forget where a lot of it came from—those green football fields all over the South and the grand enthusiastic crowds on magical Saturday afternoons with the Crimson Tide.

Sela Ward is an Emmy-Award-winning film and TV actress best known for the TV drama series Sisters *and* Once and Again.

practiced the players hard in Tuscaloosa until just two days before the game—much to the consternation of Crimson Tiders who were treated daily to newspaper photographs of Fighting Irishmen basking on Miami beaches with pretty girls. It was all to no avail. In a tight, hard-fought contest Notre Dame beat Alabama 13-11, with the Tide giving up four turnovers. Linebacker Ronnie Robertson remembered how Bryant told them afterward to "hold our heads high, show our class, show our pride, we had nothing to be ashamed of." As always, in the press conferences Bryant placed the blame squarely upon himself, saying he had not done a good enough job preparing his team. Bama could take consolation that they were still SEC champions and proudly posted Leroy Cook, Sylvester Croom, Woodrow Lowe, and Mike Washington on All-America teams. Moreover, before the next season began, the state legislature passed a resolution to rename Denny Stadium "Bryant-Denny Stadium" in honor of the coach's achievements.

The 1975 Bama team looked better than ever and therefore Tide fans were shocked when, in the season opener, they were trounced by Missouri 20-7 in a nationally televised game. Bryant, who had voted for an SEC winner tie-in with the Sugar Bowl, was doubly disappointed because he wanted to be the first SEC team to play in the new Superdome, but after the Missouri game he chafed and gnawed and confided to a Sugar Bowl official that his team wasn't good enough to go to *any* bowl that year.

Above: *Unsung heroes such as quarterback Robert Fraley played a crucial role in Crimson Tide football. Shown here in 1973, Fraley got in what playing time he could behind starting quarterbacks Richard Todd and Gary Rutledge, but he was on the All-SEC Academic Team. Graduating from the Alabama School of Law, Fraley was one of America's most prominent sports attorneys until he died in a bizarre 1999 crash of the Lear Jet owned by his client, pro-golfer Payne Stewart.* **Opposite page:** *All-American receiver Ozzie Newsome, "The Wondrous Wizard of Oz," snatching a pass.*

It was typical Bryant self-deprecation. The Crimson Tide didn't lose another single game in 1975 and blew out her opponents by an almost incredible 374-72 points. Led by quarterback Richard Todd and All-America defensive end Leroy Cook, Bama won its cherished cigars after whipping Tennessee 30-7 and destroyed the Washington Huskies by a score of 52-0. At that game were assembled all the remaining players of the 1926 Rose Bowl, in which Alabama's one-point victory over Washington had propelled them into national fame fifty years earlier. By the time Coach Bryant finished introducing them one by one to a packed Bryant-Denny Stadium there was hardly a dry eye in the house. The author James Michener was at the game, researching his book *Sports in America*. "I thought Nebraska was the most football crazed state until I came to Alabama," he wrote. "The people in the audience welcomed the [Rose Bowl] team with an absolute admiration that is hard to describe."

The final match against Auburn wasn't much of a problem either; the Tide mashed them 28-0. Now it was time for the Sugar Bowl, despite Bryant's sorrowful appraisal at the beginning of the season. The Bear was known throughout the football fraternity as a spectacular matcher of bowl teams and was straining at the bit this year to get Joe Paterno's famous Penn State team down to New Orleans. His voice carried much weight with the Sugar Bowl Committee and so the top teams in the SEC and the Northeast met on New Year's Eve night before a huge TV audience. It was still 3-3 going into the fourth quarter when Todd passed for a fifty-five-yarder to a young sophomore split end named Ozzie Newsome ("The Wondrous Wizard of Oz"), leading Bama to a touchdown and two field goals while the defense under Leroy Cook and Bob Baumhower held the Nittany Lions to two field goals. This victory finally broke the embarrassing string of post-season bowl losses Bryant had endured for the past eight years and also established the great and lasting rivalry between the two football powers. After the game the press all wanted to know why the coach hadn't worn his trademark houndstooth hat during the game. "My mama always told me never to wear a hat indoors," Bryant replied serenely.

THE NEXT YEAR HOPES RAN HIGH FOR A REPEAT performance, but this was not in the cards. With his usual pessimism, Bryant had down-played prospects for a championship season and this time he was right. Too many players had graduated—especially on the defense. With Todd gone, quarterbacking duties fell to sophomore Jeff Rutledge. To everyone's dismay Bama dropped a close opening game against Ole Miss in Jackson, losing 10-7. The old saying "Woe betide the team that has to play Alabama after a loss," applied yet again as the Tide swarmed over SMU 56-3 and went on to trounce Vanderbilt 42-14. It looked like there might be a replay of 1975 after all, but this optimism ended when the Tide went to Athens and got wiped out by Georgia 21-0. They won the next five games but then dropped a close one to Notre Dame in South Bend, 21-18. Nevertheless, after handing Auburn a 38-7 drubbing, Bryant took his team to his eighteenth consecutive bowl game. It was the Liberty Bowl in Memphis against UCLA and, among other things, it was the coldest

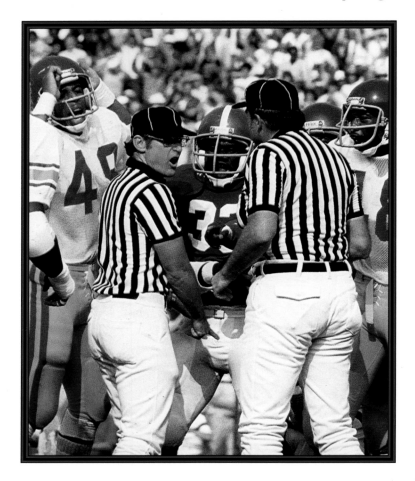

Southern Cal beat Alabama 24-14 in 1978, but not without argument.

night in memory. All-American Bob Baumhower would remember it as the coldest he'd ever been, even though the Miami Dolphins he later played for journeyed to such ice palaces as Minnesota and Green Bay. Drinks froze on the sidelines; blood from cuts simply congealed. Everybody from Bryant on down was miserable but the sunshine boys from UCLA were even more so, and Bama whipped them 36-6. The year ended with Ozzie Newsome and Bob Baumhower as All-America picks.

The 1977 season started off jerkily. The Tide pounded Ole Miss but then lost to Nebraska by a touchdown after Rutledge threw five interceptions. Gloomy appraisals of Bama's defense began to appear, but this was a team with heart, and lots of it. In a nationally televised match in Los Angeles against number one Southern Cal, Bama came out on top. It became one of the most talked-about football games of the year: a nip-and-tuck contest going into the fourth quarter. In the last moments Southern Cal scored, making it 21-20 with Bama leading. The Trojans decided to go for the two-point win. All-SEC defensive end Wayne Hamilton hit the quarterback early, forcing a bad pass that All-SEC linebacker Barry Krauss intercepted to end the game. That victory provided the glue that held the team together and after that, it was all rosy for the Tide, including a 48-21 flogging of Auburn.

As SEC champions, Bama went to the Sugar Bowl against Woody Hayes's Ohio State Buckeyes. The press was billing it as a contest between the two winningest coaches presently in the game, but Bryant was having none of that. "I don't know why you people keep making such a big deal over Woody Hayes and Paul Bryant. I assure you I'm not going to play and I hope Woody *does*," he said. Actually, it wasn't much of a contest. Bama swarmed over the Buckeyes with Jeff Rutledge hitting Bruce Bolton on a terrific twenty-seven-yard touchdown pass. Major Ogilvie and Tony Nathan did yeoman's duty for the offense, and when it was over Bama had won 35-6. At that point the thinking was that they had a good shot at the national championship, but those hopes were dashed when Notre Dame beat number-one Texas in the Cotton Bowl and jumped to the top spot over the Tide. Nevertheless, Bryant was jubilant after the game, observing to the press that "Woody is a great coach, and I ain't bad." It was about as close as Bear Bryant would come to self-promotion.

Above: *Tony Nathan scoring in the Bama-Ohio State Sugar Bowl of 1978.* **Left:** *In 1977 Alabama lost to Nebraska but won all the rest and as SEC champions whipped Ohio State in the Sugar Bowl, 35-6. Bryant shakes hands with Buckeyes coach Woody Hayes after the game.*

Above: *Steadman Shealy, All-SEC quarter-back, also earned All-SEC academic honors in '78 and '79.* **Left:** *Alabama won the SEC and AP national championships in 1978. Here, the Vanderbilt quarterback is about to receive an unwanted fraternal embrace from Bama's All-SEC defender Warren Lyles.*

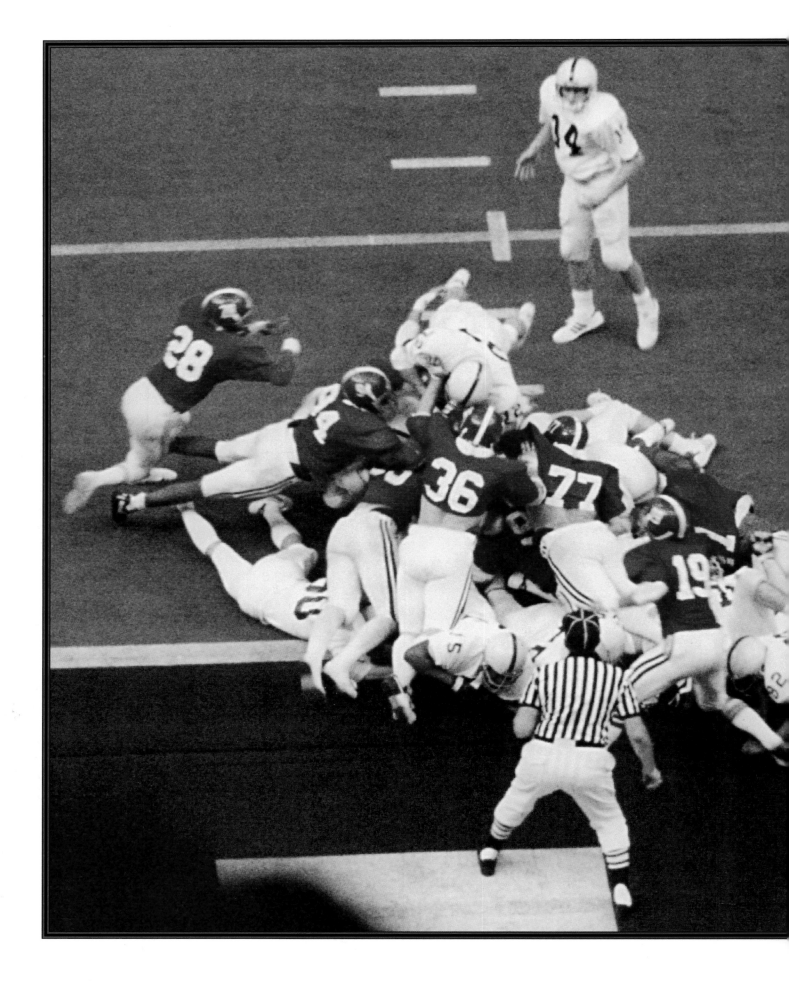

Next year the pre-season polls put Alabama in the number-one spot for 1978, and at first it looked like they were right as Bama demolished Nebraska and Missouri. Then they came up against a tough Southern Cal team and got beat 24-14. It was a disappointing loss in more ways than one, as we shall see. Nonetheless, as in the previous year's loss to Nebraska, the loss to USC seemed to cement the Tide and they didn't lose another game all season. Bama beat highly ranked LSU 31-10 in a titanic defensive struggle belied by the score. Afterwards, Tigers coach Charlie McClendon stated for the record: "Fellas, I've been in football all my life, and there has never been a better defensive team anywhere, anyplace than the one Alabama has. It strangles you." After a 36-16 victory over Auburn, the number-two-ranked Bama clinched the SEC championship and was again headed to the Sugar Bowl to face number-one-ranked Penn State. It was one of the all-time great contests, remembered for one thing: the famous Goal Line Stand.

A defensive war was under way with the score 0-0 in the closing moments of the first half when Rutledge hit Bruce Bolton for a thirty-yard pass in the end zone. The second half Bama and Penn State each scored, and as the final minutes of the game wore down it was Alabama 14, Penn State 7. Then a frightening thing happened: Penn State recovered a Bama fumble at the Tide nineteen and a few plays later it was the Nittany Lions with third and two at Alabama's goal. Penn State gained a yard but was stopped by Don McNeal a foot short of the touchdown. Now it was fourth and less than a yard and Penn State took time out. Bryant had told the team this game would most likely come down to what he called a "gut check" and in the defensive huddle safety Murray Legg told the others over and over, "gut check time!" When Penn State quarterback Chuck Fusina came over to examine the distance to the goal, Bama's All-American tackle Marty Lyons said to him, "You better pass."

He didn't. Instead he gave the ball to fullback Mike Guman who came straight at the center of the Tide's defense where future All-American linebacker Barry Krauss was waiting for him. The collision popped the rivets in Krauss's helmet but it also stopped Guman dead in his tracks outside the goal. John Forney would never forget the words of ABC's announcer Keith Jackson: "Fourth down and a foot separating top-ranked Penn State from a possible national championship! Fusina hands to Guman—He didn't make it! He didn't make it! What an unbelievable goal line stand by Alabama!"

Now it was national championship time. The National Football Foundation and the Football Writers Association both voted Bama number one, but the spiteful UPI voted Southern Cal—which had beaten the Tide early in the season—first and Alabama second. Next day, however, the Associated Press gave the Tide its number-one ranking and that cinched it for everybody.

Alabama's famous Goal Line Stand against Penn State in the 1979 Sugar Bowl. The national champion Crimson Tide was ahead 14-7 in the last moments of the game when the Nittany Lions recovered a Bama fumble and a few plays later they were third and two at the Tide goal. The next play put them inside the Bama one, but Crimson Tiders began yelling "gut check time!" to each other, and on the next play, led by All-American Barry Krauss, the Tide stopped Penn State cold at the goal to win the game.

COULD THEY DO IT AGAIN? This was on everyone's lips as the 1979 season rolled around. On paper it sure seemed so; Bama returned many starters from the championship team the year before and was ranked number one in the preseason polls. Not only that, they breezed over their first five opponents by a combined score of 219-9! Then a cloud rose on the horizon in the form of coach Johnny Majors's Tennessee Volunteers. Bama had figured on having a pretty easy time of it but walked into the dressing room at halftime down 17-7. To many other teams this would have excited panic and fear, but Bryant had instilled in these boys—many of whom had played together for three years—a supreme confidence, and about the worst emotion they were experiencing then was mystification. Bryant now went into his old "everything is okay" mode, clapping the players on the back and saying things like "We have them just where we want them" and "We've lulled them into a false sense of security"—words calculated to reassure his team. Bryant was an uncanny master at such gamesmanship.

When they returned to the field Bryant replaced his starting quarterback, Steadman Shealy, with a substitute, Don Jacobs, who led the Tide to a comeback 27-17 win. Afterward, Bryant was asked if he thought that game

Above: *Center Dwight Stephenson, #57, was a first-team All-American in 1979.*
Right: *The 12-0 Crimson Tide were national champions in 1979. Here they celebrate victory number eleven, against Auburn. Left to right: Vince Booth, Jim Bunch, Steadman Shealy, Keith Pugh.*

Above: *Bama's Alan McElroy kicks against Auburn in 1978. The holder is Kevin Jones.* **Right:** *Bama rolled over Vanderbilt 66-3 in 1979 and the starting team took the rest of the afternoon off to watch the spectacle. Left to right: Warren Lyles, E. J. Junior, Mike Brock, and Byron Braggs.*

would make Bama a better team. "I sure do," he told them. "I wouldn't take anything for it, the way it happened. I wouldn't want it to happen again, but now we know we can do it." Only LSU and Auburn gave the Tide trouble for the rest of the season, but they overcame this and, as SEC champions, again packed up for New Orleans and the Superdome to meet number-six Arkansas. Alabama mauled the Razorbacks 24-9, with Bryant even resurrecting his old charade, the quick kick. With a 12-0 season Bama remained the only unbeaten, untied team in the country and this time was elected undisputed national champion.

~

BY NOW BRYANT'S DOMINATION OF BIG-TIME COLLEGE FOOTBALL was legend. Books had been written about him. He had appeared regularly on the cover of *Sports Illustrated* and other major sports magazines and on network talk shows. But suddenly another thing loomed large in his career—perhaps largest of all. Paul Bryant was on the verge of becoming the winningest football coach of all time. Yet there was something else, too. Unknown to all but a handful of people, Bear Bryant was not a well man. The great heart he brought to the

All-American quarterback Walter Lewis sneaks through against LSU in 1980.

game, to the University, to his players, his life, and the lives of everyone he touched was failing him.

But as the autumn of 1980 approached an excitement began to ignite the national football scene. Since the 1940s, the record of college football wins belonged to the famed Amos Alonzo Stagg, who amassed a lifetime total of 314 victories over a fifty-seven-year career. As Bryant approached his sixty-seventh birthday, he was just eighteen games away from tying Stagg and nineteen from surpassing him. With Alabama playing the way it was, it seemed certain that Bear Bryant was going to do just that. Bryant mostly pooh-poohed the notion in his usual way. "That's why all this talk about Mr. Warner, Mr. Stagg and myself bothers me so much. My players have won the games, some in spite of me, and now I'm getting credit for it. I'm embarrassed by that," he said. But he also remarked on another occasion that if somebody had to hold the record, it might as well be him. Thus, the countdown began.

But of course there was still the 1980 season to think about. The team was heavy on returning starters and a lot of people were betting that Alabama would become the first school to win three national championships in a row. In the beginning it looked that way. The Tide rolled over its first seven opponents by a combined score of 257-58. A narrow 17-13 squeaker over tinymight Rutgers at the Meadowlands should have given Bama fans warning, but when they whipped Tennessee 27-0 people thought all was right with the world. It wasn't. On the first day of November the number-one-ranked Tide went to Jackson to play Mississippi State and slunk home with a 6-3 loss. They took it out next week against LSU 28-7, then dropped a heart-breaker against Notre Dame 7-0. Besides the loss itself something else was aggravating about it—Alabama had not beaten Notre Dame ever and it was looking habit-forming. Bama roared back to crush Auburn 34-18 and wound up in the Cotton Bowl where they blasted Baylor 30-2. Linebacker Thomas Boyd and defensive end E. J. Junior were named All-Americans. All in all it was a good season, but not for hard-core Crimson Tide fans, who remained foolishly convinced the team must win all of its games all of the time.

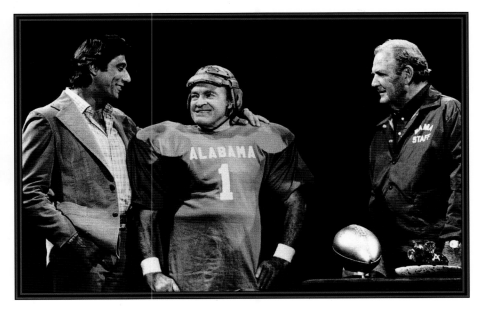

Above: *Bama defenders reach for the block on the way to a 27-0 victory over the Vols in 1980.* **Right:** *In 1980 Bob Hope came to campus and put on a show with Joe Namath and Coach Bryant.*

A great commotion attended the opening of the 1981 season. Bryant was now only eight games behind tying Stagg's record and was almost certain to surpass it. The only question was when. People were already preparing for it. The target game to tie the record was homecoming against Rutgers in Tuscaloosa and the go-ahead win was to be revenge upon Mississippi State. Naturally, it didn't work out that way. After walloping LSU the Tide took an embarrassing 24-21 loss from then nobody Georgia Tech. They rebounded the next three games, then were stymied to a vile 13-13 tie with Southern Mississippi. Winning their next three games handily, the Tide traveled to Pennsylvania to take on the highly ranked Nittany Lions. Bryant stood only one game behind the great Amos Alonzo Stagg. Playing in Joe Paterno's own backyard and engineered by the Tide's great quarterback Walter Lewis, Bama manhandled the Lions 31-16 to bring Bryant's record even with the "Father of Football." When the defensive unit finally walked off the field after holding Penn State in a last-quarter goal line stand reminiscent of the legendary one in the Sugar Bowl, Bryant tipped his hat to each of them. Walter Lewis remembered that day: "I don't guess I realized how influential Coach was, but I remember people just standing in lines on the field as he was walking on. They were just trying to get a glimpse of him. They really respected him."

Now the final hurdle, the 315th win, was at hand and it was against none other than Bama's most ardent foe, Auburn. In a nationally televised game at Legion Field, the Tide emerged from the tunnel into one of the most celebrated football events of all time. People from all over the sports world were there, including scores of Bryant's former players. Tickets were impossible to come by. Everybody knew this was most probably a once-in-a-lifetime occasion.

It got started badly for Alabama and by the fourth quarter Auburn was leading 17-14. Then with Lewis at quarterback, Bama started from its own twenty and marched down the field into Auburn territory with the efficiency of an enormous machine. All the little Xs and Os and Vs Bryant had drilled into them over the years on the chalkboard finally worked just like they were supposed to. On the Tigers' thirty-eight Lewis hit split end Jesse Bendross for the touchdown. With the crowd chanting "315, 315!" the stadium erupted; not only that, but the Tide scored again in the closing moments: Alabama 28, Auburn 17. They had done it. For themselves. For him. It couldn't have been more perfect for Bryant: a final-quarter comeback victory against Auburn. It didn't get any better than that. It still doesn't.

The team carried him off the field and the media mobbed him. Bryant said: "I ought to be carrying my players off the field on my shoulders. And I would if I were strong enough. I'd take them one at a time if I had to stay till midnight." He made sure to remember everyone he could in his long coaching career: Maryland, Kentucky, and Texas A&M, "who had as much to do with this as anyone." He especially remembered those now deceased. When Bryant finally got to the dressing room after all the hoopla, Auburn coach Pat Dye was there to congratulate him. "I'm proud of you coach," Dye told him. "I just wish you could have set the record a little later." President Ronald Reagan, the former Rose Bowl sportscaster with an affinity toward Alabama, called with congratulations. Bryant remembered him being at all of Bama's

Above: *"Big Al," the Crimson Tide mascot. It is tough duty for the students who play Big Al. Elephant suits can be hot, especially early in the season.*
Opposite page: *Walter Lewis cocked and ready to fire.*

practices when he played in the 1935 Rose Bowl. Former president Jimmy Carter also called. But All-SEC nose guard Warren Lyles probably summed it up as well as anybody when he said, "I wish I could tell you how proud I am to be an Alabama football player, but I have no idea how to do it. I feel as rich as Howard Hughes. I feel like I share that pedestal Coach Bryant stands on tonight."

Alabama was tied with Georgia for the SEC championship but the Sugar Bowl Committee opted to go with Georgia and All-American Herschel Walker's star power that year. So the Tide went to Dallas to play Texas in the Cotton Bowl, losing 14-12. Maybe it was a letdown after all the pressure that year, but in any case it was just a footnote, compared with what Bryant and his teams had accomplished.

~

AND SO IN THE SECOND YEAR OF THE NEW DECADE Bryant set at it again, as he had for more than fifty years, as a player and coach, with time out only for military service in the war. A year earlier he had told a *Tuscaloosa News* sports editor, "My life has been so tied up in football it has flown by. Practice, recruiting and games. There hasn't been anything else but football."

By now Bryant had already had the first of the heart failures that would eventually kill him. His problem was coronary artery disease. But few except his doctors knew this. After the first attack, he was given strong medication and was back at practice days later. It was to be his final season and he probably knew it then. His secretary, Linda Knowles, remembers: "His last year he was a very sick man, and he willed himself to live—that's exactly what he did. What was driving him to stay alive was to complete the season. I don't know if he himself knew how short his time was, but I think he had the drive and the will to complete that season and to have things in order before he died."

Yes, as Linda Knowles said, there were games yet to be played and Bryant set about his task as he always did. He had some fabulous defensive players, including Jeremiah Castille, Mike Pitts, and Tommy Wilcox, who would become All-Americans. The first five games suggested the Tide might well be in line again for a national championship. Bama rolled over Georgia Tech, Ole Miss, Vanderbilt, and Arkansas State and wound up mid-season with a fantastic 42-21 blowout of number-two-ranked Penn State. Then it all began to unravel. The Tide lost to Tennessee in Knoxville, rebounded against Cincinnati and Mississippi State, then spiraled downward like the stick of a spent Fourth of July rocket. LSU and Southern Mississippi both beat them, and finally a heartbreaking one-point loss to Auburn ended the regular season.

Two weeks later, Bryant announced his retirement. It was an emotional scene in Memorial Coliseum. Bryant said:

"There comes a time in every profession when you need to hang it up, and that has come to me as head football coach at the University of Alabama. My main purpose as director of athletics and head football coach here has been to field the best possible team, to improve each player as a person, and to produce citizens who will be a credit to our modern day society.

At Penn State in 1981: Coach Bryant's victory ride after winning game 314, tying the record of Amos Alonzo Stagg.

"We have been successful in most of those areas, but I feel the time has come for a change in our football leadership. We lost two big football games this season that we should have won. And we played in only four or five games like Bryant-coached teams should play. I've done a poor job coaching.

"This is my school, my alma mater, and I love it. And I love the players, but in my opinion they deserve better coaching than they've been getting from me this year. My stepping down is an effort to see that they get better coaching from someone else.

December 1982: Coach Bryant announces his retirement. "There comes a time in every profession when you need to hang it up, and that has come to me as head football coach at the University of Alabama," he said with characteristic bluntness.

"It has been a great job for me, personally, to have the opportunity to coach at my alma mater. I know I will miss coaching, but the thing I will miss most is the association I have had with the players, the coaches, the competition—all those things that have made such a strong tradition at Alabama."

~

EVEN WITH AN 8-4 SEASON—the worst in more than a decade—Alabama was still a formidable draw for the post-season bowls and this year was tapped to meet Illinois in the Liberty Bowl at Memphis. Players particularly remember an emotional moment at the last practice. They were in a projection room about to watch film when Bryant took the podium to give his usual talk—except this time it was not so usual, because it was his last as head coach of the Crimson Tide. He spoke for a few moments about football, then drifted off about how much he loved the players and the school and the game, and then he began to cry. He motioned for the lights to be turned down and the projector turned on. Everybody in the room was crying too.

It was another freezing night at the Liberty Bowl when Bryant walked onto the playing field for his final game. All-SEC center Steve Mott remembers how cold it was. "At the bowl games they give the players a lot of souvenirs. One of the packages had toiletries and things like that. And they had panty hose in them. I don't know what we were supposed to do with those,

GOODBYE TO THE BEAR

～

Howell Raines

ACCORDING TO THE UNIVERSITY OF Alabama football records, the date would have to have been September 27, 1958. I was in the back seat of a 1957 Dodge, hurtling down the long lap of Alabama from Birmingham toward the bleak gumbo prairie south of Montgomery. We were on a sporting venture of some kind, bound for a cabin in the pinelands. I was fifteen years old. My elders sat in the front seat fiddling with the radio that, on a maddeningly intermittent signal, brought astounding news from Mobile. The University of Alabama, which had won four games in the previous three years, was ahead of Louisiana State University, the predicted national champion. Finally, Alabama lost, but not before it was clear that the new coach was a serious citizen. That is my first memory of Bear Bryant.

On December 29, 1982, I watched the broadcast of Bryant's last game. It was a victory just solid enough to arouse the hope that what is called "Alabama's winning tradition" could go on without him. But after twenty-five years in the stands, in front of television sets, and, later, hunched over radios in distant cities where the signal from home was almost too faint to hear, I was tempted to announce my retirement as an Alabama fan. It could, after all, never be as good again. And believe me, to have been in the city of Tuscaloosa in October when you were young and full of Early Times and had a shining Alabama girl by your side—to have had all that and then to have seen those red shirts pour out onto the field, and, then, coming behind them, with that inexorable big cat walk of his, the man himself, The Bear—that was very good indeed.

Alabama native and Pulitzer Prize winner Howell Raines is the editorial page editor for The New York Times. *He has a master's degree from UA.*

Coach Bryant before the '81 Cotton Bowl, holding his ever-present rolled-up game plan and wearing his trademark houndstooth hat.

but a lot of the guys ended up cutting them off at about the knees and wearing them to keep warm at the game!"

Bama didn't let their coach down that night, whipping the Illini 21-15 and giving Bear Bryant an unequaled final record in college football of 323 wins, 85 losses, and 17 ties. Afterward the Illinois quarterback and Heisman Trophy candidate Tony Eason stated to the press: "Let's face it. Alabama just likes to hit you. They are the hardest hitting team I've ever played against." It was the kind of thing that made Bryant proudest of all.

～

IN LESS THAN A MONTH THE BIG HEART WAS STILLED. Bryant had agreed to stay on as athletics director until the next season but on the afternoon of January 25, 1983, became ill with chest pains and other symptoms of a heart attack. He was rushed to Druid City Hospital where it was determined there was no massive injury, but doctors still worried about a major attack occurring. Next morning Bryant was pain-free, joking and laughing with the hospital staff and visitors—including Ray Perkins, who had been named his successor— when at 12:45 p.m. his breathing became shallow and almost immediately his heart and breath stopped. Doctors and staff rushed in and began desperate measures to resuscitate him, but it was to no avail. He was pronounced dead forty-five minutes after the episode. At last the storms were over.

The sports world was stunned. Sympathy calls and tributes poured in from around the nation, from President Reagan on down. Especially meaningful was the reaction of other college coaches who spoke of how Paul Bryant had touched so positively everyone he ever met. It was so true. He had made it a rule in his life to treat all men with consideration and for this, as much as his winning record on the football field, a particular sanctity hovered over him.

The funeral was held at Tuscaloosa with burial at Birmingham's Elmwood Cemetery. Bryant's football players were the pallbearers. As the funeral cortege slowly wound its way past Bryant-Denny Stadium, past Thomas Field with his big coaching tower now forever empty, people in the thousands lined the streets and highways and overpasses all the way to Birmingham to pay their respects. Along Interstate 59 scores of huge tractor-trailer rigs, alerted to one another by CB radios, pulled over and their drivers stood by the roadside in reverent homage. Six large buses carried the players and the athletic department staff. Coach Jim Goostree, Alabama's longtime athletic trainer, remembered that Bryant had always ridden in the right front seat of the lead bus. When people began boarding, including the new head coach Ray Perkins and his wife, they passed that seat by. "It wasn't planned that way," Goostree said, "it's just the way it happened."

After graveside services at Elmwood, Bryant was laid to rest and thus he passed into legend, long linked with his name. It is generally agreed that the largest funerals ever held in the South were those of Jefferson Davis, Martin Luther King, Jr., Elvis Presley, and Paul William Bryant.

On a freezing night in Memphis, the Tide gave Bryant his final victory, a 21-15 win over Illinois in the Liberty Bowl, the place where he'd started a quarter century before.

THE DISTINGUISHED ADVERSARY

~

Willie Morris

LET ME SAY AT THE OUTSET that I am a fervid Ole Miss fan, but I am reminded of two beguiling pilgrimages my wife JoAnne and I made in recent years. During them, it was my pleasure to honor our distinguished and long-standing adversary, the Crimson Tide, for one of the most noble football traditions in American history, an achievement accompanied over the years by considerable grace and dignity, not to mention tenacity and resilience.

Our first visitation relevant to the themes of this book took place during a publishing conference we attended on Alabama's campus. I felt it incumbent to drop in on the Bryant Museum.

When I was growing up in the Delta Village of Yazoo City, Mississippi, years ago, I knew as much about SEC football as anybody in town. One of the authentic heroes of my youth was Harry Gilmer, and I remember as yesterday the way he leapt with such dexterity in the air while throwing his noteworthy passes. I even wrote him a fan letter when I was ten years old, and two months or so later I got a handwritten reply from him on a penny postcard, in which he thanked me for my compliments but said he owed it all to his teammates.

The Bryant Museum was an odyssey through time for me, a sense of childhood moments in their passing. It's a fine establishment, and my wife, who is a historian, kept remarking how impressed she was by its auspicious displays of authentic chronology and events, very accessible and well-organized. The memorabilia of the stunning Bama Rose Bowl games of 1926, 1927, 1931, 1935, 1938, and 1946 magnetized me—especially the 1926 one, when people gathered at the train depots of Dixie to celebrate the returning Bama players and coaches, whose victory over the University of Washington was a symbolic triumph for the entire whipped-down South of that day. I did not

know, until the museum told me, that Bear Bryant played the entire Tennessee game of 1935 on a broken leg!

And here was the documentation of the incredible national championships under Paul Bryant of 1961, '64, '65, '73, '78, and '79—accomplishments which will certainly never be recorded with such frequency in this nation again. And the exhibits of the Bama players I kept up with over time: the immortal Gilmer, Vaughan Mancha, Dixie Howell, Don Hutson, Bart Starr, Lee Roy Jordan, Kenny "Snake" Stabler, Pat Trammell, John Hannah, Ozzie Newsome, Dwight Stephenson, Bob Baumhower, Ray Perkins, Johnny Musso, Jim Krapf—a singular roster if ever there was one. And David "the Deuce" Palmer, who almost single-handedly defeated my beloved Ole Miss in 1993. And displays here and there of four whom I knew personally: Joe Namath when he owned his bar in New York City, Steve Sloan when he was coaching at Ole Miss, Scott Hunter on whose Mobile television programs I have appeared, and Bruce Bolton, later an ABC television producer. I was sitting in a Polish tavern in Bridgehampton, Long Island, on New Year's Day 1979 with the writer Budd Schulberg watching the historic Bama-Penn State game— the Goal Line Stand in the Sugar Bowl—and remembered Bolton's critical TD pass reception.

There was another New Year's morning a few years ago. We were visiting relatives in Birmingham. We were staying in a motel, and before the bowl games began on the tube, I concluded I had to go to Bear Bryant's grave.

"How are we going to find it?" my wife asked.

"I'll ask at the front desk."

"Will they know?"

"Hah!"

The motel man, who claimed to have named his young son Paul Bryant, drew me a map to the Elmwood Cemetery. It is a historic cemetery, and enormous, expanding far away in all directions of Birmingham, and

The Bear in winter: Coach Bryant in his tower during his final season at the university.

when we got there I discovered I did not need the hand-drawn map the motel man had given me, because once you enter the front gate there are substantial crimson arrows on the asphalt drives which lead you on the lengthy circuitous route to the grave itself.

And there he was, the Bear in repose, another authentic hero for me. He was an exceedingly tough personage, but in his indwelling heart he cared for what mattered: mainly human beings. It was a cold, crisp Ala-bama forenoon with a patina of frost on the greensward, preternaturally quiet, and we had the vicinity all to ourselves. Strangely, someone had left a distinctive offering there to the Bear—a tin of Copenhagen snuff. I too wished to pay my obeisance to this legendary American. In the car I found half-a-dozen festive peppermint holiday decorations wrapped in cellophane. I placed them on the grave. "Thank you, Coach Bryant," I whispered. And I meant it.

Esteemed Southern writer Willie Morris, who edited Harper's Magazine *in the 1960s, died in August 1999.*

Chapter Seven

FLUX

1983 ~ 1989

HUS ENDED THE BRYANT DYNASTY. He had led the Crimson Tide to six national championships, thirteen SEC championships and during twenty-five years at The University of Alabama his teams compiled a winning record of 232-46-9. He took the Tide to a bowl game every year but his first. Forty-five Bryant players were named First Team All-Americans and hundreds more received awards for athletic, leadership, and scholarship merit. Not only had the dark years of the 1950s been restored to the eras of Wallace Wade and Frank Thomas, they had been gloriously enhanced. But the achievements of Paul Bryant carried no guarantee of their perpetuation.

When Walter Ray Perkins took over the Alabama football program there were high hopes—at least as much as could be held with the realization that the Great Man was gone. A native of Petal, Mississippi, Perkins had been an All-American receiver under Bryant during the fabulous championship years of the mid-sixties. He'd played pro ball with the Baltimore Colts and was head coach of the New York Giants. Bryant did not participate in the selection of Perkins, reasoning that he had too many favorites among the possible candidates. So president Joab Thomas organized a search committee and Perkins was the man it came up with.

The first thing Perkins did was tear down Bryant's renowned coaching tower. Not only that, but he quickly tried to move himself and his regime out of the shadow of his famous mentor. Perkins could be a likable character, but he could also be mercurial and curt. His main problem with the media and fans was that he was not Bear Bryant and, knowing this, Perkins seemed to go out of his way to prove it. One woman, a longtime Bama fan, was heard to grouse, "You'd never see Bear Bryant wearing those headphones!" Never-

Alabama's All-SEC quarterback Gary Hollingsworth behind center Roger Shultz in 1989. Hollingsworth set the school record for passing yardage that year, throwing for 2,379 yards and 14 touchdowns.

theless, it must have been a difficult thing for Perkins to come in as a "replacement" for someone so beloved and admired.

His first season, 1983, wasn't too bad for a newcomer. Bryant had left Perkins some fine material in the shape of Walter Lewis, now in his last season, senior split ends Jesse Bendross and Joey Jones, and junior fullback Ricky Moore. He also recruited some stellar freshman standouts, including Cornelius Bennett, Kerry Goode, Curt Jarvis, and Wes Neighbors. The Tide went 8-4 that year, but many of its losses were close, including a 34-28 squeaker to Penn State marked by a disgraceful denial of a last-second goal line pass which the replays clearly show was an Alabama touchdown. Auburn's great Bo Jackson accounted for Bama's 23-20 loss to the Tigers in a torrential rainstorm. The Crimson Tide was invited to yet another post-season game, the Sun Bowl, where they blew out SMU 28-7. Even so there was of course grumbling among the die-hards, but all in all Perkins had done well.

~

ANY GREAT EXPECTATIONS FOR 1984 WERE QUICKLY DASHED in the season opener as the Tide not only lost 38-31 to future Heisman Trophy great Doug Flutie and his Boston College but also lost standout Kerry Goode for the season to a knee injury. Bama also dropped games to Georgia Tech, Vanderbilt, Georgia, and two excruciating nail-biters against Tennessee, 28-27, and LSU, 16-14. Thus, for the first time since the sorrowful days of Ears Whitworth back in the 1950s, The University of Alabama was assured a losing season as well as the end of its twenty-five-year consecutive streak of bowl appearances. Many wanted Perkins's head on a platter, but there was still one game left that year and it was the one that mattered.

In a nationally televised contest December 1 at Legion Field the Crimson Tide went up against the nationally ranked Auburn Tigers, who had the number one rushing defense in the country, as well as the all-time great Bo Jackson. It was said by some that Bama could only play the spoiler's role and deny Auburn the SEC championship and a Sugar Bowl bid, but this was not the way the team saw it. What they needed was vindication and the way they were to get it, Perkins had told them, was by running the ball down Auburn's throat. Wes Neighbors remembered his reaction to that news: "We looked at each other like he was crazy." Before the game, Perkins employed what Neighbors called "one of the best motivating tactics I ever saw." He brought in a score of former Bama greats to talk to the team. People like Lee Roy Jordan, Joe Namath, Major Ogilvie, Joey Jones, and Neighbors's own father, the former All-American Billy Neighbors. Some cried, some shook their fists, but when it was time for the Tide to take the field, they were fired up like wild men.

That team possibly saved Perkins's job that afternoon. They bottled up Bo Jackson so that his longest run was fifteen yards. Behind the quarterbacking of Mike Shula, running back Paul Ott Carruth scored two Tide touchdowns and Van Tiffin kicked a field goal, but Alabama was still hanging on by its fingernails to a 17-15 lead with minutes left in the fourth quarter. Then Auburn intercepted and marched down to the Bama goal line, fourth and one. In a call that is still being talked about, Tigers coach Pat Dye declined a

Coach Ray Perkins with quarterback Mike Shula. In 1985 Shula set the school record for touchdown passes, with sixteen.

field goal that would have won the game and elected to run a toss sweep to halfback Brent Fullwood. But Auburn running back Bo Jackson and fullback Tommy Agee, who were supposed to be blocking, ran the wrong way, leaving Fullwood vulnerable to Bama's free safety Rory Turner, who flattened him outside the goal. "I just waxed the dude," Turner declared merrily. Linebacker Cornelius Bennett was named All-American. The win seemed to galvanize the Crimson Tide players and carried over to the next season. Wes Neighbors put it this way: "I believe that win paid untold dividends for the future of Alabama football."

"The Kick"—Van Tiffin propels the Tide to a last-second 25-23 win over Auburn in 1985.

The payoff became apparent in the 1985 season. Bama went 9-2-1, losing only to Penn State and Tennessee by a measly two points each and tying LSU. But all that was in the future as the Crimson Tide took the field before eighty-plus-thousand Georgia Bulldog fans "Between the Hedges" on a stifling early September Saturday. It was a tense and bitterly fought contest all evening that finally came down to this: Georgia 16, Bama 13 with less than a minute left to play. Alabama had the ball first and ten on its own twenty-nine. It was with horror and amazement that the Bulldogs fans—let alone the Bulldogs themselves—watched helplessly as junior quarterback Mike Shula marched the Crimson Tide fifty-four yards in four plays and on the fifth fired a seventeen-yard touchdown pass to wide receiver Al Bell. As the final seconds wound down on the scoreboard clock, the Georgia players gaped at it, dumbfounded. This was just the spark Perkins and his team needed to set the tone for a winning season.

They were 7-2-1 going into the biggest game of the year—the fiftieth anniversary of the rivalry with Auburn. The Tigers' Bo Jackson, a week away from winning the Heisman Trophy, was still the biggest gun in the SEC. It was a struggle of much severity, seesawing back and forth until Auburn came back to lead 23-22 with less than a minute to play. It was the Georgia game all over again and again Bama was up to the task. After an incompletion and a sack with only half a minute left, Mike Shula from his own twelve made brilliant use of the clock. He passed to Gene Jelks out to the twenty-six then, on fourth down, gave off to Al Bell for twenty yards on a reverse. Shula next hit Greg Richardson on the Auburn forty-five and Richardson bulled himself out of bounds for five more yards. There were just six seconds left when Van Tiffin took the field for what is now known in Bama parlance as *The Kick*. It seemed to take an eternity, even for Tiffin, but sailed fifty-two yards cleanly through the uprights as the clock ran out. Perkins rushed onto the field shouting "I love you, Van Tiffin," and lifted him into the air. Jubilant Alabama fans danced and shouted in the stands as Auburn supporters slouched sourly for the exits. It was a hell of a win. Jelks, a freshman who years later would become infamous for his role in Alabama's first NCAA sanctions, was the game's Most Valuable Player, having rushed for 192 yards. Tackle Jon Hand was named All-American, as was Cornelius Bennett for a second time. They went to the Aloha Bowl that year and flattened Southern Cal, 24-3.

～

THE KICKOFF CLASSIC TAPPED BAMA AND OHIO STATE to start the 1986 season. It was the first time the teams had met since the 1978 Sugar Bowl. Not only was Bryant gone, but Woody Hayes had been forced to resign after striking a Clemson player in a moment of temporary stupidity. The Tide brought a dangerous arsenal into East Rutherford Stadium that night: in addition to Shula, Jelks, Tiffin, Al Bell, and Cornelius Bennett, there were the talented David Casteal, Bobby Humphrey, Curt Jarvis, Greg Richardson, and Derrick Thomas. Van Tiffin kicked three field goals and Al Bell caught a touchdown pass to close it out in the fourth quarter, 16-10. It was an auspicious beginning and Bama capitalized on it by beating Vanderbilt, Southern Miss, and Florida before coming up against their eternal nemesis, Notre Dame, which Alabama had never beaten. But revenge is sweet. It was barely a contest in Birmingham that day as millions of TV watchers saw the Tiders blow out the Fighting Irish, 28-10. Next Bama stomped Memphis State before running all over Tennessee, 56-28. There was much talk that this was the year they would go all the way, but that did not happen because on October 8 at Bryant-Denny Stadium a determined Penn State put the old masheroo on the Crimson Tide, 23-3. It was disappointing, to say the least, and seemed to set the stage for the second loss of the year. After thrashing Mississippi State 38-3, the Tide met LSU in Birmingham. It was a bitter and frustrating evening. The Bengal Tigers went into the locker room at the half leading 14-7, a score which would not ordinarily bother the Crimson Tide. This time it should have, because all Bama managed to do in the second half was put up a twenty-two-yard field goal by Van Tiffin. Four times they entered LSU territory and three times were repulsed.

In the Iron Bowl that year, Bama dropped a fierce and ardent contest to the Auburn Tigers. Going into the second half the Crimson Tide was leading

Above: *The Sack! All-American linebacker Cornelius Bennett flattens Steve Beuerlein in the 1986 Notre Dame game, a 28-10 win for Bama.* **Left:** *The Million Dollar Band in the mid-1980s.*

14-7 and added another three with a Tiffin field goal in the third. But the fortunes of the game are notoriously uncertain and in the final period the Tigers' Brent Fullwood blasted in for a touchdown. Minutes later Auburn split end Lawyer Tillman scored on a reverse to give the Tigers a heart-sickening 21-17 win.

This may or may not have been the impetus behind Perkins's decision to quit. Surely he had nothing to be ashamed of with a 32-15-1 record—especially when many of the losses could be laid on the disastrous losing season of 1984. But there was something else, too. Perkins was an extremely proud man—some said arrogant. He tended to wear his feelings on his sleeve, often snapping at reporters' hard questions. Surely it must have rankled to

Above: *Bobby Humphrey is one of Alabama's all-time leading rushers. In 1992 he was named to the Alabama all-century team.* **Right:** *All-American linebacker Derrick Thomas after Penn State's quarterback in 1988.*

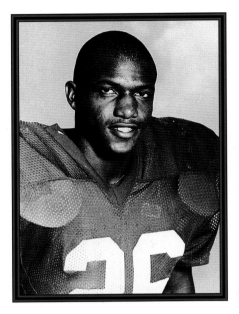

read the unhappy remarks of sportswriters, editorial letters, and unpleasant mail that usually follows a Bama loss. After all, during the three years Perkins had played at Alabama, Bear Bryant had lost only two games and the coach was revered almost as a god. It must have been a reality check for Perkins when he realized Bama fans can be disagreeable as well. Following the Auburn debacle, rumors began to circulate that Perkins was going to accept the job as head coach of the Tampa Bay Buccaneers. He denied them until the end, then resigned and went off to Florida. It could have been that Perkins, who had coached for fifteen years in the NFL, simply found it hard to adjust to dealing with college boys, many of them still teenagers, with all their youthful problems. That probably had to do with it, too. In any case, after Alabama went to the Sun Bowl and demolished the Washington Huskies 28-6, Perkins was gone, and not everyone mourned his going.

Above: *Running back Bobby Humphrey, All-American in 1986.* **Right:** *Fans were somewhat leery of Bill Curry in 1987 when he came from Georgia Tech to coach the Crimson Tide. A good coach and a good man, Curry just wasn't "family."*

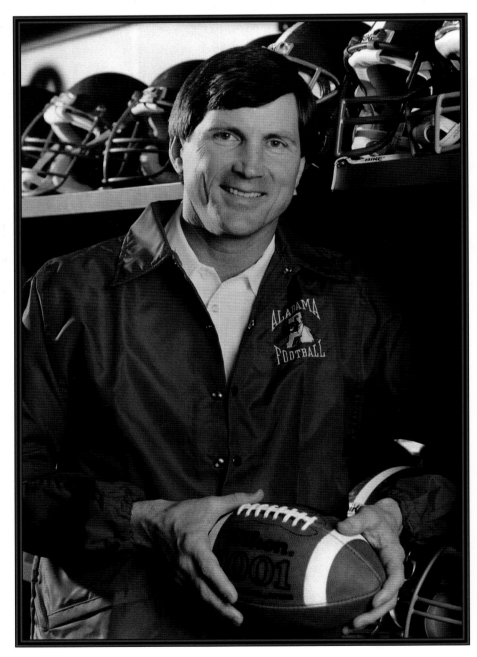

Cornelius Bennett received unanimous All-American honors; Bobby Humphrey and Van Tiffin were also on various All-American teams.

President Joab Thomas was by this time deeply involved in the football program. After Bryant declined to select his own replacement, Thomas had spearheaded the search in secret and he intended to do it again. Birmingham sportswriter Alf Van Hoose summed up the arrival of Bill Curry this way: "There were cheers for Bill Curry of Georgia Tech when Dr. Thomas ramrodded his selection through the so-called search committee. Curry had looks, presentation, academic background and experience. He bore two minuses: (1) he was from a place most Alabamians detested and (2) he had been 0-7 against Auburn."

Curry arrived for the 1987 season with a large number of assistants from Georgia Tech. This did not bode well in the minds of many Bama fans who saw this as intrusive and unwise, since Curry's seven-year record at Tech had been a disappointing 31-43-4. President Thomas was blunt in defending his decision to hire Curry. "First," he said, "we were looking for people with unquestionable integrity. Second, we wanted people who would assist in raising our academic standards, and, third, we wanted people who could win. Bill Curry is going to win."

Quarterback David Smith in 1987 about to throw with protection from center Roger Shultz in Bama's 38-6 win over Southern Miss.

Nevertheless, there was still grousing in some quarters that Curry wasn't "family," and he did not help the situation when he began holding closed practices, excluding not only favored alumni but even former star Alabama players. In the view of some he had trampled upon vested traditions. It all seemed like it was going to pay off, though, when the Crimson Tide opened its 1987 season by thrashing Southern Miss 38-6 and next week went to Penn State and thrashed them, too, 24-13. Bobby Humphrey was back with his sterling running game, as was halfback David Casteal, placekicker Philip Doyle, linebackers Greg Gilbert and Derrick Thomas, center Roger Shultz, nose guard Willie Wyatt, and Gene Jelks, now moved to cornerback. There was a new quarterback, David Smith, who had starred in both the Southern Miss and Penn State games. But Bama stumbled badly the next week against Florida. The game was tied 6-6 in the third quarter when Florida's great freshman running back Emmitt Smith simply exploded, rushing 224 yards for a school record and scoring two touchdowns. "We got whipped," Curry said afterward. "Coaches, players, we got outplayed and out-prepared by Florida."

Bama next beat Vanderbilt and Southwestern Louisiana before a shocking 13-10 upset by Memphis State started the grumbling going again. It was a poor performance marked by penalties, turnovers, and miscues on the part of the Crimson Tide. Afterward, Curry announced that he and his team "have our backs to the wall."

Bama came off the wall next week with a new quarterback, freshman Jeff Dunn, to blast Tennessee 41-22 and renew hopes that the winning tradition was still alive and well. For his part, Curry branded it "not a great performance." Alabama next defeated Mississippi State and LSU for a 4-1 record

Above: Coach Joe Paterno and Bama's Bill Curry before the 1987 Penn State game. Bama won it, 23-13. **Right:** Bama linebacker Phillip Brown (89) crushes a ball carrier in 1987.

Above: *Offensive linebacker Randy Rockwell puts on the pressure, but Memphis State came out on top, 13-10, in 1987.* **Opposite page:** *Tight end Howard Cross squeaks out some yardage in Bama's loss to Notre Dame in 1987.*

in the SEC but then came the Irish of Notre Dame, who gave Alabama the worst whipping it had taken since Nebraska's 38-6 romp in the 1971 Orange Bowl. "Fortunately we don't go out with a performance like this," Curry said. "We still have a game left, and a very big one."

It was, and Bama didn't win it. This was, of course, the Iron Bowl, and a win would have made Alabama SEC champions. The teams were scoreless late in the first half when Derrick Thomas blocked an Auburn punt, recovered it, and went out of bounds at the Tigers' nine. Bama ran it down to the one but on fourth down Dunn overthrew and Auburn not only took possession but, assisted by two personal foul penalties against the Tide, marched down the field for a touchdown. Bama got nothing going in the second half, while the Tigers kicked a field goal to win it 10-0. "Our men played their hearts out," Curry said defiantly.

The Crimson Tide was invited to the Hall of Fame Bowl that January but dropped a teeth-gritting contest against Michigan 28-24. Like Perkins before him, for his first year Curry's 7-5 season wasn't bad but it wasn't good either. At least not good enough for Alabama supporters, even though Bobby Humphrey was named All-American for the second year in a row.

VOICES OF THE TIDE

~

Clyde Bolton

A SPORTSWRITER'S JOB COVERING Alabama is difficult and touchy. If he writes good things about the Crimson Tide, nobody notices because Bama fans expect only nice things to be written; if he says things critical, he is excoriated as being cruel or unfair. Sportswriters know this when they enter the profession, or soon learn it. But their job is to tell it like it is; or at least the way they see it, or saw it, day after day, season after season.

The main problem with sportswriting, though, is timing and it works like this: the real reason for the few failing football seasons at Alabama is that all the stupid and incompetent people were selected to be football coaches while only wise men were chosen as sportswriters. The misfortune in the arrangement has been that the smart sportswriters never tell the dumb football coaches what they should have done to win until after their teams have lost the games.

I came to the *Birmingham News* in 1961, and I've covered Alabama football ever since. Joe Namath made his debut as a varsity Tidesman on September 22, 1962. He threw three touchdown passes as Alabama swamped Georgia 35-0 at Legion Field. The practice of interviewing players wasn't as commonplace then as it is now: Coach Bryant preferred to be the spokesman, but after the game I went into the dressing room and immediately sought out Namath and began asking questions.

Suddenly a voice boomed from across the festive room: "Get away from that boy!" Bryant screamed, "You'll ruin him!" The room became silent and all eyes focused on me, and I turned the color of an Alabama jersey. End of interview but, as I recall, Namath was not ruined by my attention.

Two names closely associated with newspaper coverage of the Crimson Tide are those of *Birmingham News* writers Zipp Newman and Benny Marshall. In those pre-radio, pre-TV days, Newman brought minute details of

Below: *As the Bama Rose Bowl Special headed for California, Coach Wade called a practice during a layover in Arizona. Here sportswriters accompanying the team, Charlie Outlaw, Howard Pill, Zipp Newman, and Morgan Blake, clown around in the desert.* **Opposite page:** *Tide broadcasters Eli Gold and John Forney flank Auburn announcer Jim Fyffe.*

Alabama's Rose Bowl adventures to eager fans. He wrote in the florid style of his day. His lead on the Tide's second Rose Bowl game, January 1, 1927, against Stanford:

Alabama thy name is courage—unyielding valor in all its splendor! Flow on Crimson thou has brought honors aplenty to Dixieland in twice sweeping the Pacific Coast off its feet with two comebacks that will ever live in gridiron history!

And this when Alabama didn't even win—the game ended in a 7-7 tie!

Benny Marshall was a stylist, a master of the human interest column who did more than any other writer to deify Bryant. Jimmy Bryan and Alf Van Hoose were among other *Birmingham News* men who covered Alabama for years. Bryan had the best lead on an Alabama game I ever read, after the Tide beat Vanderbilt 66-3 in 1979, and when U.S. monetary inflation was running in the double digits: "Inflation killed the Commodores Saturday. Once the football was inflated, Vanderbilt was dead."

Ray Melick is a bulldog on the Alabama beat for the *Birmingham Post Herald*. Naylor Stone and Bill Lumpkin were well-known Tide chroniclers for the P-H. Al Browning and Cecil Hurt have produced distinguished Crim-

son Tide coverage for the *Tuscaloosa News*, and George Smith of the *Anniston Star* not only wrote expertly of Bama but watched his son Barry play for Alabama.

John Forney was the beloved Voice of the Crimson Tide for years before the games were so widely broadcast on television. Keith Jackson of ABC Sports has covered dozen's of Alabama games in the past four decades. The great Mel Allen, an Alabama grad himself, was an early Bama broadcaster, too.

Eli Gold, of Bama's Crimson Tide Football Network, is the most versatile announcer in America. Anyone who listens to Alabama's games on the radio will be familiar with the names of Jerry Duncan, Maury Farrell, Doug Layton, and Kenny Stabler.

Like most people, John Forney generally trod lightly around Coach Bryant, but once mustered up enough courage to complain to him that the numbers on Alabama players' jerseys were too small for easy identification from up in the press box.

Bryant embraced Forney's shoulders—a bit too firmly for comfort—and told him: "Ole buddy, you oughta know 'em with no numbers at all."

Columnist Clyde Bolton has covered sports for the Birmingham News *since 1961.*

As Curry promised, things got better in 1988, with Bryant-Denny Stadium now enlarged to seat seventy thousand. An early season loss to Ole Miss was forgiven after big wins over Tennessee and Penn State. In the Penn State game Derrick Thomas put on an astonishing performance. He was credited with three sacks, eight individual tackles, one knocked-down pass, and forcing the Nittany Lions' quarterback to throw early on eight occasions. CBS sports announcer Brent Musburger said on air: "Folks, this is the greatest individual defensive effort I have ever witnessed." Alabama 8, Penn State 3. But then Bama dropped a one-point loss to LSU and got beaten again by Auburn 15-10. A 30-10 win over Texas A&M and a 29-28 victory over Army in the Sun Bowl capped a 9-3 season. Still, Curry hadn't beaten Auburn and so many rumors were flying that university president Roger Sayers called a hasty press conference in College Station to discount rumors that Curry might be fired.

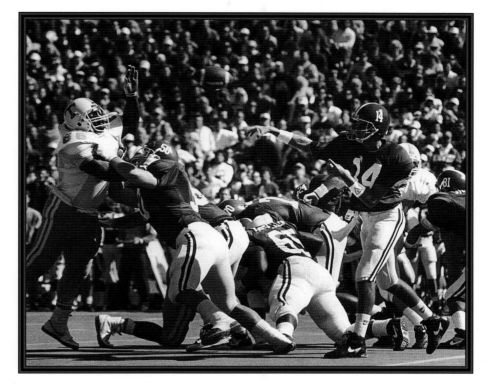

As a sidelight, the Texas A&M game was curious for the reason that it had been dubbed the Hurricane Bowl after a September matchup was postponed by Curry because of Hurricane Gilbert. A&M had a good time of it, at least until the game, electing a "Hurricane Queen" and her court, "The Seven Tropical Depressions." Derrick Thomas racked up his twenty-seventh sack of the year and the prestigious Butkus Award as the nation's finest defensive player.

Furthermore, the Army game proved to be a thoroughly entertaining contest. The schools had never played before but this year Army had developed a really fine team; in fact, going into the fourth quarter it was Army 28, Bama 20 until the Tide began to click. David Smith, coming off a knee injury, had returned as quarterback. He said of the Army footballers afterwards: "They are a little bit smaller than most of the teams we played, but they played as hard as anybody I had ever seen." Smith had a sterling afternoon for his final game, completing thirty-two passes for 412 yards against Army's 0. But Army ran all over Bama, gaining 350 yards rushing, and if Derrick Thomas hadn't blocked two field goal attempts, the Tide would surely have lost the game. Thomas, Kermit Kendrick, and Larry Rose were named All-Americans.

≈

Next year, 1989, Bama became SEC champions for the first time since Bryant's last days and it seemed that Curry was riding high. Among the standouts on this stellar team were junior quarterback Gary Hollingsworth, who had to

Above: *Gary Hollingsworth leads the team to a 47-30 defeat of Tennessee on the way to a 1989 SEC championship.*
Opposite page: *All-American Derrick Thomas was one of the greatest and most beloved players for the Crimson Tide. He lettered all four years, from 1985 to 1988. He held every Alabama linebacking record, including the most sacks in a single season, and in a career. In 1988 he won the Butkus Award, given to the nation's best linebacker. He was a nine-time Pro-Bowl player for the Kansas City Chiefs and was voted into the Senior Bowl's Hall of Fame in 1999. On January 23, 2000, he was involved in an icy automobile accident and three weeks later died of injuries suffered in the crash. Derrick Thomas was truly the spirit of Alabama football.*

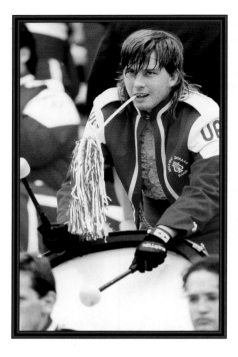

Above: *A drummer really getting into the action.* **Right:** *Fullback Martin Houston leads the way for tailback Siran Stacy in a 35-7 victory over Memphis State in 1989.*

step in for an injured Jeff Dunn, running back Siran Stacy, ends Lamonde Russell and Marco Battle, cornerback John Mangum, nose guard Willie Wyatt, and a big linebacker named Keith McCants. Mangum, a senior, would make All-American that year. So would junior Keith McCants who then packed up and left the team—the first Alabama player to do so under new rules that allowed an athlete to declare himself eligible for the NFL draft before his senior year.

Bama romped through its first nine games of the 1989 season and was destined for the Sugar Bowl and a possible national championship until it met Auburn for the first time in the Tigers' newly expanded eighty-five-thousand-seat Jordan-Hare Stadium. Since the series had been renewed four decades earlier, the Iron Bowl had by mutual agreement been played in Birmingham, supposedly neutral turf. But over the years Auburn was made to believe by the media and other sources that Birmingham was Tide territory, and this certainly had some bearing on their decision to invest so much in a huge new facility on campus.

It was a perfect day for football: fifty-two degrees, sunny, and light westerly winds. Alabama entered the game ranked number two in both wire service polls and Gary Hollingsworth was within one completed toss of surpassing Scott Hunter's single-season record for throwing yardage, which had stood for nearly twenty years. Hollingsworth moved past Hunter that long afternoon but failed to move the Crimson Tide past Auburn. In what was supposed to be a struggle of the defenses, Auburn racked up 441 yards and Alabama 427. But it was the Plainsmen who came up with the win and, yet again, Bill Curry was deeper in the doghouse with many Tide fans. In those days the Alabama Football Network carried a phone-in radio show for several hours after a game and the evening of the Auburn loss the calls became particularly vicious. These Monday morning quarterbacks did all but curse Bill Curry and some did that, too. Moreover, the media in general were critical of his handling of the game.

~

FOR CURRY, WHO DURING HIS ALABAMA CAREER endured the slings and arrows somewhat stoically—including having a rock thrown through the window of his office—it was the last straw. The University of Kentucky was looking for a coach and Curry accepted the job. It must have crossed his mind that if winning an SEC championship and taking his team to the Sugar Bowl weren't enough for these people, he was not going to stick around to find out what was. In any case, down in New Orleans Curry told his players he might take another job. Rumors of this had been floating around anyway and what effect they had on the Crimson Tide's 33-25 loss to the Miami Hurricanes that night is difficult to assess. Bama went to the dressing room at the half trailing by only three points, but Miami roared back in the final periods to clinch the national title. After Curry's final announcement that he was headed for bluegrass country, Roger Shultz, the stalwart Alabama center, quipped: "I knew Coach Curry was leaving when he came into the squad room with a blue jacket on and in its lapels were tickets to the Kentucky Derby."

Linebacker Keith McCants intercepts an Auburn pass in 1989, in Alabama's first game at Jordan-Hare Stadium. Auburn won it, 30-20.

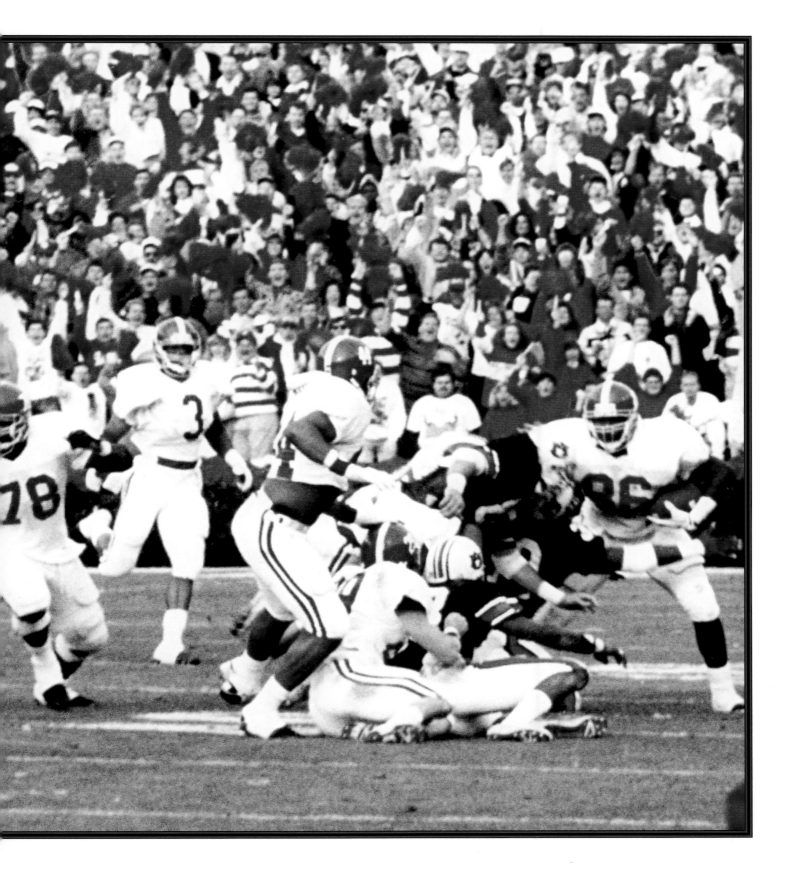

Chapter Eight

Chapter Eight

FAMILY

1990 ~ 1996

N THE DEAD OF WINTER IN 1990 GENE STALLINGS turned his gaze once more upon the Capstone. He had been hired as Curry's replacement by university president Roger Sayers, a good football fan, and by athletics director Hootie Ingram—who, after nearly forty years, still held the Alabama record for interceptions in a single season. The fifty-five-year-old "Bebes" Stallings once again was "family." He had been one of the few to endure all the horrors of Bear Bryant's infamous Junction, Texas, training camp. He had been an assistant coach at Bama under Bryant before returning as head coach of Texas A&M and later coaching the Phoenix Cardinals. No matter that he had compiled overall losing seasons at both posts. He was still family. In Gene Stallings, Alabama fans believed they had at last found the true heir to the Great Man. He was to prove them right.

Many, including Stallings, believed Bryant had wanted Stallings to replace him ahead of Perkins back in '82. In any case, he was back. Linda Knowles, Bryant's long-time secretary who remained in the athletic department, had this to say about it: "You could probably call any coach or player or staff member who has ever been at the University and ask them where they'd like to be. And once you've been associated with the football program at Alabama, it gets into your blood and just becomes 'home.' Coach Stallings just came home, the way I look at it, and it was awfully good to see him."

At first, it was not a very good homecoming. Bama dropped the opening game to a Southern Miss team led by Brett Favre in heat so intense Tide managers used more than a ton of ice on the sidelines. Next the Tide fell to Florida and Georgia but only by a combined total of five points. The grumbling began once more. At that point Stallings took stock of the kind of football his team was playing and decided to change it. He moved them from a wide-open passing offense to a power running game. Roger Shultz, the big

In 1994 the Tide beat Tennessee 17-13 in Knoxville and Coach Stallings and Jay Barker celebrate with cigars, a tradition started by Bear Bryant thirty years earlier.

Receiver Lamonde Russell with a perfect snag for the Tide in the 1990 Southern Miss. game, the first of the season.

senior center who had by then played under Perkins, Curry, and now Stallings, remembered it being a difficult adjustment. "It would be like a traditional passing team like Brigham Young changing to a running game."

Even without star tailback Siran Stacy, who was out for the season with an injury after the Southern Miss game, Stallings had replacements Derrick Lassic and Chris Anderson in the lineup. He also had star receivers for Gary Hollingsworth in ends Lamonde Russell and Steve Busky. Stallings experimented with his new game plan on Vanderbilt the next week. He was pleasantly surprised—the Tide crushed the Commodores 59-28. After rolling up a school record fifty-two points in the first half, Stallings pulled out his first string and let backups play the rest of the game. After whipping Southwestern Louisiana the Crimson Tide appeared in Knoxville before ninety-seven thousand antagonistic fans to meet the powerful Tennessee Volunteers, ranked third in the nation. The contest did not stir much interest among the sports

Above: *The "Third Saturday in October," 1990. With four seconds left on the clock, Philip Doyle kicks the game-winning field goal to beat the Tennessee Vols 9-6 in Knoxville.*
Left: *Placekicker Philip Doyle on the shoulders of his teammates.*

fraternity—one ESPN sportscaster even predicted it would be like a high school team going up against a major college power. How wrong he was.

In a game of field goals they were tied 6-6 in the fourth quarter when Stacy Harrison broke through and blocked a Tennessee field goal attempt to give the Tide possession on the Vols' thirty-seven. After three runs for seven yards, Philip Doyle, who had recently broken Van Tiffin's school record by kicking sixty field goals, trotted out and whacked a forty-seven-yarder for the Bama victory. Stallings, passing out the traditional Tennessee victory cigars, was jubilant. "This has to rank right up there with the biggest wins I've ever had in my career," he declared.

His jubilation was short-lived, however, as Penn State spoiled Alabama's homecoming game the next week by beating the Tide 9-0. It was the first time since 1955 that Bama had been shut out at home. But there were four more games left in the season and this was a team that did not quit. After whipping Mississippi State, LSU, and Cincinnati, the Crimson Tide now turned its attention toward Auburn. It had been four long fallow years since the Tigers had gone down to defeat in the Iron Bowl, and now Alabama was determined to concentrate all its strengths against them.

Bringing a less than satisfactory 6-4 record into Legion Field on a sunny cool afternoon, Bama wasn't given much of a chance. Both coaches predicted that the outcome would hinge on turnovers and both were correct. The Crimson Tide forced three fumbles and two interceptions from the bewildered Tigers. Alabama led 10-0, before Auburn scored a touchdown late in the first half. Then Bama's defense really dug in. Philip Doyle added two more field goals, smashing the SEC record with seventy-eight career goals. He was named to every All-American team. Crimson Tide fans were delirious. They were a family again, and even a displeasing 34-7 New Year's Day loss to Louisville in the Fiesta Bowl could not dampen that.

Left: *Defensive tackle Byron Holdbrooks exults after sacking Auburn's quarterback in 1990.* **Above:** *The "Big Dogs" or "Tide Guys," with their outlandish game day uniforms, have been a fixture at Bama games since the 1970s.*

THE 1991 SEASON OPENED WITH GREAT HOPES AND EXPECTATIONS that would not go unfulfilled, but at first it did not seem so. Bama was elated by the return of the great tailback Siran Stacy, as well as quarterback Danny Woodson, receiver Prince Wimbley, and fullback Kevin Turner, plus defensive stars Antonio Langham, John Sullins, George Teague, and All-American John Copeland. And there was another bright light in the lineup that most fans were unaware of—a little freshman receiver from Birmingham named David Palmer.

After trouncing Temple, the Crimson Tide traveled to Gainesville to meet its most obnoxious opponents, the Florida Gators. In a game marked by boorish behavior from Gator fans who threw liquor bottles and other objects at Tide supporters, Florida simply outplayed Alabama by an insulting 35-0. After reviewing the number of fumbles, interceptions, penalties, and other miscues, Stallings sourly reported that "about a third of the time we were making a bad play."

Florida notwithstanding, Bama went on to win all the rest of its games including big victories over Georgia, Tennessee, and LSU, in which a young freshman quarterback named Jay Barker started for the first time after Danny Woodson was suspended for violating team rules. Stallings, more confident of his basic game, had installed all sorts of trick plays this season, including double reverses, tailbacks passing the football, and letting split end David Palmer play quarterback. When Auburn time rolled around the Tide was ready and, as usual, it was a bitterly contested game. Bama wound up on top 13-6 but not before some scares. Punter Tank Williamson possibly saved the day with six kicks averaging 45.7 yards—one of them for 71 yards!

The Blockbuster Bowl in Miami came calling and Bama met the defending national champions, the University of Colorado Buffaloes. It was the Crimson Tide's forty-fourth post-season bowl, continuing to surpass all other teams in NCAA history. David Palmer was all over the field, returning a punt for a

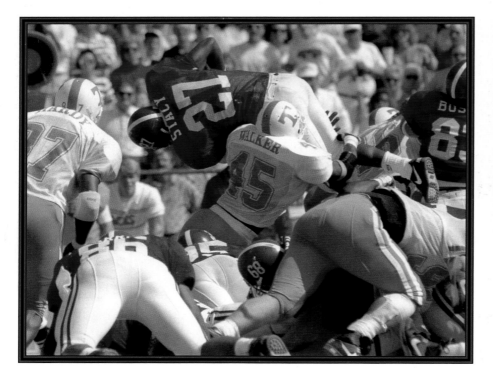

Above: *The Crimson Tide takes the field in the Stallings era.* **Left:** *Siran Stacy goes over the top for a touchdown in the 1991 Tennessee game at Legion Field. Bama won it, 24-19.*

touchdown, catching and throwing passes, and generally bamboozling the confused Buffaloes, who lost to the Tide 30-25. Now known as "The Deuce," Palmer was rewarded with the "Brian Piccolo Most Valuable Player" trophy. Siran Stacy received the CBS "Player of the Game" citation. Nose guard Robert Stewart was named All-American that year.

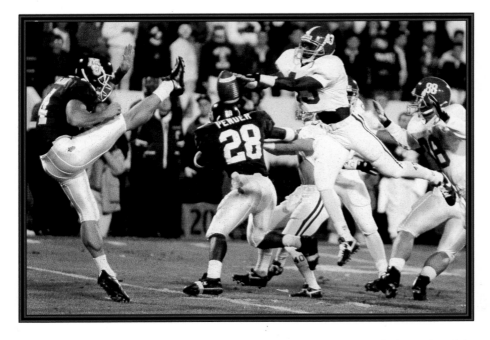

THE GLORIOUS YEAR OF 1992 HARKENED BACK to the great national championship seasons of Bear Bryant in the 1960s and 1970s. Bama played thirteen games and did not lose a one of them—a perfect season in every way except one, which we shall later see. Led by Chris Anderson, Jay Barker, Steve Busky, John Copeland, Eric Curry, Derrick Lassic, Antonio Langham, Antonio London, David Palmer, Michael Proctor, Sam Shade, George Teague, Sherman Williams, George Wilson, Prince Wimbley, and others truly too numerous to mention, the Crimson Tide steamrolled over each and every opponent. When Iron Bowl time arrived Bama was ranked number two in the nation behind the Hurricanes of Miami.

Less than twenty-four hours before game time, Auburn coach Pat Dye announced he would not be returning for the 1993 season. Perhaps he had had a premonition. It was 0-0 at the end of the first half. In the second, a sixty-one-yard interception run by Antonio Langham put the Tide ahead 7-0 and a Michael Proctor field goal moments later made it 10-0. Sherman Williams scored in the fourth quarter to ice it for the Tide 17-0. It was the first time Auburn had been shut out since Dye's arrival nearly twenty years earlier.

Now came the new Really Big One. When the SEC added Arkansas and South Carolina, bringing the total to twelve teams, it reorganized itself into East and West Divisions and scheduled a playoff game to determine the final winner. The inaugural SEC Championship Game, Alabama vs. Florida, was played December 5 at Legion Field and it was all it was billed to be. The Gators scored in the first quarter, answered by Alabama. Bama racked up another seven in the second, and in the third quarter it was Bama 21, Florida 14. In the fourth period Bama's punting game collapsed and the Gators tied it up. Now the nation's number one defense took over and with minutes to go Antonio Langham intercepted a Shane Matthews pass and ran it back for the final score: Bama 28, Florida 21. Linebacker Derrick Oden said of Langham's play that day, "He must be superman. I swear if I pulled up his shirt, I think he would have a big S under it." Jay Barker, who was now 15-0 as a starter for

Above: *David "The Deuce" Palmer hauling one in as Bama crushes Ole Miss 31-10 in 1992.* **Above left:** *Antonio Langham blocks a Mississippi State punt in 1992 in a 30-21 win over the Bulldogs in Starkville.*

the Tide, joked after the game: "I got to do my favorite play tonight. I got to get down on one knee and let the seconds run out."

Flushed with this victory, it was finally Sugar Bowl time and at stake was nothing less than the national championship against the number-one-ranked team in America, Miami. For weeks both parties had eyed one another with suspicion and, for Miami's part, contempt; numerous Hurricane players were quoted in the media with disparaging remarks about the Crimson Tide. This had the effect of rousing the underdog Tiders to the ferocity of wolves.

That chill New Year's Day in New Orleans, The University of Alabama was still celebrating its one hundredth year of college football. The team that appeared in the Superdome was a far cry from the tiny band of players William Little had assembled in front of the library on the quadrangle in the

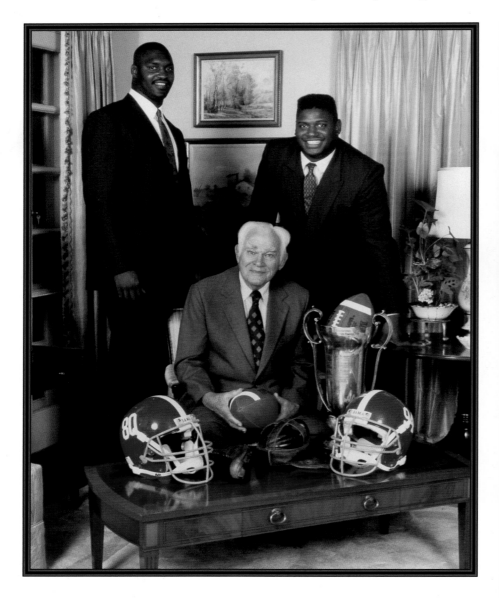

Above: *All-Americans Eric Curry and John Copeland flank "Wu" Winslett, standout Bama end in the Rose Bowls of '26 and '27.* **Right:** *Running back Derrick Lassic following Martin Houston in the Crimson Tide's spectacular 28-21 win over Florida in the SEC's first championship game in 1992.*

autumn of 1892, but the spirit of those long-gone heroes and those of the other great Crimson Tide teams must have echoed to the rafters of the fabulous indoor stadium. Here tonight would be the most-watched college game in the country; here tonight would be the final exam against the defending national champions from Florida.

Alabama was there and they were magnificent; the game itself became memorable to the height of some heroic fable. The first quarter ended in a 3-3 tie but by the half the Tide was ahead 13-6, courtesy of another Michael Proctor field goal and a touchdown by Sherman Williams. The Hurricanes seemed shocked by this unanticipated turn of events. Bama's All-American big defensive end John Copeland said afterward of Miami's Heisman-Trophy-winning quarterback Gino Torretta: "In the second quarter, I saw Torretta look over at me, and he froze for a second. I saw fear."

In the second half the Tide came out inflamed with the passions of victory. Torretta threw an interception to Bama's Tommy Johnson on the first play from scrimmage, who returned it to the Hurricanes' twenty. Six plays later Derrick Lassic scored, making it Alabama 20, Miami 6.

Smelling the fear and uncertainty of Miami's stellar quarterback, when the 'Canes set up for their first play after receiving Bama's kickoff, Stallings called an astonishing defensive alignment. When Torretta set up in the shotgun he was virtually paralyzed to discover all eleven of Bama's nationally number one defensive unit glaring at him right on the line of scrimmage.

Every one of them, right on the line! This, of course, would be enough to rattle the likes of a John Elway and so when Torretta attempted a feeble pass, George Teague intercepted and ran it back thirty-one yards for the score. Bama 27, 'Canes 6.

Not only that, a few plays later the ubiquitous Teague ran down trash-talking Miami receiver Lamar Thomas—who had just caught a pass and was headed for Bama's goal—and literally snatched the ball away from him in mid-stride. This was one of the most amazing feats ever seen in big-time college ball though, unfortunately, it was called back because of an upfield penalty. Miami opened the final period with a spectacular seventy-eight-yard punt return to bring the score to 27-13, but that was all she wrote. Late in the fourth quarter Derrick Lassic capped a twelve-play drive by Jay Barker to rush for his second touchdown, and the game ended with Alabama the undisputed national champions, 34-13.

Stallings had proven one thing at least, that a serious running game and a sterling defense will win ball games. He had learned that the hard way, from Paul "Bear" Bryant. Jay Barker threw only four times for 18 yards that night but Bama's runners gained 267 yards. Derrick Lassic was named the game's Most Valuable Player. As for the defense, Lassic probably summed it up best with this intended compliment: "Our defensive guys are so mean and like hitting people so much, they'd probably slap their own mothers!" One of the things Stallings was most proud of was the behavior of the team. "We took 145 players to New Orleans, and we didn't have one player get into trouble the whole time we were there. We had 11 p.m. curfews for four straight nights and not one player was late. You could take 145 Sunday School teachers to New Orleans, leave them for a week, and some of them are going to get in trouble."

~

STALLINGS HONESTLY BELIEVED IT WHEN HE DECLARED no player had gotten into trouble in New Orleans. But the truth was, one player had not only gotten into trouble down there, he was instrumental in getting the entire football program at The University of Alabama into the most trouble it had ever been in—worse even than the difficult years under Ears Whitworth. What had happened is a bane of college football today: a sports agent had cast a wicked shadow over the stunning Sugar Bowl victory. On December 17, after Antonio Langham's brilliant performance against Florida in the SEC Championship Game, a Washington, D.C.-based sports agent had arranged through a member of Langham's family to make Langham a "loan" of four hundred dollars. The agent's intention was to persuade Langham to sign a contract with him, forego the 1993 season at Alabama, and sign up for the NFL draft.

While declaring himself eligible for the draft was not illegal in itself under NCAA rules, if Langham signed a contract with a sports agent it certainly was. But that is what happened directly after the glorious win in the Sugar Bowl.

George Teague in the Sugar Bowl, returning a Gino Torretta pass for a Bama touchdown.

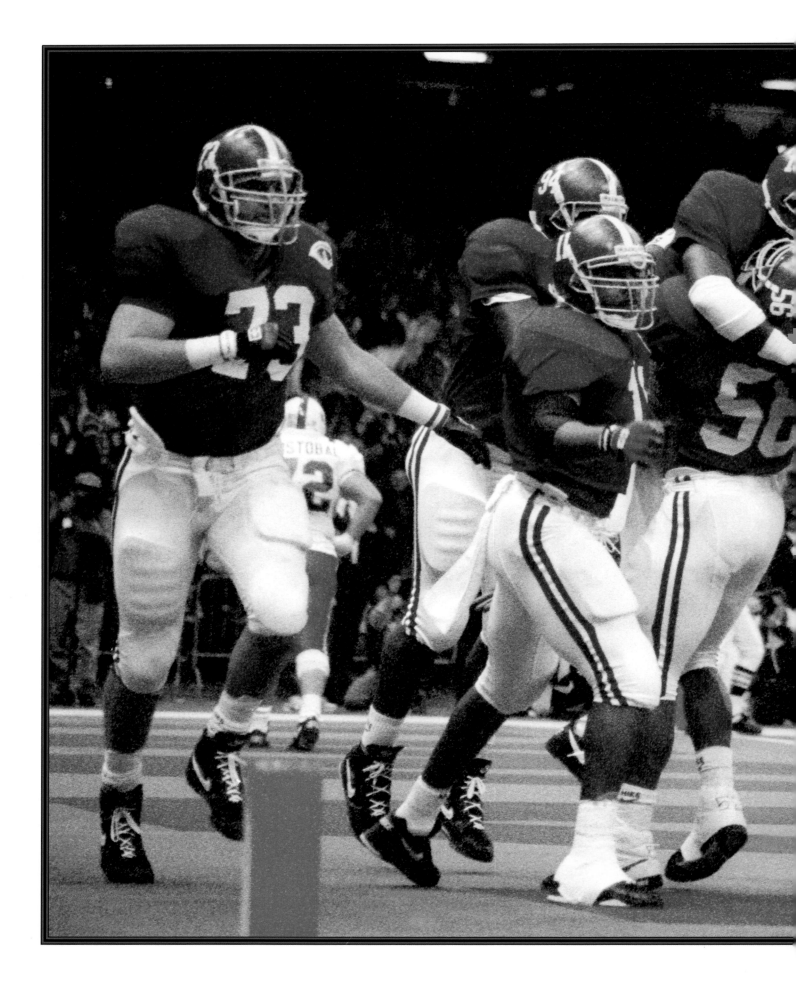

The '93 Sugar Bowl ends, and you'd almost think these players believe they've won!

PLEASE USE RAMPS TO EXIT
Escalators will be shut off-thank you

Coach Stallings gets his national championship victory ride after the
'93 Sugar Bowl. The scoreboard clock in the background tells it all.

According to NCAA records, the agent "hung around the hotel lobby after the game," and took Langham nightclubbing until the wee hours of the morning, then reappeared in his hotel room a short while afterward with what he claimed was a document Langham needed to sign to be eligible for the NFL draft. According to what Langham later said, he was told to sign in two places, but the second signature, by Langham's account, was in fact an agreement to put himself in the stable of the sports agent—though Langham declared he was unaware of this at the time because he did not read the papers.

In any event, when Langham returned home to Town Creek, Alabama, on January 3, he let it slip that he had signed something declaring himself eligible for the draft. His family were of two notions about this, but the ones who prevailed were his guardians, the Goode segment of the family, which had placed three Goodes—Kerry, Clyde, and Chris—on Bama teams. They persuaded Langham to undeclare himself and return to the University for his final year of eligibility. Langham called Stallings and told him about signing the eligibility declaration—but not about the agency contract, which he always swore he did not know he had signed. After asking Langham whether there was a sports agent or any money involved—and receiving a "no" to both questions—Stallings agreed to contact the NFL and help have his draft request annulled.

Nine months later, the NCAA investigators were in Tuscaloosa. They were there not because of Langham but because former Bama standout Gene Jelks had stirred up a great commotion by going to the media with stories that back in 1989 while at Alabama, he had received illegal loans from a bank officer in Altoona, Alabama, who was also a Crimson Tide booster. According to Jelks he used most of the proceeds of the loans to pay for athletic disability insurance policies. This revelation stank to high heaven from the start. Jelks, it seems, was still festering at being moved from running back to cornerback by coach Bill Curry. Presently unemployed, Jelks blamed his bad luck, newspaper accounts said, on the theory that as a running back he might have had a better shot at the NFL. It was also revealed in the press that Jelks was and had been in the employ of Auburn boosters who, records show, issued him checks totaling sixty to seventy thousand dollars, plus an apartment and other emoluments, which resulted in Jelks's alma mater being stabbed in the back.

Though nothing much came of the Jelks business, the NCAA enforcement people were down in Alabama when University officials told them what they had learned about the Langham case.

～

THE CRIMSON TIDE SEEMED TO BE ON A ROLL AGAIN IN 1993, though not quite of the previous season's caliber. With All-American Antonio Langham still one of its star players, after winning the first five games and a number-two national ranking, Bama drew a repellent 17-17 tie with Tennessee, then lost to LSU 17-13 in Bryant-Denny Stadium. After whipping the Mississippi State Bulldogs, the 8-1-1 Tide was gearing up for Auburn and an excellent shot at another SEC championship when all hell began to break loose. That Septem-

All-American Antonio Langham was duped into signing a contract with a sports agent which cost Alabama its first sanctions for violating NCAA rules. The Tide was forced to forfeit all games that Langham had played in 1993, as well as the loss of many scholarships and was not allowed to play in a post-season bowl.

ber, NCAA records show, the sports agent had resurfaced, harassing Langham's family and actually phoning Coach Stallings to suggest that unless Langham honored his alleged contract with him the following year, dark things could happen to the Alabama football program. Stallings vocally denounced this smack of blackmail, hung up on the man, and contacted the athletic department, which set into motion a renewed investigation of the matter.

Problem was, nobody knew exactly what the agent had, and the agent would not exactly say. Stallings had told the man to put whatever it was into writing and forward it immediately, but this was not done. The University also demanded that the agent produce for examination any agreement with Langham, but the agent hired a lawyer and refused to do so all through the first ten games of the season.

When the agent's lawyer finally coughed up the wretched document, it was, for the University, about as bad as receiving a death warrant. Not only was there Langham's signature contracting him to the sports agent, but the agent had also tape-recorded the conversation in which Langham, with an uncle orchestrating the call, had asked for the "loan/gift" of the four hundred dollars. The University at once reported all this to the NCAA authorities, worrying it could lead to forfeiture of all ten of the games Langham had participated in that year. Arguing, however, that Langham—an impressionable young man flush off one of the great football wins of all time—had been duped into signing the so-called agreement, the University asked that his eligibility be restored. The NCAA was unmoved and so Langham sat out the rest of the season.

News of this misfortune naturally leaked to the press and while it is uncertain what effect it had on the team, Bama dropped its final regular season game to Auburn 22-14. The Tide still had a shot to win the SEC but when they met Florida at Legion Field for the championship game it seemed their hearts were not in it. Florida won, 28-13. A 24-10 thrashing of North Carolina in the Gator Bowl was satisfying enough, but black clouds remained on the horizon as the season of 1994 began.

Coach Stallings, wide receiver Kevin Lee, and offensive coordinator Mal Moore during the 1993 Tennessee game. It ended in a 17-17 tie. In 1999 Mal Moore became athletics director for the University.

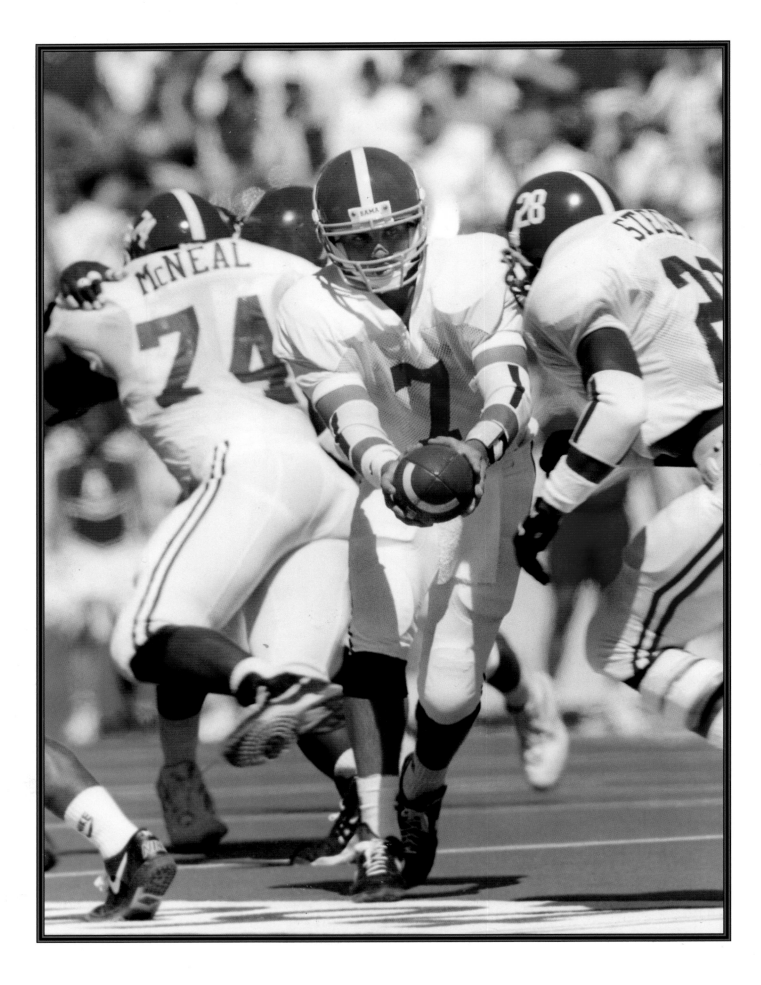

In September of 1994 the NCAA issued a formal letter of inquiry to the University in the Langham matter. Alabama responded by laying out all the facts as it saw them:

◦ A sports agent had unconscionably pressed himself upon a young player and tricked him into signing an agreement the player—even if he knew he had signed it—immediately repudiated.

◦ There was no reason for authorities at the University to have suspected anything further after Langham's December 5 declaration that all he had signed was an application to waive his senior year and enter the NFL draft, which he immediately withdrew. Members of Langham's family confirmed this account.

◦ When the sports agent contacted Stallings on September 20, after the 1993 season had begun, claiming that Langham had indeed signed a contract with him, Stallings and the University—with Langham still denying any wrongdoing—immediately did what they could to obtain a copy of the alleged document but were stonewalled by the sports agent until the season was nearly finished.

◦ When the agent's document was finally produced, the University reported the incident to the NCAA without delay.

This done, they waited for the other shoe to drop.

◦

IN A WAY, THE FANS AND PLAYERS WERE LIKE PASSENGERS ON THE *Titanic*, merrily believing the best and going about their business while the coaches and athletic staff, like ship's officers on the bridge, were deeply concerned about the worst: this was the prevailing mood as Bama began steamrolling over its opponents in 1994. And a great team it was, too: Jay Barker, Willie Gaston, Dameian Jeffries, Tommy Johnson, Chad Key, Tarrant Lynch, Toderick Malone, Sam Shade, and Sherman Williams were among the stars. The only disappointment was that David "The Deuce" Palmer, after being named an All-American in 1993, had decided to quit the team to join the pros his senior year. Nevertheless, Bama won every regular season game that year, with Jay Barker surpassing the legendary Harry Gilmer as Alabama's all-time winningest quarterback as well as edging out Gary Hollingsworth's record

Above: *The irrepressible Freddie Kitchens unloads a pass in 1996.*
Opposite page: *Quarterback Jay Barker handing off to Brian Steger.*

for all-time pass completions. Barker was also named All-American, as was placekicker Michael Proctor. When time came for the SEC championship game—now played in Atlanta—they believed they were invincible.

They weren't. It was one of the sourest losses in many years—a one-point cliff-hanger in which the Gators came out on top 24-23. Bama was ahead late in the fourth quarter when Gator quarterback Danny Wuerffel passed for the Florida go-ahead touchdown and a ticket to the Sugar Bowl. The Crimson Tide was invited to play Ohio State in the Citrus Bowl where they whipped the Buckeyes 24-17. They weren't national champs that year, or even SEC champs—though they came within two points of it—but with a 12-1 record it had been a fine season.

Linebacker Dwayne Rudd sacks Arkansas' quarterback in Little Rock in 1996. Bama beat the Razorbacks 17-7.

As THE 1995 FOOTBALL YEAR ROLLED AROUND there was still an undercurrent of agitation and foreboding over the outcome of the NCAA investigation. A sinister lull had lain over the future of Alabama's football program for a year while University officials and NCAA authorities argued and briefed and argued some more about the Langham incident. Finally it was announced: the nation's supreme athletic authority condemned The University of Alabama for not paying more specific attention in the matter—for not exercising the proper "skepticism," as the Committee on Infractions put it—regarding Langham's assertions that he had not signed with an agent.

Worse, in many ways, the committee decided that the University's Faculty Athletic Representative had lied to the NCAA back in 1993 in his letter asking that Langham's eligibility be restored. This stupendous embarrassment resulted in further sanctions for an ethical violation of the NCAA rules. The sanctions that the NCAA imposed were just short of the dreaded "death penalty." Bama was put on probation. It could not play in a bowl game in 1995. It must forfeit all ten games Langham had played in during 1993 and—most damaging of all—must give up thirty football scholarships over a three-year period. It might not have been the "death penalty," but it was sufficient—as the NCAA intended—to cripple Crimson Tide football teams for years to come.

The University fervently appealed the ethics charges against its Faculty Athletic Representative, professor Tom Jones. Though no school had ever successfully appealed a sanctions case, the NCAA, after hearing all the evidence and arguments so forcefully put by the president's executive assistant, Dr. Culpepper Clark, reversed itself entirely on that question, vindicating Jones and the University, and restored seventeen of the lost football scholarships. Furthermore, Dr. Jones himself then filed a libel suit against the NCAA for besmirching his name—and he won it.

There were to be sure some University officials connected with the athletic department who might have been more diligent. That they were not is a pity, but it is no disgrace, for there was never hard evidence to indicate that anybody in the University administration did anything intentionally wrong or covered anything up. In fact, the NCAA investigators themselves had sided with Alabama, but the Infractions Committee ignored their findings. If anyone is squarely and undoubtedly to blame it must be the sports agent who—in violation of Alabama state law—laid a trap for the apparently ignorant Antonio Langham to sign his contract. Thus, The University of Alabama, which never in its history had an NCAA penalty levied against it, now found its reputation badly tarnished. Langham went on to the pros but without the services of his one-time agent, whom he had renounced from the day he placed his signature on the dotted line.

≈

WITH THIS INDIGNITY FINALLY BEHIND IT—except the fateful loss of scholarships—Alabama prepared for the 1995 football season. After struggling for wins over its first two opponents, Vanderbilt and Southern Mississippi, the Tide lost a heartbreaker to Arkansas, 20-19. Amid controversy over who should start at quarterback, Brian Burgdorf was chosen over Freddie Kitchens. Bama still had an arsenal of stars including Curtis Brown, Chad Key, Montoya Madden, Dennis Riddle, Dwayne Rudd, Ed Scissum, Deshea Townsend, and of course All-American kicker Michael Proctor, but when Tennessee time rolled around, it became clear this was not one of the great Crimson Tide teams. Behind the passing of Tennessee standout Peyton Manning, the Volunteers crushed Bama 41-14 at Legion Field. Tennessee was leading 21-0 at halftime when Stallings replaced Burgdorf with Freddie Kitchens. Throwing forty-

Michael Vaughn catches the winning touchdown pass in the end zone to put Bama on top 17-7 over Arkansas in 1996.

three passes in the second half (compared with Burgdorf's five in the first half) Kitchens completed twenty of them, but it was to no avail, and the Tide motored back to Tuscaloosa without a whiff of cigar smoke in the buses.

With wins over Ole Miss, North Texas, LSU, and Mississippi State it looked as if Bama was going to salvage the season, even if they had already lost the SEC. But there was always Auburn to consider. It was a wide-open game, savagely fought as usual. With Kitchens now at the reins Bama led 27-24 in the final period when the Tigers' Fred Beasley broke out for a twenty-two-yard touchdown to give the Plainsmen the go-ahead with about ten minutes left. Kitchens drove the Tide seventy-seven yards in a series of desperation plays, but once on the Tigers' twenty-two he stalled, throwing four incomplete passes, one of which, photographs later revealed, had been caught in the end zone by Curtis Brown. Since the NCAA penalty had banned Alabama from a bowl game, the 8-3 season of 1995 ended in disappointment there and then on the field as Auburn ran out the final seconds on the clock. Auburn 31, Bama 27.

~

NINETEEN-NINETY-SIX LOOKED TO SHAPE UP AS A GOOD YEAR for the Crimson Tide. With Kitchens at the helm and such stars as Curtis Alexander, John Causey, Dennis Riddle, Ed Scissum, and Michael Vaughn on offense and a defensive lineup that included Fernando Bryant, Chris Hood, Dwayne Rudd, and Deshea Townsend they were a formidable bunch. They proved it, too, breezing through the first seven games, including the sweet retribution of a 17-7 win over Arkansas that marked the one-thousandth football game played by The University of Alabama. Now came the fabulous Third Saturday in October up in Knoxville, and they almost pulled it off. The underdog Tide was leading 13-6 in the fourth quarter before a record crowd of 106,000 hostile Tennessee fans when Peyton Manning tied the game at thirteen-all with three minutes left to play. Bama had been leading in most of the statistics all day but suddenly Tennessee running back Jay Graham broke out for a seventy-nine-yard touchdown run that locked up the game for the Volunteers, 20-13.

Disheartening as the Tennessee loss was, Bama rebounded nicely the next week to whip LSU 26-0 down in Baton Rouge, where red-shirt freshman Shaun Alexander set the all-time single game rushing mark. But the Tide slipped badly against Mississippi State next week in Starkville. Alabama was leading nicely in the final minutes when State hit on a sixty-nine-yard pass to put the Bulldogs close enough for a game-winning field goal. It was a shocking loss for the Tide.

But next week came the "One That Mattered," the game that could erase any and all indignities of the season. On November 23 the Crimson Tide met the Auburn Tigers on Legion Field. It was a seesaw contest that Bama had to win to get into the SEC championship game. In the first quarter Alabama scored seventeen points. In the second, Auburn scored seventeen points, but with just thirty seconds remaining in the game, delirious Auburnites were dancing in jubilation with the Tigers beating Bama 23-17. Then, with the suddenness of a thunderclap from the blue, Freddie Kitchens unloaded a

Alabama's All-American Shaun Alexander ran all over LSU for 291 yards down in Baton Rouge in a 26-0 Tide victory in 1996.

pass to Dennis Riddle who went in for the game-tying score. Moments later Jon Brock calmly kicked the ball through the goal to give Alabama the win, 24-23. It wasn't the way Bama liked to do it, but for Tide fans, it was heaven.

~

THE CRIMSON TIDE WENT TO ATLANTA ON DECEMBER 7, Pearl Harbor Day, to meet the Florida Gators for the conference championship. It was billed up big: Florida's number-one-in-the-SEC passing offense behind Heisman Trophy

Dennis Riddle scores Bama's winning touchdown in the last seconds of the '96 Auburn game at Legion Field.

candidate Danny Wuerffel versus Bama's number-one passing defense. It was Florida 24, Bama 14 at the start of the third quarter when it all began to come apart for the Tide. Kitchens got into a throwing contest with Wuerffel and lost it 45-30.

It was a distasteful way to end what might have been yet another championship season, but at least they had come away 9-3 and had beaten Auburn. This time the Outback Bowl came courting and the Tide met the University of Michigan Wolverines on New Year's Day in Tampa. It was a close and exciting game. Jon Brock kicked a field goal and Dwayne Rudd made a spectacular eighty-eight-yard touchdown run after intercepting a Michigan pass to put Bama ahead 10-6 in the final period. Then Shaun Alexander made it

17-6 on another touchdown run. Michigan was still in the contest, however, and on its next possession not only scored but converted for two points, cutting Alabama's lead to three. An on-sides kick by Michigan was recovered by the Tide and that iced the game, 17-14. Kevin Jackson, Michael Myers, and Dwayne Rudd were named All-Americans that year.

Meantime, an event had convulsed players and fans of Alabama football for the past several weeks. Minutes after the great win against Auburn, Coach Gene Stallings announced he was retiring from the game. Stallings was sixty-one years old—just eight years shy of Bear Bryant's age at his death—and he had a grown son, John Mark, with Down's Syndrome. John Mark went to all the Bama games, served the team as a trainer, and is still possibly the most devoted fan of the Crimson Tide in its hundred-plus years of history, but Stallings felt his coaching duties took too much time away from John Mark. It was whispered in some quarters that Stallings also saw the handwriting on the wall now that the loss of scholarships from the NCAA sanctions was about to take its toll in the next few years, but there is no real evidence of this. Stallings had given The University of Alabama seven seasons during which his teams compiled a proud winning record of 70-16-1.

In any case, Stallings was gone and the man chosen to replace him was defensive coordinator Mike DuBose. This decision was made primarily by the University's new president, Dr. Andrew Sorensen, and the new athletics director, Bob Bockrath. A native of Opp, Alabama, DuBose was, ironically, the only Crimson Tide head coach to have actually been born in the state. He had played standout ball as a defensive end on the great SEC and national championship teams of Bear Bryant from 1972 to 1974. What was more, he was still family.

Last game: Coach Gene Stallings and his son John Mark at Bryant-Denny Stadium. Stallings retired in 1997 after seven winning seasons and a national championship for the Crimson Tide.

Chapter Nine

MILLENNIUM

1997 ~ 2000

Below: *Coach Mike DuBose in the locker room before his first game as Alabama's head coach in 1997. The Tide beat Houston 42-17 at Legion Field.* **Opposite page:** *Bama players lift helmets in a salute to the crowd.*

RUEL DAYS LAY AHEAD AS THE TWENTIETH century drew nearer to its close. It was always Mike DuBose's passionate dream to be head football coach at The University of Alabama, but this quickly turned into a nightmare. Though blessed with forty-nine returning lettermen from the Stallings regime, DuBose found himself with a depth chart that seemed pitifully small as a result of the NCAA scholarship penalty. Still there were hopes for the 1997 season when Bama whipped Houston 42-17 in the opening game and smashed Vandy 20-0 in the second. Then things began to go sour. Arkansas came to Tuscaloosa and beat the Tide 17-16 with a last-second touchdown. Bama beat Southern Miss next week but then, astonishingly, lost to Kentucky 40-34. Next, Tennessee rolled over the Tide but Bama bounded back again with a 29-20 victory over Ole Miss.

Still, the season seemed salvageable. With the irrepressible Freddie Kitchens as quarterback, the Tide had returned runners Curtis Alexander, Shaun Alexander, Montoya Madden, Ed Scissum, and, of course, Dennis Riddle. To catch passes were Chad Goss, Calvin Hall, Rod Rutledge, Michael Vaughn, and Clint Waggoner. Also back were defensive stars Fernando Bryant, Chris Hood, Kelvin Sigler, and Deshea Townsend.

Despite this, the 1997 season became a disaster of almost epic proportions, and DuBose seemed hapless and helpless against the onslaught. At homecoming lowly Louisiana Tech thrashed Alabama 26-20. Next it was LSU's turn to humiliate the Tide 27-0—in Bryant-Denny Stadium, no less—followed by a thumping from Mississippi State. Finally a heart-stopping 18-17 loss to

Auburn completed the miserable 4-7 season. The Crimson Tide had not played so badly since Ears Whitworth's 1957 team went 2-7-1. Never mind that four of the seven defeats were by less than a touchdown and thus chalked up by optimists to "bad luck." If one had to describe the season in a single word, it would have to be "mistakes." It wasn't that the players didn't play hard, but the interceptions, penalties, fumbles, and broken plays seemed to hover over the Crimson Tide like a pall at almost every game, most especially when they played at home.

Everyone was mortified, from the players to the fans and of course Mike DuBose. This just wasn't, well, the Crimson Tide, not at least for the past forty years, it wasn't.

≈

THE 1998 SEASON OPENED ON YET ANOTHER sour note. After more than thirty years Bryant Hall, the splendid athletic dormitory, was shut down, closed to players, courtesy of the NCAA, which had decided it was unfair to smaller colleges that larger schools could afford to house their athletes in such facilities. Bama athletes were thus turned

Alabama's Fernando Bryant runs for a touchdown after stealing a pass meant for Houston's #16 Jason McKinley.

out to fend for themselves among the various student housing options. Earlier, the NCAA had banned Bama and other schools from furnishing players the trademark "Crimson Tide" blazers for on-the-road games. This was based on the cockeyed theory that it amounted to giving the players compensation—never mind that the blazers always remained the property of the athletic department, and the travelling squad not only had to turn them back in at the end of their trips, but for good when their eligibility had expired.

Fans, players, and coaches waited with trepidation as the 1998 season began. Bryant-Denny Stadium had again been enlarged to seat nearly eighty-four thousand, including eighty-one posh sky boxes, and Bama was playing more of its games at home. The season opened in Tuscaloosa with a 38-31 win over Brigham Young, with Shaun Alexander scoring five touchdowns and being named SEC Player of the Week. Next the Tide rolled over Vanderbilt 32-7, with Alexander named Player of the Week for the second time in a row, and things were looking rosy until the team went to Fayetteville the following week to play Arkansas. It was miserable, the worst game Bama had played in more than forty years. The Tide managed to score only two field goals and racked up thirteen penalties, tying the school record for the dubious distinction of most infractions in one game. Arkansas, on the other hand, scored forty-two points—twenty-one in the fourth quarter! Something, obviously, had gone wrong again and, what was worse, next on the schedule was Florida.

DuBose replaced quarterback John David Phillips with freshman Andrew Zow and though Florida won by only six points, 16-10, statistics show the Tide was far inferior to the Gators, whose total offense was nearly twice that of Alabama. The only good thing to be said was that Bama held down their penalties to five. Next week was a homecoming game against Ole Miss that went down to the wire. It was 17-17 when the clock ran out and the game went into overtime. Then Shaun Alexander set the Tide up for a twenty-two-yard field goal win by Ryan Pflugner—the first overtime win in Bama history. Next, Alabama squeaked by East Carolina 23-22, blowing a 21-0 half-time lead, and winning only on a two-point blocked kick score by Kecalf Bailey.

The Third Saturday in October the Tide dutifully journeyed to Knoxville to meet the soon-to-be national champs, the Tennessee Volunteers. It was not a brilliant performance and Alabama came out on the losing end, 35-18, though they outplayed the Vols in almost every statistical category but the final score. The season was looking weird again.

Bama opened the 1998 season in a newly renovated Bryant-Denny Stadium, beating Brigham Young 38-31.

Bama's Quincy Jackson for a Tide touchdown in a 22-17 victory over LSU in 1998.

Bama won the next two games, against Southern Mississippi, 30-20, and LSU (in Tiger Stadium), 22-16. This last was truly an inspired performance as the Tide went into the final period losing 16-7, then Andrew Zow (again named SEC Player of the Week) unleashed two touchdown passes to win it for Bama after a perfect onsides kick which the Tide recovered. But next week they ran up against a determined Mississippi State in Starkville and got whipped 26 to 14, even though they piled up a total offense of 456 to the Bulldogs' 295. Weirder and weirder.

The last contest, of course, was against Auburn and people were saying that if the Tide lost this one, drastic changes would be made. They needn't have worried; Bama pulled the Tigers' tail to the tune of 31-17, despite being outplayed in total offense and turning over the ball four times—Triumph of the Weird! And so 1998 closed on a happier note with a winning 7-4 regular season—the exact reverse of 1997—and the Tide got invited to play Virginia Tech in the new Music City Bowl in Nashville— Bama's forty-ninth bowl appearance. It was a dreadful and humiliating performance. In freezing rain and a sleet storm, the Tide fumbled, let passes be intercepted, and managed just fifty rushing yards to get itself thoroughly shellacked by the Hokies, 38-7. Since Virginia Tech had no real tradition as a football power as Bama did, it was all the more mortifying, but Tide fans could at least take some consolation next season when the Hokies went on to play for the national championship.

Again the cry rang out, "Next year, next year!" as it had in '97. By now the crippling scholarship losses caused by the NCAA penalty were beginning to abate and Bama had a great recruiting season. It would be returning veteran players such as All-SEC Shaun Alexander and a more seasoned Andrew Zow as well as many lettermen on both sides of the line. Off-season talk was that Alabama was going to have a smash-up team in 1999 and was even picked by pre-season sportswriters to win the SEC West division. Then, only days before fall practice started, two events both vexed and elated the University, the fans, and the news media.

During the spring, Coach DuBose was rumored to have been involved with a female secretary, rumors he denied at the time. But three months later, DuBose admitted that he had not told the truth about "inappropriate" behavior that led the University to settle a complaint for several hundred thousand dollars, money DuBose would ultimately repay from his pocket. This turn of events also came at an unfortunate time for the Crimson Tide, which had struggled through two uncomfortable seasons; nevertheless, DuBose was popular with his players, and university officials, including President Sorensen, stood behind him. DuBose was retained as coach, though his contract was shortened by two years and other sanctions were levied.

Coming just on the heels of this bad news was the happy publication of *Sports Illustrated*'s "Team of the Century," which not only named three Bama standouts, John Hannah, Don Hutson, and Lee Roy Jordan, as first teamers, but Paul "Bear" Bryant was selected Coach of the Century. These splendid accolades took some of the edge off an otherwise shaky opening of the Crimson Tide's final football season before the millennium.

It nearly got off to a bad start when Vanderbilt outplayed and outscored the Tide for three quarters before Bama woke up and put the Commodores away, 28-17, behind the rushing and pass catching of Shaun Alexander. Next week Houston fell prey to the Tide 37-10 with the passing of Andrew Zow and Shaun Alexander rushing for 167 yards and two touchdowns. Freshman quarterback Tyler Watts saw action for the first time.

Things were going about as planned when a total calamity befell Alabama: they *lost* to lowly Louisiana Tech. One sportswriter called it the "most improbable defeat occurring under absolutely impossible circumstances."

Alabama was leading the Bulldogs 28-22 with less than three minutes on the clock. Tech's much heralded quarterback Tim Rattay then led his team from its own twenty-three to deep in Bama territory. With thirty-eight seconds left to play Rattay was sacked by

Darius Gilbert and taken off the field on a stretcher with an ankle injury, and substitute quarterback Brian Stallworth entered the game. He was sacked by Cornelius Griffin but on the next play rifled a pass that took the Bulldogs out of bounds with nine seconds to go and facing a fourth and 22 on Bama's twenty-eight-yard line. Just before they wheeled Rattay into the tunnel the injured quarterback told the stretcher-bearers to stop so he could watch the last play of the game. For Tech fans, what happened next was like the final scene of a wonderful movie; for Bama fans, it was a nightmare come true. Stallworth heaved a hail-Mary into the end zone toward his 6'4" receiver Sean Cangelosi, who was totally surrounded by four Crimson Tide defend-

Above: *DuBose gathers his captains in the showers for a last-minute strategy session before hitting the field against Florida at the dreaded Swamp.*
Opposite page: *Running back Shaun Alexander (left) and quarterback Andrew Zow were a potent one-two punch for Alabama in 1999.*

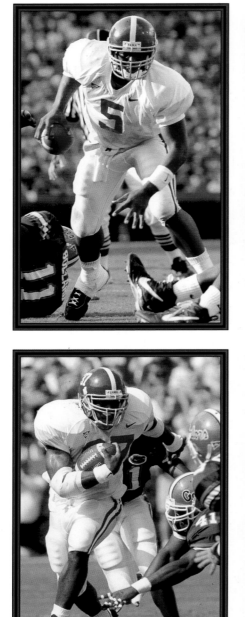

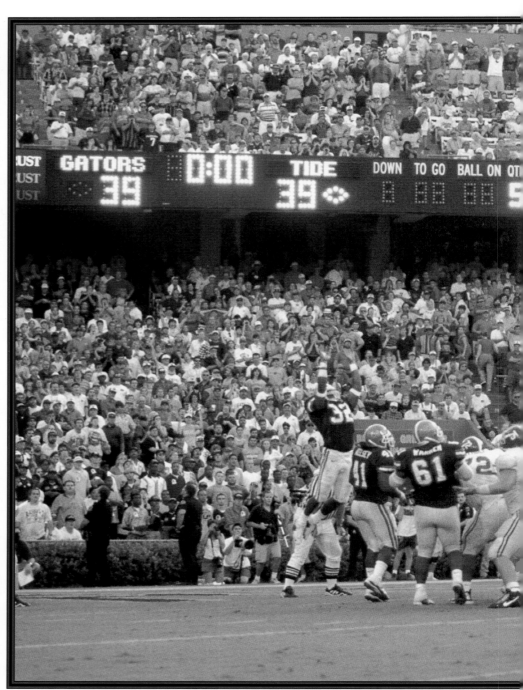

ers. Cangelosi leapt into the air and came down with the ball. Louisiana Tech 29, Bama 28. It was a revolting development.

People started calling for DuBose's scalp again; athletics director Bob Bockrath was replaced by Mal Moore, who had coached under Bear Bryant. Penalties and turnovers cost the Tide dearly in the Louisiana Tech game, and the next week was against Arkansas at Bryant-Denny. Bama was leading 35-28 in the final seconds when Razorback quarterback Clint Stoerner threw an almost duplicate hail-Mary pass into the end zone and for a breath-catching instant it looked like a replay of the awful defeat the previous week. But the ball hit the ground and the stadium erupted. Linebacker Marvin Constant said, "I was thinking, please God, not again!"

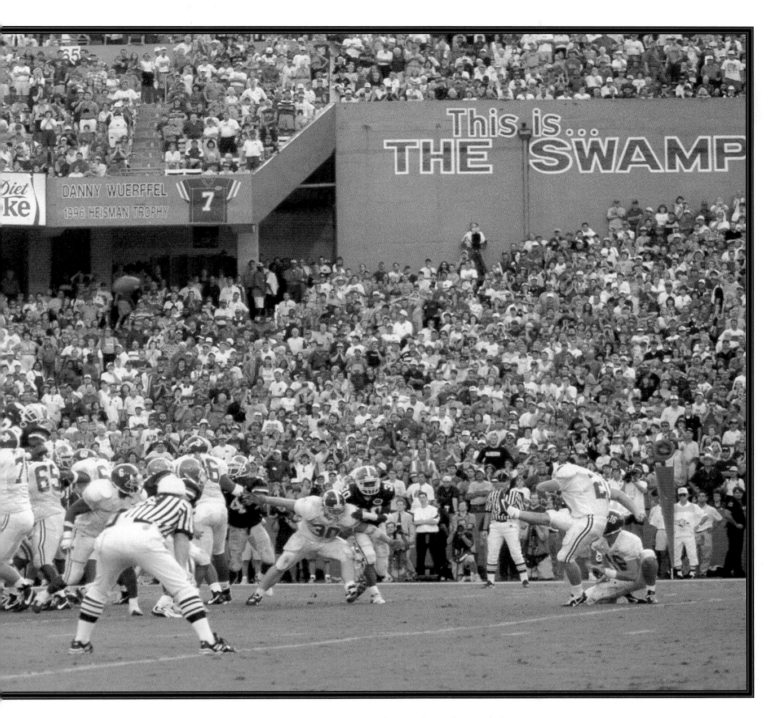

Once more it was penalties and turnovers, six of them, that plagued the Crimson Tide, and worse, Bama had to journey next week to Gainesville to play the number-three-ranked Florida Gators, who had not lost in their vaunted "Swamp" for thirty games. It was a splendid and miraculous performance by The University of Alabama. The lead changed hands no less than eight times, and at the end of regulation play the score was tied 33-33. Florida led off in overtime with a touchdown but missed the extra point. Now it was Bama's turn. On the first play Shaun Alexander faked out every Gator on the field and dashed twenty-five yards into the end zone. To win it the Tide needed the extra point, but Chris Kemp's try went wide, blowing a chance to put the game away. Now the miracle part came into play: Florida's end had been

Bama's Chris Kemp with the game-winning last minute 1999 kick that beat the Gators in their own backyard!

offside and Bama was given a second chance. This time the kick was straight through the uprights and Alabama won it, 40-39. Suddenly things were looking bright again.

Bama, now eleven in the national polls, went to Oxford and put a whipping on Ole Miss, 30-24. Shaun Alexander scored three touchdowns and ran for 214 yards, and much talk of the Heisman followed him around. This was good news for the Tide. Alabama had never had a Heisman winner before and, unlike many other schools, did not have a policy of promoting players for the trophy. Nevertheless, next week was the Third Saturday in October.

Disaster came to Bryant-Denny Stadium in the form of the Tennessee Volunteers, who had not played in Tuscaloosa since 1930. The Vols simply outplayed Bama 21-7 and, almost worse, both Andrew Zow and Shaun Alexander suffered crippling ankle injuries.

At homecoming next week there was concern that Bama would have to struggle against Southern Miss. People were concerned that after the losses to Louisiana Tech and Tennessee the heart might have gone out of this team, but they needn't have worried. Back-up running back Shaun Bohanon stepped comfortably into Shaun Alexander's shoes and Tyler Watts fit nicely into Andrew Zow's. At halftime Alabama led 20-7. In the third quarter Freddie Milons grabbed a Southern Miss punt and raced it back sixty-five yards for a touchdown. When all was said and done, Bama was on top 35-14.

LSU was geared to beat the Tide in 1999 with a go-ahead last-second touchdown, but linebacker Marvin Constant and others stopped the Tigers' quarterback in mid-air to end the game.

The next week Alabama endured a long and difficult ordeal to break its home-field jinx with LSU. Both Zow and Alexander played in the game, but not for long, and it was back to Tyler Watts and Shaun Bohanon. The game was a thorough cliff-hanger at the end. In the third quarter Bama led 23-7, but the Tigers fought back until they were just six points behind. With ten seconds left in the game and LSU at the Bama one-yard line, quarterback Josh Booty rolled right but was smacked down by Reggie Myles and Marvin Constant. A

controversy then ensued. LSU had no more time-outs, but Constant was hurt on the play, and it appeared that the referee had called an injury time-out. Bama players, however, flooded the field in celebration and after two minutes of hollering and finger-jabbing, the referees ruled that the game was over. LSU complained of "hometown" refereeing and said the game would have been theirs if they'd played in Baton Rouge, never mind that these same referees would have been on the field there, too. It wasn't a pretty win, but a win it was.

Red-shirt freshman quarterback Tyler Watts came on strong in the 1999 season, shown here throwing a pass during Alabama's 23-17 win over LSU.

Above: *Crunch time for the Bulldogs as Alabama's Miguel Merritt and Kenny King take down a runner in the game's first half.* **Right:** *Wide receiver Freddie Milons can just about do it all: run, catch, throw. Here he scampers past a hapless Mississippi State player toward a 19-7 upset over the Bulldogs at Bryant-Denny, giving the Tide the SEC West championship.*

Next week was the battle for the SEC West championship against undefeated Mississippi State. The Bulldogs came into Bryant-Denny with blood in their eyes and left with their tails between their legs after a 19-7 shellacking. Shaun Alexander scored two touchdowns and moved ahead of Auburn's fabled Bo Jackson into fourth place in the SEC's all-time-scoring records. Darius Gilbert, Milo Lewis, and Reggie Myles each intercepted the Bulldogs and freshman linebacker Saleem Rasheed blocked a punt.

Next week was the Big One again, the finale at Auburn, and as usual it was a nail-biter. Alabama had not won against Auburn on their home field for four straight meetings. Bama was losing 14-6 in the third quarter when Tyler Watts, who had stepped in for a lackluster Andrew Zow, generaled a twelve-play drive to the Auburn six, where Shaun Alexander was repelled four times in a row. This did not bode well.

But on the very next play Bama sacked Auburn's quarterback Ben Leard in the end zone for a two-point safety. The Tigers then had to kick off and Freddie Milons raced it back thirty yards into Auburn territory. Meantime, Shaun Alexander had been getting a pep talk on the sidelines where DuBose told him he'd "been blessed by God with a lot of talent and that he was capable of taking this game over"—which he did.

Alexander broke through what seemed to be certain tackles to carry the ball to the Tigers' sixteen. Freddie Milons lined up as quarterback on fourth down and burst up the middle for eight yards. On the next play Alexander waltzed into the end zone unmolested to give Bama a 15-14 go ahead. It was all Shaun Alexander's game after that. He became Alabama's all-time leading rusher with another touchdown and, as if that weren't enough, scored again with just a minute left to play. Twelve thousand Crimson Tide fans would not leave the stadium and kept chanting, "SEC, SEC," for twenty minutes until the players finally ran out of the dressing room and back onto the jubilant field. It was an exhilarating ending to the last Alabama-Auburn game of the century.

≈

THUS, TWO WEEKS LATER THE CURTAIN LIFTED on one of the great confrontations in SEC football. Even if the players had no misgivings, many Bama fans harbored doubts as to whether this Crimson Tide team could beat the fierce Florida Gators, no matter that they'd already done so by a lone point earlier in the season. Florida had beaten Bama's arch rival Tennessee, which had in turn thrashed the Tide and remained ahead of Alabama in the national rankings. Bookies picked Florida to win it by at least a touchdown and Gator fans were screaming "payback time" because of the earlier Bama win.

But that night at the Georgia Dome a hard and indisputable fact became evident: that through all the glory days of Wallace Wade, Frank Thomas, Bear Bryant, and Gene Stallings, there was never a more splendid football team in University of Alabama history than the one that stepped onto the field in Atlanta on December 4, 1999, to settle the SEC championship. Plagued with crippling injuries and the relentless media focus on the earlier Mike DuBose difficulty, these men and their coaches proved up to any task.

It began with a fright. The game was less than two minutes old when, with the score already Florida 7, Alabama 0, the Tide missed an easy field goal. Doomsayers on air and off began predicting a rout but the atmosphere in Atlanta's Georgia Dome became electric with Bama pride. After that it all belonged to the men in red.

To the astonishment of sportswriters and the ecstasy of Bama fans, with DuBose alternating his two sterling quarterbacks Andrew Zow and Tyler Watts, the Tide not only skinned the Gators, they made belts, shoes, and handbags out of them. Coach Steve Spurrier's Florida defense was keying on Shaun Alexander as DuBose knew it would and Bama was thus able to show the Gators things they never dreamed they'd see in their worst nightmare. With shades of David Palmer, Bama's great Stallings-era flanker, wide receiver Freddie Milons lined up as quarterback on several occasions and on a quarterback keeper in the last period streaked for a seventy-seven-yard touchdown, leaving a trail of flattened and faked-out Gators in his wake. That seemed to be the play that broke Florida's back. To add insult to injury, big

Cornelius Griffin, #97, with a little help from Kindal Moorehead, #54, takes down Auburn quarterback Ben Leard in the end zone for a safety that helped turn the game around in Bama's favor.

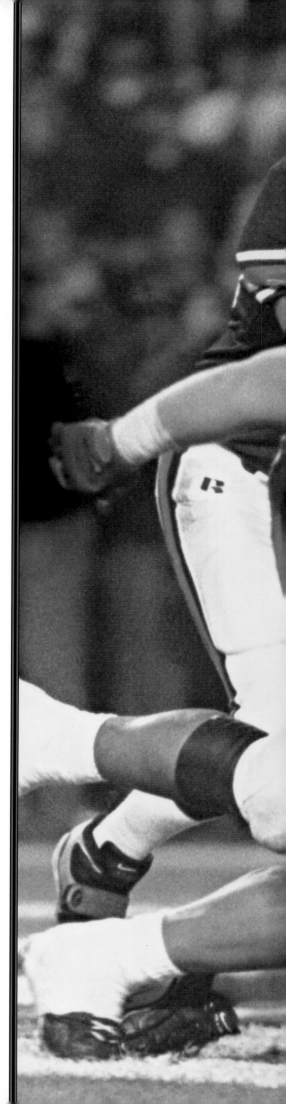

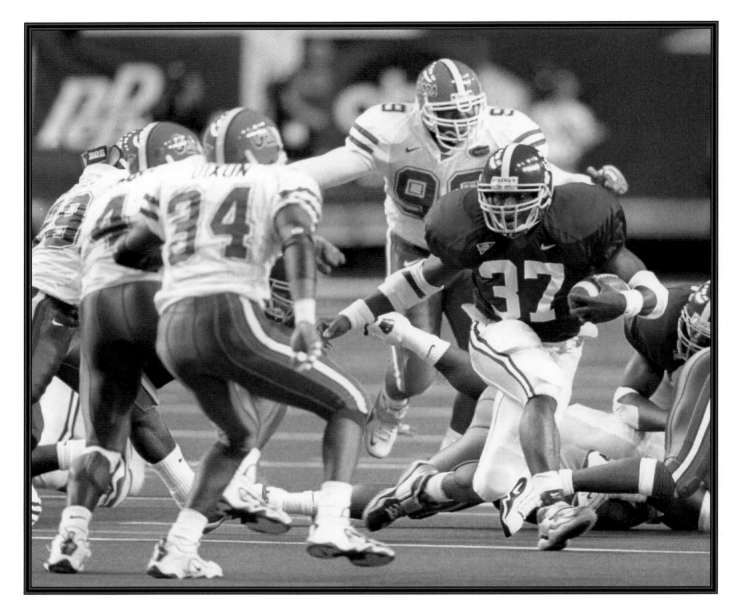

tackle Reggie Grimes then snatched a Gator pass tipped by noseguard Jarett Johnson and bear-hugged it thirty-eight yards for a touchdown. The final score: Alabama 34, Florida 7. If anyone had questions as to whether the Crimson Tide was "back," that settled it.

As it had in the earlier meeting that season, Bama hogged the time-of-possession to an amazing 40:11 to 19:49 and outgained Florida 462 to 114 in offensive yards. Ryan Pflugner kicked three field goals and tied the SEC championship game record with a forty-eight-yarder in the second quarter. Freddie Milons set SEC championship records for the longest run and for most yards gained per play (17.6). He was selected Most Valuable Player of the game.

By late in the fourth quarter the Georgia Dome was empty of Gator fans, who skulked off while their team endured its final humiliation alone. Characteristically, Gator coach Spurrier blamed almost everybody, singling out for odium his quarterbacks, his offensive line, and his offense in general. "We've got to find some players who want to play," he told reporters. Ever the gentle-

The great Shaun Alexander dragging a host of Florida Gators into the goal with him in the SEC win.

man, All-American Shaun Alexander, who in the role of stalking horse didn't get his usual two or three touchdowns that day, had this to say afterward: "I didn't come back to win the Heisman Trophy. I came back to play in games like this. The guys on this team wanted this championship so badly."

And that, ladies and gentlemen, is what The University of Alabama and its football team are all about.

⁓

THE MONDAY AFTER THE GAME MIKE DUBOSE was chosen SEC Coach of the Year and Shaun Alexander was named SEC Player of the Year. Left tackle Chris Samuels, who did not allow a single quarterback sack all year, won the Outland Trophy as the nation's best lineman as well as the Jacobs Trophy as the best blocker in the conference. Alexander, Samuels, and Freddie Milons were named All-SEC. None of these was a real surprise but an announcement that same day out of New York was a total shocker. A week before the deadline for the Heisman votes to even be mailed in, the Downtown Athletic Club announced that Shaun Alexander was not going to be considered for the Heisman Trophy. To many this seemed an insult, considering that Alexander had become the nation's top scorer (24 touchdowns, 144 points) and had the highest national scoring average (13.9 points per game). Moreover, his accomplishments were all the more astonishing when one factors in the injury that forced Alexander to sit out an entire game and play only sparingly in another. Not only that, he became Alabama's all-time leading rusher with 3,566 career yards. *Mobile Register* sports editor John Cameron summed up the indignity by branding the Heisman Committee's decision a "cruel outrage."

⁓

AND SO AS THE CENTURY CLOSED it was on to the Orange Bowl against the University of Michigan, one of the few football teams with a history so star-studded as the Crimson Tide. The two schools had only met twice before and each had a win. It would mark Alabama's fiftieth appearance in a post-season bowl, by far outreaching all other teams. The contest was joined on the evening of the first day of the year 2000.

One of the longest games in football history, it started on January 1 and did not end until January 2. An entertaining but interminable halftime show featuring Gladys Knight didn't help, but what held the thing up most was penalties: the Tide lost more than 130 yards in penalties and Michigan wasn't far behind. Taking into consideration all the time it takes to dispose of twenty-eight penalties, many of them "holding" calls, it probably added nearly an hour to the game. In this writer's opinion, they should either make "holding" legal and let the linemen jostle around like Sumo wrestlers, or go back to the old days when linemen couldn't use their hands. At present, "holding" is mostly a subjective interpretation on the part of referees and mostly it just "holds" up the games.

DuBose continued his practice of alternating Andrew Zow and Tyler Watts at quarterback but they were both hampered by the loss of star offensive tackle Chris Samuels, sidelined with a knee injury. The first half belonged to

Reggie Grimes celebrates with fans after scoring on a pass interception in the last quarter of the SEC Championship Game. The big tackle just bear-hugged the ball and lumbered thirty-eight yards across the goal line, punctuating a dramatic win over the Gators.

Bama, with Shaun Alexander scoring two touchdowns, one of them set up by a twenty-seven-yard punt return by Freddie Milons.

But Michigan roared back in the second half and the game seesawed back and forth with Wolverines quarterback Tom Brady tossing three more touchdown passes. Shaun Alexander rushed for his third Bama score and Freddie Milons made an electrifying sixty-seven-yard punt return for another touchdown. By the end of the fourth period, with everyone on their feet in delirium, it had come down to a 28-28 tie with only six seconds left on the clock, and Michigan was on the verge of winning it with an easy field goal.

But that was not to be. Bama linebacker Phillip Weeks leaped high to block Hayden Epstein's kick, throwing the game into overtime. On their first play Michigan scored with a pass, putting them ahead for the first time in the game. But Bama came right back with a score of its own and was prepared to tie it up again when the unthinkable happened; Ryan Pflugner's extra-point kick sailed just wide to the right and the game was suddenly over: Michigan 35, Bama 34. It was a heartbreaking loss, especially for Pflugner, who literally collapsed on the field when he watched his kick fail.

But this you can etch in stone about the team of 1999: it was a *team* with a capital "T." Mike DuBose had remarked earlier in the week how proud he was that they'd all worked as a team, how when one player failed, or was injured, or something else bad happened to him, his teammates would all step in and help him. And that is precisely what the Crimson Tide did with Ryan Pflugner: they went over and hauled him to his feet and hugged him off the field. It was a sight to make the most disappointed critic choke up in tears.

Despite Bama's loss, this was one of the great college games of all time, and Michigan coach Lloyd Carr summed it up with characteristic graciousness, saying that no matter how much he liked to win, in this case "it was a shame somebody had to lose."

∼

THUS THE OLD MILLENNIUM ENDED AND THE NEW ONE BEGAN with a winning season for The University of Alabama, just as it had a hundred years earlier in 1899. During the entire century in between, the Crimson Tide had only ten losing seasons, the rest winning ones for ninety-two years, excluding the two sea-

Freshman quarterback Tyler Watts breaks out for yardage against Florida in the SEC Championship Game at the Georgia Dome. Bama stomped the mortified Gators 34-7, and in the final quarter the Florida fans deserted the stadium, leaving their team to endure its humiliation alone.

sons' time-out for wars. It has been invited to more post-season bowl games than any other college. It is the only school that mentions the Rose Bowl in its fight song and the only college team to be memorialized in a rock 'n roll song: "They got a name for the winners in the world/I want a name when I lose/They call Alabama the Crimson Tide/Call me Deacon Blues" (from Steely Dan's "Deacon Blues").

But the history of Alabama football is far more than this. The Crimson Tide has given immeasurable excitement, pleasure, and pride to people not only throughout the state, but throughout the nation. It has done this not at the expense of its players, but to their everlasting benefit. They come as boys; they leave as men.

Some day late in the twenty-first century a geologist might walk out of Smith Hall to the main quadrangle and with his spade begin to turn the soil to see what scientific discovery he can dig up. A foot or so into the dirt he starts to uncover strange artifacts: cracked teeth, broken cleats, bits of bone and sinew, and wonders what on earth went on here? Since the University prides itself on the integration of academic disciplines, the geologist brings the items to the archaeology department for further identification, and the archaeologist says these are the residue of some organized human endeavor. The two take them next to the biology department for forensic testing, where DNA examination reveals the artifacts contain blood, sweat, and tears. More sophisticated tests disclose they are also rife with superhuman amounts of courage, character, and unbridled determination. The geologist, archaeologist, and biologist now take their little box of artifacts to the history department where it is concluded they must have belonged to pioneers: the members of Alabama's original football teams who practiced and played their games on the quad two centuries ago beneath the shadows of all the great academic buildings of the University.

At about that same time, a lone figure might be seen from a distance on the field inside Bryant-Denny Stadium. In the lengthening shadows we see the figure walking slowly across the grass, stopping every so often to look up at the empty grandstands as if to hear the echoes of long-ago cheering. It might be an aging player or a coach, a former cheerleader, a waterboy, or perhaps a member of the Million Dollar Band. It could be a team manager or a guy who once dressed up in the Big Al suit. It may be a former student, a teacher, or an old-time referee. Possibly, it is only a ghost, but most likely it's just a plain-old football fan with enduring memories of the glory that is Alabama's Crimson Tide.

An officer of the University Police watches from one of the gates but does not disturb the intruder. He perfectly understands the impulse to come back once again, to relive the anxious moment or victory's old sweet song. To be a part of it all, just one more time.

Reggie Grimes hoists the SEC championship sign in celebration of Bama's big win over Florida, which marked the pinnacle of a dramatic turnaround season.

ALL-TIME LETTERMEN

1892 ~ 1999

Courtesy UA Athletics Media Relations

A

ABBOTT, Eli (T)
  Tuscaloosa, Ala., 1892-93-94
ABERNATHY, Thad (FL)
  Enterprise, Ala., 1997
ABNEY, Larry (SE)
  Slidell, La., 1984-85-86-87
ABRAMS, Charlie (TE)
  Demopolis, Ala., 1986-87-89
ABRAMS Jason (TE)
  Demopolis, Ala., 1992
ABRUZZESE, Raymond (HB)
  Philadelphia, Pa., 1960-61
ABSTON, Bill (RH)
  Peterson, Ala., 1948-49
ADAMS, George (E)
  Montgomery, Ala., 1935
ADAMS, J.J. (p)
  Katy, Tex., 1993
ADCOCK, Mike (OT)
  Huntsville, Ala., 1981-82-83
ADKINSON, Wayne (HB)
  Dothan, Ala., 1970-71-72
AIKEN, Tom (FS)
  Stone Mountain, Ga., 1995
ALAND, Jack (T)
  Birmingham, Ala., 1942
ALBRIGHT, Carl (H)
  Tuscaloosa, Ala., 1994
ALBRIGHT, George (HB)
  Tuscaloosa, Ala. 1944
ALEXANDER, Curtis (TB)
  Memphis, Tenn., 1994-95-96-97
ALEXANDER, Shaun (TB)
  Florence, Ky., 1996-97-98-99
ALLEN, Charles G. (T)
  Athens, Ala., 1957-58-59
ALLEN, Doug (FB)
  Cantonment, Fla., 1985-86-87
ALLEN, John (T)
  Birmingham, Ala., 1907
ALLEN, Steve (G)
  Athens, Ala., 1961-62-63
ALLEN, Wes (SE)
  Cottondale, Ala., 1997-98

ALLISON, Scott (OT)
  Titusville, Fla., 1978-79-80
ALLMAN, Phil (DB)
  Birmingham, Ala., 1976-77-78
AMELONG, William (LB)
  Los Angeles, Calif., 1988-89
ANDERSON, Andy (OG)
  Lithia Springs, Ga., 1986
ANDERSON, Chris (RB)
  Huntsville, Ala., 1990-91-92-93
ANDREWS, Mickey (HB)
  Ozark, Ala., 1963-64
ANGELICH, James Dykes (HB)
  Indiana Harbor, Ind.,
  1933-34-35
ARANT, Hershel W. (G)
  Notasulga, Ala., 1908
ARTHUR, Paul (E)
  Birmingham, Ala., 1949
ATKINS, Sam (OT)
  Mobile, Ala., 1988
AUGUST, Johnny (HB)
  Shadyside, Ohio, 1942-46-47
AUSMUS, Michael (CB)
  Mobile, Ala., 1992-93
AUSTILL, Huriescsco (E)
  Springhill, Ala., 1904
AUSTILL, Jere (B)
  Springhill, Ala., 1908
AVERITTE, Warren (C)
  Greenville, Miss., 1938-39-40
AVINGER, Clarence "Butch"
  (QB)
  Montgomery, Ala., 1948-49-50
AYDELETTE, William Leslie
  "Buddy" (TE-OT)
  Mobile, Ala., 1977-78-79
AYERS, Calvin (RB)
  Decatur, Ala., 1989

B

BAILEY, David (SE)
  Bailey, Miss., 1969-70-71
BAILEY, Kecalf (CB)
  Tuscaloosa, Ala., 1997-98-99

BAKER, George (T)
  Cleveland, Ohio, 1921
BAKER, Joseph (Mgr.)
  East Amherst, N.Y., 1941
BALLARD, Clarence Bingham
  (T) Birmingham, Ala., 1901-02
BANKHEAD, M. H. (B)
  Fayette, Ala., 1895
BANKHEAD, Wm. Brockman
  (FB) Fayette, Ala., 1892-93
BANKS, R. R. (B)
  Columbus, Miss., 1901
BARGER, William (OG)
  Birmingham, Ala.,
  1990-91-92-93
BARKER, Jay (QB)
  Trussville, Ala., 1991-92-93-94
BARKER, Troy (G)
  Lineville, Ala., 1931-32-33
BARNES, Emile "Red" (HB)
  Grove Hill, Ala., 1925-26
BARNES, Gary (SS)
  Nashville, Tenn., 1999
BARNES, Ronnie Joe (DE)
  Abbeville, Ala., 1973-74
BARNES, W. A. (T)
  Dothan, Ala., 1912
BARNES, Wiley (C)
  Marianna, Fla., 1978-79
BARNETT, Henry Herndon (C)
  Fitzpatrick, Ala., 1911
BARRON, Marvin (G-T)
  Troy, Ala., 1970-71-73
BARRON, Randy (DT)
  Dadeville, Ala., 1966-67-68
BARRY, Dick (FB)
  Cordele, Ga., 1951
BARTLETT, Charles (HB)
  Marlin, Texas, 1920-21-22
BASWELL, Ben (T)
  Pell City, Ala., 1935
BATES, C. F. (B)
  Mobile, Ala., 1914
BATES, Tim (LB)
  Tarrant, Ala., 1964-65

BATEY, Joseph Dwight "Bo"
  (OG) Jacksonville, Ala., 1976
BATTLE, Bill (E)
  Birmingham, Ala., 1960-61-62
BATTLE, Marco (WR)
  Phenix City, Ala., 1987-88-89
BATY, William C., Jr. (HB)
  Bessemer, Ala., 1921-22-23
BAUGHMAN, Bill (C)
  Jeanette, Pa., 1946
BAUMHOWER, Robert Glenn
  (DT) Tuscaloosa, Ala.,74-75-76
BEALLE, Sherman "Bucky" (E)
  Elyria, Ohio 1929
BEAN, Dickie (HB)
  Childersburg, Ala., 1966
BEARD, Brad (QB)
  Pleasant Grove, Ala., 1999
BEARD, Jeff (DT)
  Bessemer, Ala., 1969-70-71
BEARD, Ken (T)
  Bessemer, Ala., 1963
BEARD, Silas "Buddy" (HB)
  Guntersville, Ala., 1937-38
BEARDEN, Lane (P)
  Pelham, Ala., 1999
BEAZLEY, Joe (DT)
  Woodbridge, Va.,
  1979-80-81-82
BECK, Ellis (HB)
  Ozark, Ala., 1971-72-73
BECK, Willie (E)
  Northport, Ala., 1956-57
BEDDINGFIELD, David (QB)
  Gadsden, Ala., 1969
BEDWELL, David (DB)
  Cedar Bluff, Ala., 1965-66-67
BELL, Albert (F)
  Los Angeles, Calif., 1985-86
BELL, Stanley (E)
  West Anniston, Ala., 1959
BELSER, Maurice (OG)
  Cordova, Ala., 1992-93-94-95
BENDROSS, Jesse (SE)
  Hollywood, Fla., 1980-81-82-83

BENNETT, Cornelius (OLB)
Birmingham, Ala.,
1983-84-85-86
BENTLEY, Edward K., Jr. (DB)
Sylacauga, Ala., 1970
BENTLEY, Jeff (OG)
Alabaster, Ala., 1986-87
BERREY, Fred Benjamin
"Bucky" (K) Montgomery,
Ala., 1974-75-76
BETHUNE, George (LB-DE)
Ft. Walton Beach, Fla.,
1986-87-88
BEVELLE, Willis (S-WR)
Bessemer, Ala., 1989-90-92
BIBLE, Tom (T)
Piedmont, Ala., 1961
BILLINGSLEY, Randy (HB)
Sylacauga, Ala., 1972-73-74
BIRD, Ron (T)
Covington, Ky., 1963
BIRES, Andy (E)
Ambridge, Pa., 1942
BISCEGLIA, Steve (FB)
Fresno, Calif., 1971-72
BLACKBURN, Darrell (LB)
Huntsville, Ala., 1993-94-95-96
BLACKMON, Sumpter (QB)
Columbus, Ga., 1941
BLACKWELL, Gene (E)
Blytheville, Ark., 1937-38-39
BLACKWOOD, J. E. (G)
Birmingham, Ala., 1921
BLAIR, Bill (DB)
Nashville, Tenn., 1968-69-70
BLAIR, Elmer (B)
Birmingham, Ala., 1917
BLAIR, J. W. (T)
Clayton, Ala., 1897
BLALOCK, Ralph (E)
Cullman, Ala., 1956-57
BLEVINS, James Allen (T)
Moulton, Ala., 1957-58-59
BLITZ, Jeff (DB)
Montgomery, Ala., 1972
BLUE, Al (DB)
Maitland, Fla., 1981-82
BOBO, Mike (FB)
Crossville, Ala., 1985
BODDEN, Vann (DE)
Moss Point, Miss.,
1993-94-95
BOHANON, Shaun (TB)
Oak Ridge, Tenn., 1999
BOLDEN, Hirchel (CB)
Dothan, Ala. 1999
BOLDEN, Ray (DB)
Tarrant, Ala., 1974-75
BOLER, Clark (T)
Northport, Ala., 1962-63
BOLER, Thomas (OT)
Northport, Ala., 1980
BOLES, John "Duffy" (HB)
Huntsville, Ala., 1973-75
BOLT, Scott (OT)
Alexander City,-Ala., 1990
BOLTON, Bruce (SE)
Memphis, Tenn., 1976-77-78
BOMAN, Atokie (FL)
Bigbee, Ala., 1997

BOMAN, T. D. (T)
Heflin, Ala., 1914-15
BOOKER, David (SE)
Huntsville, Ala., 1979
BOOKER, Steve (LB)
Huntsville, Ala., 1981-82-83
BOONE, Alfred Morgan "Dan"
(E) Samantha, Ala., 1917-18-19
BOONE, Isaac M. "Ike" (E)
Samantha, Ala., 1919
BOOTH, Baxter (E)
Athens, Ala., 1956-57-58
BOOTHE, Vince (OG)
Fairhope, Ala., 1977-78-79
BOOZER, Young (HB)
Dothan, Ala., 1934-35-36
BORDERS, Tom (T)
Birmingham, Ala., 1939
BOSCHUNG, Paul (DT)
Tuscaloosa, Ala., 1967-68-69
BOSTICK, Lewis (G)
Birmingham, Ala., 1936-37-38
BOSWELL, Charley (HB)
Ensley, Ala., 1938-39
BOWDOIN, James L. "Goofy"
(G) Coffee Springs, Ala.,
1927-28
BOWDOIN, Jimmy (HB)
Elba, Ala., 1954-55-56
BOWENS, Tim (FL)
Killen, Ala., 1996-97-98-99
BOWMAN, Steve (FB)
Pascagoula, Miss., 1963-64-65
BOX, Jimmy (E)
Sheffield, Ala., 1960
BOYD, Thomas (LB)
Huntsville, Ala., 1978-79-80-81
BOYKIN, Gideon Frierson (G)
Brewton, Ala., 1894
BOYKIN, Dave (FB)
Parrish, Ala., 1928-29
BOYLE, R. E. (G)
Birmingham, Ala., 1892-93
BOYLES, J. V. (E)
Thomasville, Ala., 1904
BOYLSTON, Robert W. (T)
Atlanta, Ga., 1959-60
BRADFORD, James J. "Jim"
(OG) Montgomery, Ala., 1977
BRADFORD, Vic (QB)
Memphis, Tenn., 1936-37-38
BRAGAN, Dale (LB)
Birmingham, Ala., 1976
BRAGGS, Byron (DT)
Montgomery, Ala.,
1977-78-79-80
BRAGGS, Chester (RB)
Greensboro, Ala., 1983-84-85-86
BRAMBLETT, Dante (OLB)
Morrow, Ga., 1984
BRAMBLETT, Gary (OG)
Dalton, Ga., 1979-80-81-82
BRANNAN, Troy Crampton
(FB) Mobile, Ala., 1914
BRANNEN, Jay, (LB)
Gainesville, Fla., 1993
BRANNEN, Jerre Lamar (E)
Anniston, Ala., 1957-58
BRASFIELD, Davis (HB)
Birmingham, Ala., 1927

BREWER, Richard (SE)
Sylacauga, Ala., 1965-66-67
BRITT, Gary (LB)
Mobile, Ala., 1977
BROCK, Jim (OG)
Montgomery, Ala., 1981
BROCK, John (PK)
Hutnington Beach, Calif., 1996
BROCK, Mike (OG)
Montgomery, Ala., 1977-78-79
BRODIE, Brooks (C)
Tifton, Ga., 1997-98
BROOKER, Johnny (PK)
Demopolis, Ala., 1982
BROOKER, Wm. T. "Tommy"
(E) Demopolis, Ala.,
1959-60-61
BROOKS, Wm. S. "Billy" (C)
Tuscaloosa, Ala., 1954-55-56
BROWN, Bill (DB)
DeKalb, Miss., 1982
BROWN, Billy (HB)
Dothan, Ala., 1928
BROWN, Carl Abercrombie (G)
Birmingham, Ala., 1898-99
BROWN, Curtis (SE)
John's Island, S.C.,
1991-92-94-95
BROWN, Dave (HB)
Birmingham, Ala., 1940-41-42
BROWN, Elverett (NT)
Montgomery, Ala.,
1991-92-93-95
BROWN, Halver "Buddy" (G)
Tallahassee, Fla., 71-72-73
BROWN, Jack (QB)
Selma, Ala., 1948-49-50-51
BROWN, Jerry (TE)
Fairfax, Ala., 1974-75
BROWN, Johnny Mack (HB)
Dothan, Ala., 1923-24-25
BROWN, Larry (TE)
Pembroke Pines, Fla.,
1979-80-81-82
BROWN, Marshall (FB)
Ladysmith, Wis., 1955-56-57
BROWN, Marvin (FB)
Hyattsville, Md., 1998-99
BROWN, Phillip (LB)
Birmingham, Ala., 1983-86-87
BROWN, Randy (T)
Scottsville, N.Y., 1968
BROWN, Rick (FL)
Ft. Worth, Tex., 1991-92-94
BROWN, Robert C. (B)
Ensley, Ala., 1916-17
BROWN, Shannon (DE)
Millbrook, Ala., 1992-93-94-95
BROWN, Tolbert "Red" (HB)
Dothan, Ala., 1926-27
BROWN, T. L. (B)
Jasper, Ala., 1919-20
BROWN, Randall R. (B)
Tuscaloosa, Ala., 1908-09
BROWN, Will (OLB)
Syracuse, N.Y., 1991-92-93
BRUNGARD, David A. (FB)
Youngstown, Ohio, 1970
BRYAN, Richard (DT)
Verona, N.J., 1972-74

BRYANT, Fernando (CB)
Murfreesboro, Tn.,
1995-96-97-98
BRYANT, Paul W. "Bear" (E)
Fordyce, Ark., 1933-34-35
BUCHANAN, Richard Woodruff
"Woody" (FB)
Montgomery, Ala., 1976
BUCHANAN, Shamari, (SE)
Atlanta, Ga., 1996-97-98-99
BUCK, Oran (K)
Oak Ridge, Tenn., 1969
BUCKLER, Wm. E. "Bill" (G)
St. Paul, Minn., 1923-24-25
BUCKNER, Tyrell (LB)
Dennison, Tex., 1993-94-95-96
BUMGARDNER, Robert H. (E)
Bessemer, Ala., 1909-10
BUNCH, Jim (OG)
Mechanicsville, Va.,
1976-77-78-79
BURGDORF, Brian (QB)
Cedartown, Ga., 1992-93-94-95
BURGETT, J.I., (T), 1893
BURKHART, C. T. (E)
Hanceville, Ala., 1920
BURKETT, Jim (FB)
Dothan, Ala., 1949-50
BURKS, Auxford (HB)
Tuscaloosa, Ala., 1903-04-05
BURKS, Basil Manly (T)
Tuscaloosa, Ala., 1913-14
BURKS, Henry Thomas (T)
Tuscaloosa, Ala., 1906-07-08
BURNETT, Hunter Tennille (B)
Tuscaloosa, Ala., 1914-15
BURNS, Harmon Theron (B)
Wedowee, Ala., 1901-02
BURR, Borden (B)
Talladega, Ala., 1893-94
BURROUGHS, Anthony (FB)
Rogersville, Ala., 1994
BURTON, Kendrick (DE)
Hartselle, Ala., 1993-94-95
BUSBEE, Kent (DB)
Meridian, Miss., 1967
BUSBY, Max (OG)
Leeds, Ala., 1977
BUSH, Jeff (B)
Tuscaloosa, Ala., 1933-34
BUSH, Jim (G)
Columbus, Ga., 1945-46
BUSKY, Steve (TE)
Suitland, Md., 1990-91-92
BUTCHER, C.P. (T)
Urbana, Ohio, 1904
BUTLER, Webb (SS)
Charleston, SC., 1999
BUTLER, Clyde (OT)
Scottsboro, Ala., 1970

C
CADENHEAD, Billy (RH)
Greenville, Miss., 1946-47-48-49
CAIN, Jim (E)
Eudora, Ark., 1945-46-47-48
CAIN, Johnny (FB)
Montgomery, Ala., 1930-31-32
CALDWELL, Blackie (B)
Tallassee, Ala., 1936

CALDWELL, Herschel (HB)
Blytheville, Ark., 1925-26
CALLAWAY, Neil (LB-DE-OT)
Macon, Ga., 1975-77
CALLIES, Kelly (DT)
Fairhope, Ala., 1977
CALVERT, John (G)
Cullman, Ala., 1965-66
CALVIN, Tom (FB)
Athens, Ala., 1948-49-50
CAMP, Joseph "Pete" (T)
Manchester, Ala., 1923-24-25
CAMPBELL, John (QB)
Durant, Miss., 1928-29-30
CAMPBELL, Mike (DB)
Pinson, Ala., 1988-92
CAMPBELL, Tilden "Happy"
(QB) Pine Bluff, Ark., 1934-35
CANALE, Blair (FS)
Memphis, Tenn., 1993-94-95
CANTERBURY, Frank (HB)
Birmingham, Ala., 1964-65-66
CARGILE, C. J. (B)
Bessemer, Ala., 1914
CARRIGAN, Ralph (C)
Oak Park, Ill., 1951-52-53
CARROLL, Jimmy (C)
Enterprise, Ala., 1965-66
CARROLL, Travis (LB)
Jacksonville, Fla., 1997-98
CARRUTH, Paul Ott (RB)
Summit, Miss., 1981-82-84
CARTER, Antonio (FL)
Tallahassee, Fla., 1999
CARTER, Jamie (DT)
Philadelphia, Miss.,
1996-97-98-99
CARTER, Joe (RB)
Starkville, Miss., 1980-81-82-83
CARY, Robert H., Jr. "Robin"
(DB) Greenwood, S.C., 1972-73
CASH, Danny (OT)
Spartanburg, S.C., 1987-89
CASH, Jeraull Wayne "Jerry" (E)
Bogart, Ga., 1970-71
CASH, Steve (LB)
Huntsville, Ala., 1980
CASHIO, Gri (G)
Gadsden, Ala., 1947
CASSADY, Michael (SE)
Florala, Ala., 1996
CASSIDY, Francis (T)
Neff, Ohio, 1944-45-46-47
CASSIMUS, John (DB-RB-WR)
Birmingham, Ala., 1987-88-89
CASTEAL, David (HB)
Eglin AFB, Fla., 1986-87-88
CASTILLE, Jeremiah (DB)
Phenix City, Ala., 1979-80-81-82
CAVAN, Peter Alexander (HB)
Thomaston, Ga., 1975-76-77
CAUSEY, Joe (HB)
Douglas, Ariz., 1931
CAUSEY, John (C)
Hayneville, Ala., 1993-94-95-96
CAYAVEC, Bob (OT)
Largo, Fla., 1980-81-82
CHAFFIN, Phil (FB)
Huntsville, Ala., 1968-69-70
CHAMBERS, Jimmy (C)

Fort Payne, Ala., 1967
CHAMBERS, Lee (QB)
Enterprise, Ala., 1999
CHANDLER, Thornton (TE)
Jacksonville, Fla., 1983-84-85
CHAPMAN, Herb (C)
Elmore, Ala., 1947
CHAPMAN, Roger (K)
Hartselle, Ala., 1977-78
CHAPPELL, Howard (B)
Sylacauga, Ala., 1931-32-33
CHATMAN, Terrill (OT)
Childersburg, Ala.,
1987-88-89-90
CHATWOOD, David (FB)
Fairhope, Ala., 1965-66-67
CHILDERS, Morris (B)
Birmingham, Ala., 1960
CHILDS, Bob (LB)
Montgomery, Ala., 1966-67-68
CHIODETTI, Larry (LH)
Philadelphia, Pa., 1950-51
CHRISTIAN, Hunter (LB)
Tuscaloosa, Ala., 1995
CHRISTIAN, Knute Rockne (C)
Tuscaloosa, Ala., 1954-55
CHRISTIAN, Myles (FB)
Tuscaloosa, Ala., 1999
CIEMNY, Richard (K)
Anthony, Kan., 1969-70
CLARK, Brent (NT)
Plainview, Ala., 1991
CLARK, Cotton (HB)
Kansas, Ala., 1961-62
CLARK, Frank Barnard (B)
Mobile, Ala., 1903-04
CLARK, Phil (G)
Columbus, Ga., 1956
CLARK, Tim (SE)
Newnan, Ga., 1978-79-80-81
CLAY, Hugh Stephen (G)
Gadsden, Ala., 1969
CLAY, John (LB-OG)
Nashville, Tenn., 1990-91-92-93
CLEMENS, Al (E)
Scottsboro, Ala., 1921-22-23
CLEMENT, C. B. "Foots" (T)
Rower, Ark., 1928-29-30
CLEMENTS, Mike (DB)
Center Point, Ala., 1978-79-80
CLINE, Jackie (DT)
McCalla, Ala., 1980-81-82
CLONTS, Steve (C)
Rome, Ga., 1989
CLORFELINE, Julius (G)
Anotpol, Russia, 1911
COCHRAN, Bob (LH)
Hueytown, Ala., 1947-48-49
COCHRAN, Chris (LB)
Germantown, Tenn., 1989-90
COCHRAN, Donald G. (G)
Birmingham, Ala., 1957-58-59
COCHRAN, Ralph (QB)
Hueytown, Ala., 1949
COCHRANE, David (B)
Tuscaloosa, Ala., 1931
COCHRANE, Henry (QB)
Paducah, Ky., 1937
COHEN, Andy (B)
El Paso, Texas, 1923-24

COKELY, Donald (T)
Chickasha, Okla., 1970-71
COLBURN, Rocky (DB)
Cantonment, Fla., 1982-83-84
COLBURN, Roman (FL)
Fort Payne, Ala., 1992-93-94
COLE, Jason (LB)
Albertville, Ala., 1994
COLE, Lorenzo (FL)
Florence, Ala., 1990-93
COLE, Richard (DT)
Crossville, Ala., 1965-66
COLE, Steve (PK)
Fayetteville, Ga., 1991-92
COLE, Tommy (NG-DT)
Jasper, Ala., 1985-86-87-88
COLEMAN, Michael (SE)
Anaheim, Calif., 1978
COLEY, Ken (DB-QB)
Birmingham, Ala., 1979-80-81-82
COLLINS, Danny (DE)
Birmingham, Ala., 1976-77
COLLINS, Earl (FB)
Mobile, Ala., 1980-81
COLLINS, Sam (SE)
Fayette, Ala., 1999
COMPTON, Ben E. (LG)
Greensboro, Ala., 1923-24-25
COMPTON, Charley (T)
Sylacauga, Ala., 1942-46-47
COMPTON, Joe (FB)
Sylacauga, Ala., 1949-50-51
COMSTOCK, Charles Dexter (B)
Birmingham, Ala., 1895-96
COMSTOCK, Donald (HB)
Lincoln, Neb., 1956
CONDON, Bill (OG)
Mobile, Ala., 1984-85-86-87
CONN, Mickey (CB)
Snellville, Ga., 1992-93-94
CONNOR, Don (C)
Gadsden, Ala., 1955
CONSTANT, Marvin (MLB)
Tuscaloosa, Ala., 1999
CONWAY, Bob (RH)
Fort Wayne, Ind., 1950-51-52
CONWAY, William P. "Bill" (G)
Birmingham, Ala., 1944
COOK, Elbert (LB)
Jacksonville, Fla., 1960-61-62
COOK, Jackson (C)
Cullman, Ala., 1994-95
COOK, Leroy (DE)
Abbeville, Ala., 1972-73-74-75
COOK, Ted (E)
Birmingham, Ala., 1942-46
COOK, Wayne (TE)
Montgomery, Ala., 1964-65-66
COOPER, Britton (DB)
Mobile, Ala., 1983-84-85-86
COOPER, Ernest "Shorty" (T)
St. Stephens, Ala., 1921-22-23
COPE, Robert (RG)
Union Springs, Ala., 1892-93
COPELAND, John, (DE)
Lanett, Ala., 1991-92
CORBITT, James "Corky" (RH)
Nashville, Tenn., 1945-46
COSTIGAN, Chris (SE)
Danville, Calif., 1989

COUCH, L. B. (C)
Alexander City, Ala., 1949-50
COUNTESS, C. C. (C)
Duncanville, Ala., 1907-08
COURTNEY, Earlando (DB)
Thomasville, Ala., 1986-87
COWELL, Vince (OG)
Snellville, Ga., 1978-79-80
COX, Adam (TB)
Jasper, Ala., 1998-99
COX, Allen (OT)
Satsuma, Ala., 1972
COX, Brent (LB)
State Road, SC., 1998
COX, Carey (C)
Bainbridge, Ga., 1937-38-39
COX, Tony (LB)
LaGrange, Ga., 1988
COYLE, Dan Joseph, Jr. (E)
Birmingham, Ala., 1954-55
CRAFT, Russ (HB)
Beach Bottom, W.Va.,
1940-41-42
CRANE, Paul (C-LB)
Prichard, Ala., 1963-64-65
CRENSHAW, Curtis (T)
Mobile, Ala., 1961
CREEN, Cecil L. (B)
Anniston, Ala., 1916
CRIM, Travis (SS)
Clanton, Ala., 1996-97
CROOM, Sylvester (C)
Tuscaloosa, Ala., 1972-73-74
CROSS, Andy (LB)
Birmingham, Ala., 1972
CROSS, Howard (TE)
New Hope, Ala., 1985-86-87-88
CROW, John David, Jr. (HB)
El Cahon, Calif., 1975-76-77
CROWSON, Roger (FB)
Jackson, Miss., 1968
CROYLE, John (DE)
Gadsden, Ala., 1971-72-73
CRUMBLEY, Allen (DB)
Birmingham, Ala., 1976-78
CRUTCHFIELD, Rance (LB)
Birmingham, Ala., 1996
CRUTCHFIELD, Rhett (TE)
Birmingham, Ala., 1997-98
CRYDER, Robert J. (OG)
O'Fallon Township, Ill.,
1975-76-77
CULLIVER, Calvin (FB)
East Brewton, Ala.,
1973-74-75-76
CULPEPPER, Ed (T)
Bradenton, Fla.,
1951-52-53-54
CULWELL, Ingram (HB)
Tuscaloosa, Ala., 1961-62
CUMMINGS, Joe (E)
Muleshoe, Texas, 1952-53
CUNNINGHAM, Brian (PK)
Birmingham, Ala., 1996-97-98
CUNNINGHAM, Derek (CB)
Birmingham, Ala., 1997
CUNNINGHAM, E. A. "Jim" (T)
Winfield, Ala., 1955-56
CURRY, Eric (DE)
Thomasville, Ga., 1990-91-92

CURTIS, Joe (E)
  Birmingham, Ala., 1950-51-52
CURTIS, Nathan Stephenson (B)
  Carrollton, Ala., 1906
CUTHBERT, Will (OT)
  Ft. Pierce, Fla., 1997-98-99

D
DARE, Charlie (OG)
  Enterprise, Ala., 1989-90-91
DASHER, Bob (OG)
  Plymouth, Mich., 1981
DAVIS, Alvin "Pig" (FB)
  Green Forest, Ark., 1937-38
DAVIS, Bill (K)
  Columbus, GA., 1971-72-73
DAVIS, Charley (RH)
  Uniontown, Pa., 1948-49
DAVIS, Danny (SS)
  Memphis, Tenn., 1992-93
DAVIS, Fernando (LB)
  Aberdeen, Miss., 1993-94-95-96
DAVIS, Fred (T)
  Louisville, Ky., 1938-39-40
DAVIS, Fred, Jr. (T)
  Louisville, Ky., 1964
DAVIS, Jim (LG)
  Hamilton, Ala., 1951-52-53
DAVIS, John (R)
  Dallas, Texas, 1987-89
DAVIS, Johnny Lee (FB)
  Montgomery, Ala., 1975-76-77
DAVIS, Mike (K)
  Columbus, Ga., 1975
DAVIS, Ricky (S)
  Bessemer, Ala., 1973-74
DAVIS, Steve (K)
  Columbus, Ga., 1965-66-67
DAVIS, Terry Ashley (QB)
  Bogalusa, La., 1970-71-72
DAVIS, Terry Lane (E)
  Birmingham, Ala., 1970
DAVIS, Tim (K)
  Columbus, Ga., 1961-62-63
DAVIS, Vantreise (LB)
  Phenix City, Ala., 1986-87-88-89
DAVIS, Wayne (LB)
  Gordo, Ala., 1983-84-85
DAVIS, William (DT)
  Fort Deposit, Ala., 1978
DAVIS, William "Junior" (T)
  Birmingham, Ala., 1967-68
DAVIDSON, James Lafayette (C)
  Centreville, Ala., 1900
DAWSON, Jimmy Dale (LB)
  Excel, Ala., 1973
DEAN, Louis (DB)
  Foley, Ala., 1984
DEAN, Mike (DB)
  Decatur, Ga., 1967-68-69
DEAN, Steve (HB)
  Orlando, Fla., 1972-73
DEASON, Dennis (C)
  Vestavia, Ala., 1992-93
DeLAURENTIS, Vincent (C)
  Hammonton, N.J., 1952-53
DEMOS, Joe (OG)
  Clearwater, Fla., 1989
DEMPSEY, Benny (C)
  Brantley, Ala., 1956-57

DEMYANOVICH, Joe (FB)
  Bayonne, N.J., 1932-33-34
DEWBERRY, John Robert (RG)
  Brundidge, Ga., 1894-95
DeNIRO, Gary (DE)
  Youngstown, Ohio, 1978-79-80
DeSHANE, Charley (QB)
  Grand Rapids, Mich., 1940
DIEHL, Bryne (P)
  Oakman, Ala., 1992-93-94
DICHIARA, Ron (K)
  Bessemer, Ala., 1974
DILDY, Jim (T)
  Nashville, Ark., 1931-32-33
DILDY, Joe (C)
  Nashville, Ark., 1933-34
DILL, Jimmy (E)
  Mobile, Ala., 1962-63
DiMARIO, Pete, (OG)
  Tuscaloosa, Ala., 1993-94-95-96
DISMUKE, Joe (OT)
  Gadsden, Ala., 1982-83
DIXON, Dennis (TE)
  Orange, Calif., 1967-68
DIXON, Gerald (CB)
  Burtonsville, Md., 1999
DIXON, Tony (FS)
  Reform, Ala., 1997-98-99
DOBBS, Edgar (E)
  Collinsville, Ala., 1928-30
DOMNANOVICH, Joe (C)
  South Bend, Ind., 1940-41-42
DONALD, Joseph Glenn (C)
  Marion Junction, Ala., 1905-06
DONALDSON, Paul (E)
  Florala, Ala., 1954
DONNELLY, Chris (SS)
  Germantown, Tenn., 1992-93
DORAN, Stephen Curtis (TE)
  Murray, KY., 1969-70
DOTHEROW, Autrey (E)
  Brooksville, Ala., 1930-31
DOVER, Don (C)
  Birmingham, Ala., 1992
DOWDELL, Anthony (DE)
  Columbus, Ga., 1994-95-96
DOWDY, Cecil (OT)
  Cherokee, Ala., 1964-65-66
DOYLE, Philip (PK)
  Birmingham, Ala., 1987-88-89-90
DRAPER, Shawn (TE/DE)
  Huntsville, Ala., 1997-98-99
DRENNEN, Earl (QB)
  Birmingham, Ala., 1900-01
DRINKARD, Reid (OG)
  Linden, Ala., 1968-69-70
DUBOSE, Mike (DE)
  Opp, Ala., 1972-73-74
DUKE, Jim (DT)
  Columbus, Ga., 1967-68-69
DUNCAN, Conley (LB)
  Hartselle, Ala., 1973-74-75
DUNCAN, Jerry (OT)
  Sparta, N.C., 1965-66
DUNN, Jeff (QB)
  Greensboro, N.C., 1987-88-89
DURBY, Ron (T)
  Memphis, Tenn., 1963-64
DYAR, Warren E. (TE)
  Florence, Ala., 1972-73

DYE, George (C)
  Birmingham, Ala., 1927
DYESS, Johnny (RB)
  Elba, Ala., 1981
DYESS, Marlin (HB)
  Elba, Ala., 1957-58-59

E
EBERDT, JESS (C)
  Blytheville, Ark., 1929-30
ECKENROD, Michael Lee (C)
  Chattanooga, Tenn., 1973
ECKERLY, Charles (G)
  Oak Park, Ill., 1952-53-54
EDWARDS, Bryant B. (RE)
  Union Springs, Ala., 1906-07-08
EDWARDS, Chris (LB)
  Bessemer, Ala., 1995-96-97-98
EDWARDS, Marion "Buddy" (T)
  Attalla, Ala., 1944
EDWARDS, Randy (DT)
  Marietta, Ga., 1980-81-82-83
ELDER, Venson (LB)
  Decatur, Ga., 1982-83
ELIAS, Johnny (MG)
  Columbus, Ga., 1981-82
ELLARD, Butch (Mgr.)
  Tuscaloosa, Ala., 1982
ELLETT, Alvin (T)
  Owen Cross Roads, Ala., 1955
ELLINGTON, Dante (OT)
  Leighton, Ala., 1999
ELLIS, Billy (B)
  Florence, Ala., 1928
ELLIS, Raiford (C)
  Birmingham, Ala., 1934
ELLIS, Victor (C)
  Chattanooga, Tenn., 1998-99
ELMORE, Albert, Sr., (E)
  Reform, Ala., 1929-30
ELMORE, Albert, Jr. (QB)
  Troy, Ala., 1953-54-55
ELMORE, Grady (K-HB)
  Ozark, Ala., 1962-63-64
EMERSON, Ken (DB)
  Columbus., Ga., 1969-70
EMMETT, J. H. (HB)
  Albertville, Ala., 1919-20-21-22
EMMONS, James Thomas (T)
  Atmore, Ala., 1954
ENIS, Ben (E)
  Fayette, Ala., 1926
EPPS, Craig (OLB)
  Miami, Fla., 1984-85-86-87
ETTER, Scott (QB)
  Lexington, Ky., 1990

F
FAGAN, Jeff (RB)
  Hollywood, Fla., 1979-80-81-82
FAUST, Donald W. (FB)
  Fairhope, Ala., 1975-76-77
FAUST, Douglas (DT)
  Fairhope, Ala., 1972
FAVORS, Michael (G)
  Mobile, Ala., 1994
FEAGIN, Michael (FL)
  Greenville, Ala., 1995-96-97-98
FEDAK, Frank (HB)
  Short Creek, W.Va., 1945

FELDER, Shannon (DB)
  Willis, Tex., 1985-87
FELL, Howie (LB)
  Birmingham, Ala., 1995
FERGUSON, Burr (LE)
  Birmingham, Ala., 1892-93
FERGUSON, Charles M. (OG)
  Cuthbert, Ga., 1968-69
FERGUSON, Hill (B)
  Birmingham, Ala., 1895-96
FERGUSON, Lee (TE)
  Albertville, Ala., 1997
FERGUSON, Mitch (RB)
  Augusta, Ga., 1977-79-80
FERGUSON, Richard (OG)
  Fort Payne, Ala., 1969
FICHMAN, Leon (T)
  Los Angeles, Calif., 1941-42
FIELDS, Paul (QB)
  Gardendale, Ala., 1982-83
FIELDS, William H. (E)
  Nashville, Tenn., 1944
FILIPPINI, Bruno (G)
  Powhatan Point, Ohio,
  1944-45-46-47
FINKLEY, Donnie (WR)
  Fairhope, Ala., 1989-90-92
FINLAY, Louis Malone (T)
  Pollard, Ala., 1909-10
FINNELL, Edward Judson (B)
  Tuscaloosa, Ala., 1911
FLANAGAN, Thad (SE)
  Leighton, Ala., 1974-75-76
FLETCHER, Maurice (QB)
  Clarksdale, Miss., 1937
FLORENCE, Craige (DB)
  Enterprise, Ala., 1981-82
FLORETTE, Anthony Ray (E)
  Cleveland, Ohio, 1920
FLOWERS, Dick (T)
  Mobile, Ala., 1946-47
FLOWERS, Lee (T)
  Mobile, Ala., 1945
FLOWERS, Kevin (DE)
  Troy, Ala., 1997
FLOYD, Chad (PK)
  Cullman, Ala., 1999
FLOYD, Lamont (LB)
  Orange Park, Fla., 1993-94-95-96
FORBUS, Roy (E)
  Alexander City, Ala., 1956
FORD, Brad (CB)
  Dadeville, Ala., 1994-95
FORD, Danny (OT)
  Gadsden, Ala., 1967-68-69
FORD, Mike (DE)
  Tuscaloosa, Ala., 1966-67-68
FORD, Steven (DB)
  Tuscaloosa, Ala., 1973-74
FORMAN, James R. (T)
  Ashville, Ala., 1901-02
FORTUNATO, Steve (G)
  Mingo Junction, Ohio,
  1946-47-48
FOSHEE, Jeff (LB/FB)
  Millbrook, Ala., 1991-92-93-94
FOSHEE, Jess (G)
  Clanton, Ala., 1937-38
FOUST, Warren (QB/FS)
  Midwest City, Ok., 1995-96-97-98

FOWLER, Conrad (SE)
Columbiana, Ala., 1966-67-68
FOWLER, Les (DB)
Hartselle, Ala., 1976
FRACCHIA, Mike (FB)
Memphis, Tenn., 1960-61-63
FRALEY, Robert (QB)
Winchester, Tenn., 1974-75
FRANCIS, Kavanaugh "Kay" (C)
Timson, Tex., 1933-34-35
FRANK, Milton (G)
Huntsville, Ala., 1958-59
FRANK, Morris
Huntsville, Ala., 1962
FRANKLIN, Arthur (RT)
Greensboro, N.C., 1906
FRANKO, Jim (G)
Yorkville, Ohio, 1947-48-49
FRAZER, Thomas Sydney (B)
Union Springs, Ala., 1892-83
FREEMAN, Wayne (OG)
Fort Payne, Ala., 1962-63-64
FRENCH, Buddy (K)
Decatur, Ala., 1963-64
FREY, Calvin (G)
Arkadelphia, Ark., 1931-32-33
FRIEND, Will (OG)
Philadelphia, Miss.,
1994-95-96-97
FRUHMORGEN, John (OG)
Tampa, Fla., 1986-87-88
FUHRMAN, Darrel (OLB)
Gadsden, Ala. 1987
FULLER, Jimmy (T)
Fairfield, Ala., 1964-65-66
FULLER, Leon (HB)
Nederland, Texas, 1959-60

G
GAGE, Fred Harrison (B)
Hampton, N.H., 1916
GALLOWAY, Ahmaad (TB)
Millington, Tenn., 1999
GAMBRELL, D. Joe (C)
Talladega, Ala., 1945-46
GAMMON, George (HB)
Cullman, Ala., 1941-42
GANDY, Joseph Maury (T)
Pell City, Ala., 1912-13
GANDY, Ralph (E)
Birmingham, Ala.,
1932-33-34-35
GANTT, Greg (K)
Birmingham, Ala., 1971-72-73
GARDNER, Charles (DB)
Carson, Calif., 1988-89-90-91
GARRETT, Broox Cleveland (E)
Thomasville, Ala., 1909
GARRETT, Coma, Jr. (E)
Thomasville, Ala., 1905-06
GARTMAN, Randy (FS)
Chicago, Ill., 1993
GASTON, Willie (FS)
Mobile, Ala., 1992-93-94
GAY, Stan (DB)
Tuskegee, Ala., 1981-82-83
GELLERSTEDT, Sam (NG)
Montgomery, Ala., 1968
GERASIMCHUK, Davis (OG)
Lomita, Calif., 1975-76

GERBER, Elwood (G)
Napierville, Ill., 1940
GERMANOS, Nicholas "Nick"
(E) Montgomery, Ala., 1954-55
GETCHELL, Billy (SE)
Queens, N.Y., 1984
GIANGROSSO, James (DE)
Chalmette, La., 1991
GIBBONS, James Booth (T)
Tuscaloosa, Ala., 1914
GIBSON, Richard (E)
Mobile, Ala., 1945
GIBSON, Rondi (WR)
Brewton, Ala., 1994-95
GILBERT, Danny (DB)
Geraldine, Ala., 1968-69-70
GILBERT, Darius, (LB)
Oxford, Ala., 1998-99
GILBERT, Greg (LB)
Decatur, Ala., 1985-86-87-88
GILDER, Andrew (FB)
Elmore, Ala., 1983
GILLILAND, Rickey (LB)
Birmingham, Ala., 1976-77-78
GILLIS, Grant (QB)
Grove Hill, Ala., 1923-24-25
GILMER, Creed (DE)
Birmingham, Ala., 1964-65
GILMER, David (OG)
Attalla, Ala., 1984-85
GILMER, Harry (HB)
Birmingham, Ala., 1944-45-46-47
GLADDEN, Chad (C)
Centre, Ala., 1991-93
GLOVER, Martin (FL)
Sumiton, Ala., 1999
GODFREE, Newton (T)
Alexander City, Ala.,
1930-31-32
GODWIN, Joe (LB)
New Brocton, Ala., 1984-85-86
GOODE, Chris (DB)
Town Creek, Ala., 1986
GOODE, Clyde (CB)
Town Creek, Ala., 1989-91
GOODE, Kerry (RB)
Town Creek, Ala., 1983-86-87
GOODE, Pierre (WR)
Town Creek, Ala., 1987-88-89
GORNTO, Jack "Red" (E)
Valdosta, Ga., 1938
GOSS, Chad (FL)
Warner Robbins, Ga.,
1995-96-97
GOSSETT, Don Lee (MG)
Knoxville, Tenn., 1969
GOTHARD, Andrew "Andy" (DB)
Alexander City, Ala., 1975-76
GOTHARD, Preston (TE)
Montgomery, Ala., 1983-84
GRAHAM, Glen W. (C)
Florence, Ala., 1955-56
GRAMMER, James W. (C)
Hartselle, Ala., 1969-71
GRAMMER, Richard (C)
Hartselle, Ala., 1967-68-69
GRANADE, James Napoleon (E)
Frankville, Ala., 1898-99
GRANT, Fred (FB)
Christianburg, Va., 1944-45-46

GRANTHAM, Jim (E)
Plano, Texas, 1945-46
GRAVES, Bibb
Montgomery, Ala., 1892
GRAY, Alan (QB)
Tampa, Fla., 1979-80-81
GRAY, Charles (E)
Pell City, Ala., 1956-57-58
GRAYSON, David Allison (RE)
Gurley, Ala., 1892-93
GREEN, Jack (G)
Centre, Ala., 1945
GREEN, Louis E. (OG)
Birmingham, Ala., 1974-76-77
GREENE, Edgar D. (RT)
Waverly, Ala., 1907-08
GREENE, Hamp (PK)
Montgomery, Ala., 1991-92
GREENWOOD, Darren (CB)
Lanett, Ala., 1989-90
GREER, Charles West (B)
Marion, Ala., 1910-11
GREGORY, James (NG)
St. Louis, Mo., 1990-91-92-93
GRESHAM, Owen Garside (T)
Prattville, Ala., 1908-09
GRIFFIN, Cornelius (DT)
Brundidge, Ala., 1998-99
GRIMES, Reggie (DT)
Nashville, Tenn., 1996-97-98-99
GROBE, Mark (FS)
Cullman, Ala., 1995
GROGAN, Jay (TE)
Cropwell, Ala., 1981-82-83
GRYSKA, Clem (HB)
Steubenville, Ohio, 1947-48
GUINYARD, Mickey (RB)
Atlanta, Ga., 1981-82
GUNNELLS, Ross (LB)
Aliceville, Ala., 1999
GWIN, James C. C. (C)
East Lake, Ala., 1903

H
HAGAN, James "Dink" (QB)
1913-14-15-16-17
HAGLER, Ellis (C)
Blue Springs, Ala., 1927-28
HALL, Calvin (SE)
Gallatin, Tenn., 1995-96-97-98
HALL, Lemanski (S, LB)
Valley, Ala., 1990-91-92-93
HALL, Mike (LB)
Tarrant, Ala., 1966-67-68
HALL, Randy Lee (DT)
Huntsville, Ala., 1972-73-74
HALL, Wayne (LB)
Huntsville, Ala., 1971-72-73
HAMER, Norris (DE)
Tarrant, Ala., 1967-68
HAMILTON, Wayne (DE)
Okahumpka, Fla., 1977-78-79
HAMMOND, Matt (OT)
Fort Payne, Ala., 1990-91-92-93
HAMMOND, Spencer (LB)
Rome, Ga., 1987-88-89-90
HAMNER, Robert Lee (B)
Fayette, Ala., 1925-26-27
HAND, Jon (DT)
Sylacauga, Ala., 1982-83-84-85

HAND, Mike (LB-OG)
Tuscumbia, Ala., 1968-69-70
HANEY, James (RB)
Rogersville, Ala., 1979
HANNAH, Charles (DT)
Albertville, Ala., 1974-75-76
HANNAH, David (OT)
Albertville, Ala., 1975-77-78-79
HANNAH, Herb (G)
Athens, Ga., 1948-49-50
HANNAH, John (OG)
Albertville, Ala., 1970-71-72
HANNAH, William C. (T)
Indianapolis, Ind., 1957-58-59
HANNON, Emile "Chick"
Montgomery, Ala., 1907
HANRAHAN, Gary (OG)
Pompano Beach, Fla., 1973
HANSEN, Cliff (T)
Gary, Ind., 1940-41
HANSON, John (FB)
Roanoke, Ala., 1939-40
HAPE, Patrick, (TE)
Killen, Ala., 1993-94-95-96
HARKINS, Grover (G)
Gadsden, Ala., 1937-38
HARKNESS, Fred (MG)
Winfield, Ala., 1980
HARPOLE, Allen "Bunk" (DG)
Columbus, Miss., 1965-66-67
HARRELL, Billy (HB)
Opelika, Ala., 1940
HARRIS, Charles (DE)
Mobile, Ala., 1965-66-67
HARRIS, Craig (RB)
Panama City, Fla., 1989-90-91-92
HARRIS, Don (DT)
Vincent, Ala., 1968-69-70
HARRIS, Hudson (HB)
Tarrant, Ala., 1962-63-64
HARRIS, Jim Bob (DB)
Athens, Ga., 1978-79-80-81
HARRIS, Joe Dale (SE)
Uriah, Ala., 1975
HARRIS, Paul (DE)
Mobile, Ala., 1974-75-76
HARRIS, Steven (LB)
Town Creek, Ala., 1995-96-97
HARRISON, Bill (DT)
Ft. Walton Beach., Fla., 1976
HARRISON, Monroe (TE)
Biloxi, Miss., 1990-91
HARRISON, Matt (C)
Dadeville, Ala., 1997
HARRISON, Stacy (DB)
Atlanta, Ga., 1988-89-90-91
HARSH, Griffin R. (QB)
Birmingham, Ala., 1914
HARSH, William L. (HB)
Birmingham, Ala., 1914-15
HARVILLE, Joey (OT)
Moulton, Ala., 1991-92-93-94
HAYDEN, Neb (QB)
Charlotte, N.C., 1969-70
HEARD, Victor John (B)
Camp Hill, Ala., 1910
HEARD, Vigil Willis (B)
Camp Hill, Ala., 1910-11
HEATH, Donnie (C)
Anniston, Ala., 1960

HECHT, George (G)
  Chicago Heights, Ill., 1940-41-42
HELMS, Sandy (G)
  Tuscaloosa, Ala., 1949-50
HELTON, Rodney (LB)
  Knoxville, Tenn., 1989
HENDERSON, Josh (DB)
  Panama City, Fla., 1982
HENDERSON, Wm. T. "Bill" (TE)
  Tuscaloosa, Ala., 1975-77
HENDERSON, S. W.
  Talladega, Ala., 1892
HENRY, Butch (E)
  Selma, Ala., 1961-62-63
HEWES, Willis (C)
  Russellville, Ark., 1931-32
HICKERSON, Ed (G)
  Ventura, Calif., 1938-40
HICKS, Billy (QB)
  Abilene, Texas, 1928-29
HICKS, J. W. (G)
  Ozark, Ala., 1912-13
HIGGINBOTHAM, Robert (DB)
  Hueytown, Ala., 1967-68
HIGGINBOTHAM, Steve (DB)
  Hueytown, Ala., 1969-70-71
HIGH, Tracy (CB)
  Pontotoc, Miss., 1993-94-95
HILL, John (RB)
  Centre, Ala., 1979-80
HILL, Marvin "Buster" (QB)
  Huntsville, Ala., 1952-54
HILL, Murry (RB)
  Atmore, Ala., 1988-89
HILL, Roosevelt (LB)
  Newnan, Ga., 1982-83
HILL, Thomas (CB)
  Meridian, Miss., 1996
HILMAN, R. G. (E)
  Epes, Ala., 1895
HINES, Edward T. (DE)
  LaFayette, Ala., 1970-72
HINTON, Robert Poole (B)
  Uniontown, Ala., 1922-23
HITE, John H. (HB)
  Nashville, Tenn., 1944
HOBBS, Sam (G)
  Selma, Ala., 1907
HOBSON, Clell (QB)
  Tuscaloosa, Ala., 1950-51-52
HODGES, Bruce (DE-T)
  Sarasota, Fla., 1977
HODGES, Norwood (FB)
  Hueytown, Ala., 1944-45-46-47
HOGAN, Paul (C)
  Valdosta, Ga., 1997-98-99
HOLCOMBE, Danny (OG)
  Marietta, Ga., 1980-81-82
HOLDBROOKS, Byron (DT)
  Haleyville, Ala., 1987-88-89-90
HOLDER, Harry (B)
  Birmingham, Ala., 1927
HOLDNAK, Ed (G)
  Kenvil, N.J., 1948-49
HOLLEY, Hillman D. (B)
  Tuscaloosa, Ala., 1930-31-32
HOLLIDAY, Joel (OT)
  Six Mile, S.C., 1994-95-96-97
HOLLINGSWORTH, Gary (QB)
  Hamilton, Ala., 1989-90

HOLLIS, William C. (HB)
  Biloxi, Miss., 1954-55
HOLLOWAY, Steven (OT)
  Hoover, Ala., 1999
HOLM, Bernard "Tony" (FB)
  Ensley, Ala., 1927-28-29
HOLM, Charlie (FB)
  Ensley, Ala., 1937-38
HOLMES, Gordon "Sherlock" (C)
  Springville, Ala., 1924-25-26
HOLOMAN, Desmond (LB)
  Hampton, Va., 1985-86
HOLSOMBACK, Roy (G)
  West Blocton, Ala., 1959-60
HOLT, Darwin (LB)
  Gainesville, Texas, 1960-61
HOLT, James Jay "Buddy" (P)
  Demopolis, Ala., 1977-79
HOMAN, Dennis (SE)
  Muscle Shoals, Ala., 1965-66-67
HOMAN, Scott (DT)
  Elkhart, Ind., 1979-80-81-82
HOOD, Bob (T)
  Gadsden, Ala., 1946-47-48
HOOD, Chris (DE)
  Town Creek, Ala., 1995-96-97
HOOD, E. P. (T)
  Woodlawn, Ala., 1919-20
HOOD, Sammy (DB)
  Ider, Ala., 1982-83
HOPE, Alvin (DB)
  Mobile, Ala., 1990-92
HOPPER, Mike (E)
  Huntsville, Ala., 1961-62-64
HORNE, Chris, (LB)
  Sandersville, Ga., 1997-98-99
HORSTEAD, Don (HB)
  Elba, Ala., 1982-84-85
HORTON, Jimmy (DE)
  Tarrant, Ala., 1971
HOUSTON, Ellis "Red" (C)
  Bessemer, Ala., 1930-31-32
HOUSTON, Martin (FB)
  Centre, Ala., 1989-90-91-92
HOVATER, Dexter Louis (B)
  Russellville, Ala., 1914-15
HOVATER, Jack (E)
  Russellville, Ala., 1919-20-21
HOVATER, Walter E. (RH)
  Russellville, Ala., 1917-18-19
HOVEN, Michael (TB)
  Chronelle, Ala., 1993
HOWARD, Frank (G)
  Barlow Bend, Ala., 1928-29-30
HOWARD, Johnny (OT)
  Bessemer, Ala., 1989-90-91-92
HOWELL, Millard "Dixie" (HB)
  Hartford, Ala., 1932-33-34
HOWLE, G. D. (FB)
  Wetumpka, Ala., 1907
HUBBARD, Colenzo (LB)
  Mulga, Ala., 1974-75-76
HUBERT, A. T. S. "Pooley" (FB)
  Meridian, Miss., 1922-23-24-25
HUDSON, Ben A. (E)
  Montgomery, Ala., 1923-24-25
HUDSON, H. Clayton (E)
  Montgomery, Ala., 1921-22
HUFSTETLER, Thomas R., Jr.
  (C) Rossville, Ga., 1977-78

HUGHES, Hal (QB)
  Pine Bluff, Ark., 1937-38
HUGHES, Howard (T)
  Little Rock, Ark., 1941
HUGHES, Larry (B)
  Tuscaloosa, Ala., 1931-32-33
HUMPHRIES, Marvin (OLB)
  Montgomery, Ala., 1984
HUMPHREY, Bobby (HB)
  Birmingham, Ala.,
  1985-86-87-88
HUNDERTMARK, John (T)
  Washington, Pa., 1933
HUNT, Ben (G)
  Scottsboro, Ala., 1920-21-22
HUNT, Morris Parker (OT)
  Orlando, Fla., 1972-73
HUNT, Travis (T)
  Albertville, Ala., 1950-51-52
HUNTER, Antoine (CB)
  Valdosta, Ga., 1997-98
HUNTER, Eddie (LB)
  LeFlore, Ala., 1995-98
HUNTER, Scott (QB)
  Prichard, Ala., 1968-69-70
HUPKE, Tom (G)
  East Chicago, Ind., 1931-32-33
HURD, Clarence S. (E)
  Bessemer, Ala., 1908-09
HURLBUT, Jack (QB)
  Houston, Texas, 1962-63
HURST, Tim (OT)
  DeArmandville, Ala., 1975-76-77
HURT, Cecil A. (E)
  Chattanooga, Tenn., 1927-28-29
HUSBAND, Hunter (TE)
  Nashville, Tenn., 1967-68-69
HUSBAND, Woodward A.
  "Woodie" (LB)
  Nashville, Tenn., 1969-70
HUTSON, Don (E)
  Pine Bluff, Ark., 1932-33-34
HUTT, John (LB)
  Tuscaloosa, Ala., 1993

I

IKNER, Lou (RB)
  Atmore, Ala., 1977-78
INGRAM, Cecil "Hootie" (DB)
  Tuscaloosa, Ala., 1952-53-54
ISRAEL, Jimmy Kent (QB)
  Haleyville, Ala., 1966
ISRAEL, Thomas Murray (G)
  Haleyville, Ala., 1969
IRVIN, Bobby Joe (LB)
  Sulligent, Ala., 1954
IVY, Hyrle, Jr. (E)
  Fort Wayne, Ind., 1951-52
IVY, Jim (DT)
  Birmingham, Ala., 1983-84

J

JACK, Jason (QB)
  Oxford, Ala., 1993
JACKSON, Billy (RB)
  Phenix City, Ala., 1978-79-80
JACKSON, Bobby (QB)
  Mobile, Ala., 1957-58
JACKSON, Kevin (SS)
  Dothan, Ala., 1995-96

JACKSON, Mark (C)
  Houston, Texas, 1981-82-83
JACKSON, Max (T)
  Notasulga, Ala., 1930-31
JACKSON, Quincy (FL)
  Brundridge, Ala., 1997-98
JACKSON, Wilbur (HB)
  Ozark, Ala., 1971-72-73
JACOBS, Donald (QB)
  Scottsboro, Ala., 1979-80
JAMES, Kenneth Morris (T)
  Columbus, Ga., 1969-70
JARVIS, Curt (NG)
  Gardendale, Ala., 1983-84-85-86
JEFFRIES, Dameian (DE)
  Sylacauga, Ala., 1991-92-93-94
JELKS, Gene (HB-DB)
  Gadsden, Ala., 1985-86-87-88-89
JENKINS, John Felix (E)
  Camden, Ala., 1894-95
JENKINS, Jug (E)
  Eufaula, Ala., 1949-50-51
JENKINS, Tom "Bobby" (FB)
  Talladega, Ala., 1942
JILLEBA, Pete (FB)
  Madison, N.J., 1967-68-69
JOHNS, Bobby (DB)
  Birmingham, Ala., 1965-66-67
JOHNSON, Billy (C)
  Selma, Ala., 1965-66-67
JOHNSON, Comell (HB)
  High Point, N.C., 1959-60
JOHNSON, D. B.
  DeSotoville, Ala., 1892
JOHNSON, Forney (QB)
  Birmingham, Ala., 1899
JOHNSON, Harold (C)
  Greensboro, Ala., 1951
JOHNSON, Hoss (OT)
  Huntsville, Ala., 1984-85-86
JOHNSON, James (HB)
  Tuscaloosa, Ala., 1924-25
JOHNSON, J. Goree (FB)
  Wetumpka, Ala., 1915-16
JOHNSON, Jarret (DT)
  Chiefland, Fla., 1999
JOHNSON, Tommy (CB)
  Niceville, Fla., 1991-92-93-94
JOHNSON, Tony (TE)
  Como, Miss., 1992-93-94-95
JOHNSTON, Donny (HB)
  Birmingham, Ala., 1966-69
JOHNSTON, Sidney (G)
  Athens, Ala., 1919-20
JOHNSTON, Wm. McDow (HB)
  Meridian, Miss., 1914
JONES, Amos (RB)
  Aliceville, Ala., 1980
JONES, Brice Sidney (E)
  Tuscaloosa, Ala., 1906-07
JONES, Bruce (RG)
  Jasper, Ala., 1923-24-25
JONES, H. H. (T)
  Centreville, Ala., 1901
JONES, Howard Criner (LG)
  Huntsville, Ala., 1914
JONES, Jason (SS)
  Tuscaloosa, Ala., 1997-99
JONES, Joe (RB)
  Thomaston, Ga., 1978-79-80

JONES, Joey (SE)
Mobile, Ala., 1980-81-82-83
JONES, Kevin (QB)
Louisville, Ky., 1977-78
JONES, Paul B. (RHB)
Selma, Ala., 1907
JONES, Ralph (E)
Florence, Ala., 1944
JONES, Ralph Lee (G)
Jones Mills, Ala., 1917-18-19
JONES, Raymond Wm. (E)
Huntsville, Ala., 1912
JONES, Robbie (LB)
Demopolis, Ala., 1979-80-81-82
JONES, Robert (RB)
Birmingham, Ala., 1989
JONES, Terry, Jr., (TE)
Tuscaloosa, Ala., 1998-99
JONES, Terry Wayne (C-NG)
Sandersville, Ga., 1975-76-77
JOPLIN, Charles West (QB-HB-
E) Gurley, Ala., 1911-12
JORDAN, Alex (SS)
Hueytown, Ala., 1991-92
JORDAN, Chris (OT)
Jackson, Ala., 1995-96
JORDAN, Lee Roy (LB)
Excel, Ala., 1960-61-62
JORDAN, Lint (E)
Monticellow, Ga., 1950-51
JUNIOR, E. J. III (DE)
Nashville, Tenn., 1977-78–79-80

K
KEARLEY, Dan (DT)
Talladega, Ala., 1962-63-64
KELLER, Phillip Brooks (LG)
Montgomery, Ala., 1911
KELLER, Thomas B. "Red" (LE)
Cullman, Ala., 1937
KELLEY, Joe (QB)
Ozark, Ala., 1966-67-68
KELLEY, Leslie (FB)
Cullman, Ala., 1964-65-66
KELLEY, Max (FB)
Cullman, Ala., 1954-55-56
KELLY, William Milner (E)
Birmingham, Ala., 1920-21
KEMP, Chris (PK)
Jacksonville, Fla., 1999
KENDRICK, Kermit (S)
Meridian, Miss., 1985-86-87-88
KENNEDY, President John F.
(Honorary)
Washington, D.C., 1961
KENT, William (RB)
Rome, Ga., 1988
KERLEY, Eric (DT)
Birmingham, Ala.,
1994-95-96-97
KERR, Dudley (K)
Reform, Ala., 1966-67
KEY, Chad (SE)
Parrish, Ala., 1993-94-95
KILGROW, Joe (HB)
Montgomery, Ala., 1935-36-37
KILLGORE, Terry (C)
Annandale, Va., 1965-66-67
KILROY, William (FB)
Philadelphia, Pa., 1952

KIM, Peter (KS)
Honolulu, Hi., 1980-81-82
KIMBALL, Morton (G)
South Bend, Ind., 1941
KINDERKNECHT, Donald H.
(FB) Hays, Kansas, 1955-56
KING, Emanuel (DE)
Leroy, Ala., 1982-83-84
KING, Joe (OT)
Gadsden, Ala., 1985-86-87
KING, Kenny (DT)
Daphne, Ala., 1999
KING, Tyrone (DB)
Docena, Ala., 1972-73-74-75
KIRBY, Lelias E. (HB)
Albertville, Ala., 1920-21
KIRKLAND, B'Ho (G)
Columbia, Ala., 1931-32-33
KITCHENS, Freddie (QB)
Attalla, Ala., 1993-95-96-97
KNAPP, David (HB)
Birmingham, Ala., 1970-71-72
KNIGHT, Canary (LB)
Tallahassee, Fla., 1998-99
KNIGHT, William (HB)
Homewood, Ala., 1957
KOMISAR, Kevin (LB)
Nashville, Tenn., 1994
KRAMER, Michael T. (DB)
Mobile, Ala., 1975-76-77
KRAPF, James Paul (C)
Newark, Del., 1970-71-72
KRAUSS, Barry (LB)
Pompano Beach, Fla.,
1976-77-78
KROUT, Bart (TE)
Birmingham, Ala., 1978-79-80-81
KUBELIUS, Skip (DT)
Morrow, Ga., 1972-73
KULBACK, Steve Joseph (DT)
Clarksville, Tenn., 1973-74
KYSER, G. H. (E-RH)
Richmond, Ala., 1893

L
LaBUE, John (RB)
Memphis, Tenn., 1976
LaBUE, Joseph II (HB)
Memphis, Tenn., 1970-71-72
LAMBERT, Buford (OT)
Warner Robins, Ga., 1976
LAMBERT, Jerry (E)
Alabama City, Ala., 1952
LAMBERT, Randolph (C)
Athens, Ga., 1973-74
LANCASTER, John (DE)
Tuscaloosa, Ala., 1979
LANEY, Greg (SS)
Coral Springs, Fla., 1993
LANGHAM, Antonio (CB)
Town Creek, Ala.,
1990-91-92-93
LANGHORNE, Jack (T)
Uniontown, Ala., 1922-23-24
LANGDALE, Noah (T)
Valdosta, Ga., 1940-41
LANGSTON, Griff (SE)
Birmingham, Ala., 1968-69-70
LANIER, M. B. (B)
Birmingham, Ala., 1905

LARY, Al (E)
Northport, Ala., 1948-49-50
LARY, Ed (E)
Northport, Ala., 1949-50-51
LASLIE, Carney (T)
Charlotte, N.C., 1930-31-32
LASSIC, Derrick (RB)
Haverstraw, N.Y., 1989-90-91-92
LAUER, Larry (C)
Wilmette, Ill., 1948-49-50
LAW, Phil (OT)
Montgomery, Ala., 1971
LAWLEY, Lane (SE)
Citronelle, Ala., 1970
LAWSON, Kirk (OT)
Florence, Ala., 1993
LAYTON, Dale (E)
Sylacauga, Ala., 1962
LAZENBY, K. J. (OT)
Monroeville, Ala., 1974-75-76
LEACH, Foy (E)
Siloam Springs, Ark., 1931-32-33
LEDBETTER, Bradley (SN)
Pelham, Ala., 1998-99
LEE, Bill (T)
Eutaw, Ala., 1932-33-34
LEE, Harry C. (G-LB)
Birmingham, Ala., 1951-52-53-54
LEE, Kevin (WR)
Mobile, Ala., 1990-91-92-93
LEE, Mickey (FB)
Enterprise, Ala., 1968-69
LEE, Shon (DB)
Deatsville, Ala., 1985-86
LEETH, Wheeler (E)
Boaz, Ala., 1941-42
LEGG, Murray (DB)
Homewood, Ala., 1976-77-78
LELAND, Billy (FB)
Birmingham, Ala., 1996
LENOIR, David (DE-TE)
Memphis, Tenn., 1987-88-89
LENOIR, E. B. "Mully" (HB)
Marlin, Texas, 1917-18-19-20
LEON, Tony (G)
Follansbee, W.Va., 1941-42
LETCHER, Marion (C)
Shorter, Ala., 1893-94
LETT, Frank Montague (G)
Good Hope, Ala., 1901-02
LEWIS, Al (G)
Covington, Ky., 1961-62-63
LEWIS, Butch (C)
Mobile, Ala., 1985-87-88
LEWIS, Chester (SN)
Tuscaloosa, Ala., 1994-95-96
LEWIS, Milo (CB)
Mountain View, Calif., 1999
LEWIS, Tommy (FB)
Greenville, Ala., 1951-52-53
LEWIS, Walter (QB)
Brewton, Ala., 1980-81-82-83
LITTLE, Poc (FB)
Birmingham, Ala., 1920
LITTLE, William G. (G)
Livingston, Ala., 1892-93
LOCKE, Eric (WR)
Murfreesboro, Tenn., 1998
LOCKETT, Victor (LB)
Mobile, Ala., 1990-91-92

LOCKRIDGE, Doug (C)
Jasper, Ala., 1948-49
LOFTIN, James (DB)
Dothan, Ala., 1956-57
LOMBARDO, John (DB)
Birmingham, Ala., 1984
LONDON, Antonio (LB)
Tullahoma, Tenn., 1989-90-91-92
LONG, Charles Allen (B)
Bessemer, Ala., 1913-14
LONG, Leon (HB)
Haleyville, Ala., 1929-30-31
LOPEZ, Alan (PK)
Dothan, Ala., 1987
LOVE, Henry Benton (G)
New Market, Ala., 1912
LOWE, Eddie (LB)
Phenix City, Ala., 1980-81-82
LOWE, Woodrow (LB)
Phenix City, Ala., 1972-73-74-75
Lowery, Jackson (SS)
Huntsville, Ala., 1993
LOWMAN, Joseph Allen (E)
Birmingham, Ala., 1916-17
LUMLEY, Wade H. (RG)
Stanton, Ala., 1907
LUMPKIN, Billy Neal (HB)
Florence, Ala., 1955
LUNA, Robert K. "Bobby" (HB)
Huntsville, Ala., 1951-52-53-54
LUSK, Thomas Joseph III (DE)
Clarksville, Tenn., 1970-72
LUTZ, Bill (TE)
Tuscaloosa, Ala., 1987
LUTZ, Harold "Red" (E-K)
Clinton, Iowa, 1949-50-51
LYLES, Warren (NG)
Birmingham, Ala., 1978-79-80-81
LYNCH, Curtis R. (E)
Wadley, Ala., 1953-54-55
LYNCH, Tarrant (RB)
Town Creek, Ala.,
1990-91-92-93-94
LYON, Samuel Hamilton (T)
Meridian, Miss., 1934-35
LYONS, Martin A. "Marty" (DT)
St. Petersburg, Fla., 1977-78

M
MACHTOLFF, Jack (C)
Sheffield, Ala. 1937
MADDEN, Montoya (RB)
Town Creek, Ala., 1995-96-97-98
MADDOX, Sam H. (TE)
Orlando, Fla., 1976-77
MALCOLM, Charles (FB)
Birmingham, Ala., 1952
MALLARD, James (SE)
Tampa, Fla., 1980
MALONE, Alex (FB)
Huntsville, Ala., 199
MALONE, Toderick (SE)
Attalla, Ala., 1993-94-95
MANCHA, Vaughn (C)
Birmingham, Ala.,
1944-45-46-47
MANGUM, John (DB)
Magee, Miss., 1986-87-88-89
MANGUM, Kris (TE)
Magee, Miss., 1992

MANLEY, Harold (E)
Winfield, Ala., 1950-51
MANN, Frank (K)
Birmingham, Ala., 1968-69-70
MANNING, Thomas (C)
Talladega, Ala., 1910-11
MARCELLO, Jerry (DB)
McKeesport, Pa., 1973
MARCUS, Van J. (T)
Birmingham, Ala., 1950-51-52
MARDINI, Georges (PK)
Damascus, Syria, 1980
MARLOW, Bobby (HB)
Troy, Ala., 1950-51-52
MARKS, Keith (SE)
Tuscaloosa, Ala., 1979-82
MARR, Charles (G) All-SE
Pine Bluff, Ark., 1933-34
MARSH, Griffith (QB)
Birmingham, Ala., 1913-14-15
MARSH, William "Bill" (LH)
Birmingham, Ala., 1915-16
MARSHALL, Fred H. (C)
Montgomery, Ala., 1970-71
MARSHALL, Jeff
Winfield, Ala., 1990
MARTIN, Darrell (T)
Blountsville, Ala., 1987
MARTIN, Gary (HB)
Dothan, Ala., 1961-62-63
MARTIN, Kenny (FB)
Hemet, Calif., 1966-67
MASON, George L. (T)
Langdale, Ala., 1952-53-54
MAURO, John (DE)
South Bend, Ind., 1978-79-80
MAXWELL, Raymond Edward
(OT) Flat Rock, Ala., 1973-74-75
MAY, Walter (B)
Mobile, Ala., 1949
MAYFIELD, Dave (T)
Jacksonville, Fla., 1949-50
MAYNOR, E. W. (C)
Oneonta, Ala., 1915-16
MEADOWS, Brenon (OG)
Birmingham, Ala., 1996-97
MELTON, James "Bimbo" (HB)
Wetumpka, Ala., 1949-50-51
MERRILL, Walter (T)
Andalusia, Ala., 1937-38-39
MERRILL, William Hoadley (G)
Eufaula, Ala., 1910
MERRITT, Miguel (LB)
Hopkinsville, Ky., 1998-99
MIKEL, Bobby (DE)
Ft. Walton Bch., Fla., 1976
MILLER, Andrew McMurray (C)
Nanafalia, Ala., 1914
MILLER, Floyd (T)
Oneonta, Ala., 1948-49
MILLER, Hugh (G)
Round Mountain, Ala., 1929-30
MILLER, John (G)
Hazelhurst, Miss., 1928-29-30
MILLER, Noah Dean (LB)
Oneonta, Ala., 1973
MILLS, Wayne (TE)
Arab, Ala., 1991
MILONS, Freddie (SE)
Starkville, Miss., 1998-99

MIMS, Carl (HB)
Sylacauga, Ala., 1941
MIMS, Fred (G)
Birmingham, Ala., 1950-51-52
MILNER, Jason (DE)
Broken Bow, Ok., 1993
MITCHELL, David Dewey (LB)
Tampa, Fla., 1975-76-77
MITCHELL, John (DE)
Mobile, Ala., 1971-72
MITCHELL, Ken "Tank" (G)
Florence, Ala., 1964
MITCHELL, Lydell (LB)
Prichard, Ala., 1985-86-87
MITCHELL, Ripp (DB)
Mobile, Ala., 1989-90
MIZERANY, Mike (G)
Birmingham, Ala., 1948-49-50
MOHR, Chris (P)
Thomson, Ga., 1985-86-87-88
MOLLICONE, Marc (TE)
Fall River, Mass., 1999
MONTGOMERY, Greg (LB)
Macon, Ga., 1972-73-74-75
MONTGOMERY, Robert M.
(DE) Shelbyville, Ky., 1970
MONTGOMERY, Wm. Gabriel
(T) Birmingham, Ala.,
1920-21
MONSKY, Leroy (G)
Montgomery, Ala., 1936-37
MOODY, Farley (B)
Tuscaloosa, Ala., 1912
MOODY, Wash (RG)
Tuscaloosa, Ala., 1906
MOONEYHAM, Marlin (FB)
Montgomery, Ala., 1962
MOORE, Harold (FB)
Chattanooga, Tenn., 1965-66
MOORE, Jimmy (E)
Anniston, Ala., 1928-29-30
MOORE, John (HB)
Montgomery, Ala., 1962
MOORE, Kelvin (DE)
Daphne, Ala., 1993-94-95-96
MOORE, Mal (QB)
Dozier, Ala., 1962
MOORE, Michael (OG)
Fayette, Ala., 1996-97
MOORE, Pete (FB)
Hopkinsville, Ky., 1968-69
MOORE, Randy (TE)
Montgomery, Ala., 1970-73
MOORE, Ricky (FB)
Huntsville, Ala., 1981-82-83-84
MOORE, Robert "Bud" (E)
Birmingham, Ala., 1958-59-60
MOOREHEAD, Kindal (DE)
Memphis, Tenn., 1998-99
MOORER, Jefferson (G)
Evergreen, Ala., 1953-54
MORGAN, Ed (FB)
Hattiesburg, Miss.,
1966-67-68
MORGAN, Patrick (P)
Birmingham, Ala., 1999
MORING, Marcus (FB)
Columbus, Ga., 1993
MORRIS, Mario (LB)
Decatur, Ala., 1991-92-93

MORRISON, Duff (HB)
Memphis, Tenn., 1958-59-61
MORRISON, William (FB)
Selma, Ala., 1926
MORROW, Bob Ed (G)
Selma, Ala., 1934
MORROW, Hugh (QB)
Birmingham, Ala., 1944-45-46-47
MORROW, Hugh (B)
Birmingham, Ala., 1893
MORTON, Farris (E)
Sardis, Ala., 1962
MORTON, L. D. (E)
Birmingham, Ala., 1916
MOSELEY, Elliott (C)
Selma, Ala., 1960
MOSELEY, Frank "Chesty" (B)
Montgomery, Ala., 1931-32-33
MOSLEY, Herschel "Herky"
(HB) Blytheville, Ark.,
1937-38-39
MOSLEY, John (HB)
Thomaston, Ala., 1964-65-66
MOSLEY, Norman "Monk" (HB)
Blytheville, Ark., 1942-46-47
MOSLEY, Russ (HB)
Blytheville, Ark., 1941-42
MOSS, Clay (SE)
Tuscaloosa, Ala., 1983
MOSS, Stan (LE)
Birmingham, Ala., 1965-66-67
MOSS, Stan (P)
Brent, Ala., 1990-92
MOTT, Steve (C)
New Orleans, La., 1980-81-82
MOYLE, Lamar (C)
Decatur, Ala., 1934-35-36
MUDD, Joseph Paul (B)
Birmingham, Ala., 1908-09
MULLINEX, Scott (OG)
Jacksonville, Fla., 1993
MURPHY, Philip (HB)
Anniston, Ala., 1973
MUSSO, Johnny (HB)
Birmingham, Ala., 1969-70-71
MYERS, Michael (DT)
Vicksburg, Miss., 1996
MYLES, Reggie (CB)
Pascagoula, Miss., 1998-99

Mc

MacAFEE, Ken (E)
North Easton, Mass., 1951
MacCARTEE, Allen Graham
(HB) Washington, D.C.,
1922-23
McADDLEY, Jason (SE)
Oakridge, Tenn., 1998-99
McALPINE, Frank (FB)
Boligee, Ala., 1944
McBEE, Jerry (HB)
Birmingham, Ala., 1955
McCAIN, George (HB)
Clanton, Ala., 1950-51
McCANTS, A. G. (RH)
Meridian, Miss., 1892-94
McCANTS, Keith (LB)
Mobile, Ala., 1988-89
McCLENDON, Frankie (T)
Guntersville, Ala., 1962-63-64

McCLINTOCK, Dustin (FB)
Quinlan, Tex., 1997-98-99
McCLINTOCK, Graham (E-B)
Laurel, Miss., 1922-23-24-27
McCOLLOUGH, Gaylon (C)
Enterprise, Ala., 1962-63-64
McCOMBS, Eddie (OT)
Birmingham, Ala., 1978-79-80
McCONVILLE, John (E)
Wheeling, W.Va., 1944
McCORQUODALE, John C.
(LT) Salitpa, Ala., 1902
McCORVERY, Gessner T. (B)
University, Ala., 1900-01
McCRARY, Tom (DT)
Scottsboro, Ala., 1982-83-84
McCULLOUGH, Jeff (OT)
Oneonta, Ala., 1994
McDONALD, James T. (T)
Sylacauga, Ala., 1927
McDONALD, Jason (OT)
Theodore, Ala.,
1996-97-98-99
McDOWELL, Holt Andrews (B)
Ensley, Ala., 1911-12
McELROY, Alan (PK)
Tuscaloosa, Ala., 1978-79
McGAHEY, T. A. "Son" (T)
Columbus, Miss., 1934-35
McGEE, Barry (OG)
Birmingham, Ala., 1975
McGHEE, Chad (FS)
Rainbow City, Ala., 1998
McGILL, Larry (HB)
Panama City, Fla., 1962-63
McGRIFF, Curtis (MG)
Cottonwood, Ala., 1977-78-79
McINTOSH, John (OG)
Dalton, Ga., 1983-84-85
McINTOSH, S.W. (T), 1894
McINTYRE, David (OT)
Columbus, Miss., 1975-76
McKEWEN, Jack, (T)
Birmingham, Ala., 1941-42
McKEWEN, Jack II (T)
Birmingham, Ala., 1968
McKINNEY, Robert B., Jr. (DB)
Mobile, Ala., 1970-71-72
McKOSKY, Ted (G)
Monessen, Pa., 1941-42-46
McLAIN, Rick (TE)
Walnut Hill, Fla., 1974-75
McLEOD, Ben (DE)
Pensacola, Fla., 1965
McLEOD, Ben W. (HB)
Leeksville, Ala., 1934-35-36
McMAKIN, David (DB)
Tucker, Ga., 1971-72-73
McMILLIAN, Mark (CB)
Los Angeles, Calif., 1990-91
McMILLIAN, Thomas E. (E)
Brewton, Ala., 1933
McNATT, Drew, (SN)
Aurora, Mo., 1998
McNEAL, Don (DB)
McCullough, Ala., 1977-78-79
McNEAL, Kareem (OT)
Tuskegee, Ala., 1992-93-94-95
McQUEEN, Mike (OT)
Enterprise, Ala., 1981-82-83

McRAE, Scott (LB)
  Huntsville, Ala., 1982-83-84
McRIGHT, Ralph (HB)
  Mt. Hope, Ala., 1928-29-30
McSORLEY, Joey (FB)
  Birmingham, Ala., 1999
McWHORTER, Jim (QB)
  Athens, Ga., 1942

N
NAMATH, Joe Willie (QB)
  Beaver Falls, Pa., 1962-63-64
NATHAN, R. L. (QB)
  Sheffield, Ala., 1912-13
NATHAN, Tony (HB)
  Birmingham, Ala.,
  1975-76-77-78
NEAL, Rick (TE)
  Birmingham, Ala., 1976-77-78
NEIGHBORS, Billy (T)
  Northport, Ala., 1959-60-61
NEIGHBORS, Keith (LB)
  Huntsville, Ala., 1990
NEIGHBORS, Sidney (T)
  Northport, Ala., 1956-57
NEIGHBORS, Wes (C)
  Huntsville, Ala.,
  1983-84-85-86
NELSON, Benny (HB)
  Huntsville, Ala., 1961-62-63
NELSON, Charles (QB)
  Opp, Ala., 1956
NELSON, Jimmy (HB)
  Live Oak, Fla., 1939-40-41
NELSON, Rod (K)
  Birmingham, Ala., 1974-75-76
NESMITH, C. C. (HB)
  Vernon, Ala., 1892-93-94
NEWBERRY, Gene (TE)
  Blytheville, Ark., 1988
NEWMAN, Hal (E)
  Birmingham, Ala., 1938-39
NEWSOME, Ozzie (SE)
  Leighton, Ala., 1974-75-76-77
NEWTON, Tom (E)
  Birmingham, Ala., 1920-21-22
NIBLETT, Josh (FB)
  Demopolis, Ala., 1993-94-95
NICHOLS, Mike (SE)
  Andalusia, Ala., 1988
NISBET, James "Bubba" (FB)
  Bainbridge, Ga., 1934-35-36
NIX, Mark (RB)
  Altoona, Ala., 1979-80-81
NOLAND, John Phillip
  Tuscaloosa, Ala., 1917-18
NOOJIN, Augustus Young (B)
  Gadsden, Ala., 1908
NOONAN, L. W. "Red" (FB)
  Mobile, Ala., 1945-47-48-49
NORMAN, Haywood Eugene
  "Butch" (DE)
  Luverne, Ala., 1973
NORRIS, Lanny S. (DB)
  Russellville, Ala., 1970-71-72
NORTHINGTON, M. P. (G)
  Prattville, Ala., 1893
NUNLEY, Jeremy (DE),
  Winchester, Tenn.,
  1990-91-92-93

O
OATES, W. C. (G)
  Montgomery, Ala., 1906
O'DELL, Richard (E)
  Lincoln, Ala., 1959-60-62
O'CONNOR, J. T. (B)
  St. Louis, Mo., 1919-20
ODEN, Derrick (LB)
  Tuscaloosa, Ala., 1989-90-91-92
ODOM, Ernest Lavont (E)
  Birmingham, Ala., 1973
OGDEN, Ray (HB)
  Jesup, Ga., 1962-63-64
OGILVIE, Morgan Oslin "Major"
  (RB) Birmingham, Ala.,
  1977-78-79-80
OLENSKI, Mitchell (T)
  Vestal, N.Y., 1942
O'LINGER, John (C)
  Scottsboro, Ala., 1959-60-61
OLIVER, William (HB)
  Panola, Ala., 1952-53
OLIVER, William "Brother"
  (DB) Livingston, Ala., 1960-61
OLIVER, W. S. "Country" (B-T)
  Panola, Ala., 1922-23-25
ORCUTT, Ben (RB)
  Arlington Heights, Ill., 1981
O'REAR, Jack (QB)
  Tarrant, Ala., 1974-76-77
OSER, Gary (C)
  New Orleans, La., 1976
O'STEEN, Robert "Gary" (FB)
  Anniston, Ala., 1957-58-59
O'SULLIVAN, Pat (LB)
  New Orleans, La., 1947-48-49-50
O'TOOLE, Mike (DB)
  Palmerdale, Ala., 1982
OTTEN, Gary (OT)
  Huntsville, Ala., 1983-84-86
OWEN, Wayne (LB)
  Gadsden, Ala., 1966-67-68
OWENS, Donald (E)
  Memphis, Tenn., 1956-57
OZMINT, Lee (DB)
  Anderson, S.C., 1986-87-88-89

P
PAGET, Manchester (LG)
  El Paso, Texas, 1920
PALMER, Dale (LB)
  Calera, Ala., 1978
PALMER, David (SE)
  Birmingham, Ala., 1991-92-93
PALMER, Thomas W. (B)
  Tuscaloosa, Ala., 1908-09
PANKS, Heath (DT)
  Slidell, La., 1996-97
PAPIAS, Julius (HB)
  Hammond, Ind., 1941
PAPPAS, Peter George (SE)
  Birmingham, Ala., 1973
PARKER, Calvin (DE)
  Eastoboga, Ala., 1976-78
PARKER, Matt (DT)
  Lawton, Okla., 1994-95
PARKHOUSE, Robin (DE)
  Orlando, Fla., 1969-70-71
PARSONS, Don (G)
  Houston, Texas, 1958

PATRICK, Linnie (RB)
  Jasper, Ala., 1980-81-82-83
PATTERSON, Jim (OG)
  Annandale, Va., 1971
PATTERSON, Roosevelt (OT)
  Mobile, Ala., 1991-92-93
PATTERSON, Steve (OG)
  Omaha, Neb., 1972-73-74
PATTERSON, Trent (OG)
  Syracuse, N.Y., 1987-88-89-90
PATTON, David Dane (E)
  Coatopa, Ala., 1898-99-1900
PATTON, James "Jap" (E)
  Tuscumbia, Ala., 1959-61
PATTON, William Pratt (E)
  Fosters, Ala., 1906-07
PAYNE, Brian (LB)
  Enterprise, Ala., 1989
PAYNE, Greg (SE)
  Montgomery, Ala., 1984-87-88
PAYNE, Leslie (T)
  Bay Minette, Ala., 1925-26-27
PEARCE, Clarke "Babe" (T)
  Winfield, Ala., 1926-27-28
PEARL, James H. (E)
  Connellsville, Pa., 1944
PEAVY, John Roberts (RB)
  Thomasville, Ala., 1902-03-04
PEEBLES, Emory Bush (QB)
  Vienna, Ala., 1908-10
PELL, Charles B. (T)
  Albertville, Ala., 1960-61-62
PENNINGTON, Jeremy (OG)
  Vernon, Ala., 1993-94-95-96
PEPPER, Raymond W. (FB)
  Albany, Ala., 1926-27
PERKINS, Ray (E)
  Petal, Miss., 1964-65-66
PERRIN, Benny (DB)
  Decatur, Ala., 1980-81
PERRY, Anthony "Lefty" (DB)
  Hazel Green, Ala., 1973
PERRY, Claude (T)
  Jasper, Ala., 1925
PERSON, Carlton, (LB)
  North Jackson, Ala., 1997
PETER, G. F.
  Brierfield, Ala., 1892
PETERS, William E. (G)
  Hammond, Ind., 1936-37
PETTEE, Robert A. "Bob" (G)
  Bradenton, Fla., 1960-61-62
PETTUS, Gordon (HB)
  Birmingham, Ala., 1945-46-48
PFLUGNER, Ryan (PK)
  Sarasota, Fla., 1998-99
PHARO, Edward (FB)
  Birmingham, Ala., 1952-56
PHILLIPS, Gary (G)
  Dothan, Ala., 1958-59-60
PHILLIPS, Greg, (SS)
  Mobile, Ala., 1998
PHILLIPS, John (NT)
  Atlanta, Ga., 1992
PHILLIPS, John David (QB/FS)
  Anniston, Ala., 1994-96-98
PICKETT, Darryl (LB)
  Montgomery, Ala., 1988-89
PICKETT, Paul (LB)
  LaGrange, Ga., 1994-96-97

PICKHARD, Frederick (T)
  Mobile, Ala., 1926-27
PIERCE, Billy (DB)
  Crossett, Ark., 1983-84
PINE, Matthew (C)
  Gadsden, Ala., 1990-91-92-93
PIPER, Billy (HB)
  Poplar Bluff, Mo., 1960-62-63
PITTS, Mike (DE)
  Baltimore, Md., 1979-80-81-82
PITTMAN, Alex Noel (LB)
  New Orleans, La., 1970
PIVER, Mike (LB)
  Chapel Hill, N.C. 1989
PIZZITOLA, Alan (DB)
  Birmingham, Ala., 1973-74-75
POE, Monte, (QB)
  Nashville, Tenn., 1999
POOLE, John Paul (E)
  Florence, Ala., 1955-58
POPE, Daniel (P)
  Alpharetta, Ga., 1997-98
POPE, Herman "Buddy" (OT)
  Bradenton, Fla., 1973-74-75
POPE, Myron (LB)
  Sweetwater, Ala., 1992
PORTIS, Marico (C)
  Prichard, Ala., 1999
POTTS, Douglas (G)
  Evergreen, Ala., 1954-55-56
POWE, Frank Houston (E)
  Talladega, Ala., 1899-1900-01
POWELL, Harold Mustin (T)
  Birmingham, Ala., 1910-11
POWELL, Ozell (DE)
  Greenville, Ala.,
  1993-94-95-96
PRATT, Derrill B. (E)
  Pell City, Ala., 1908-09
PRATT, G. W. (G)
  Pell City, Ala., 1907-09
PRATT, Henry Merrill (RG)
  Prattville, Ala., 1892-93-94
PRESTWOOD, Thomas A. (DE)
  Chattanooga, Tenn., 1975
PRICE, Scott (DB)
  Jasper, Tenn., 1977
PRITCHETT, Bart (NT)
  Mobile, Ala., 1992
PRITCHETT, James P. (E)
  Birmingham, Ala., 1955
PROCTOR, Michael (PK),
  Pelham, Ala., 1992-93-94-95
PROM, John (G)
  Jacksonville, Fla., 1951
PROPST, Clyde "Shorty" (C)
  Ohatchee, Ala., 1922-23-24
PROPST, Eddie (DB)
  Birmingham, Ala., 1966-67
PRUDHOMME, John Mark (DB)
  Memphis, Tenn., 1973-74-75
PRUITT, Jeremy (FS)
  Rainsville, Ala., 1995-96
PUGH, Ed (TE)
  Opelika, Ala., 1984
PUGH, George (TE)
  Montgomery, Ala.,
  1972-73-74-75
PUGH, Keith Harrison (SE)
  Evergreen, Ala., 1977-78-79

Q

QUICK, Cecil Van (DE)
Collins, Miss., 1970

R

RABURN, Gene (FB)
Jasper, Ala., 1965-66
RADFORD, James Solomon (T)
Hartford, Ala., 1935-36
RAINES, Billy (G)
Moulton, Ala., 1956-57
RAINES, James Patrick (C)
Montgomery, Ala., 1970-71-72
RAINES, Vaughn Michael (DT)
Montgomery, Ala., 1972-73
RAMIL, Mike (DT)
Corona, Calif., 1988-89
RANAGER, George (SE)
Meridian, Miss., 1968-69-70
RANKIN, Carlton (QB)
Piedmont, Ala., 1962
RANSON, Brad (DT)
Huntsville, Ala., 1994
RASHEED, Saleem (LB)
Birmimngham, Ala., 1999
RAST, Holt (E)
Birmingham, Ala., 1939-40-41
RAY, Chris, (OG)
Piedmont, Ala.,, 1999
RAY, David (SE-K)
Phenix City, Ala., 1964-65
RAY, Michael (C)
Boaz, Ala., 1995-96-97
RAY, Shontua (CB)
Montevallo, Ala., 1999
RAYAM, Thomas (DT)
Orlando, Fla., 1987-88
REAVES, Pete (G)
Bessemer, Ala., 1958
REDDEN, Guy (G)
Sulligent, Ala., 1904-05
REDDEN, Jake (G)
Vernon, Ala., 1937-38
REDMILL, Griff (DT/OG)
Jasper, Ala., 1997-98-99
REED, Wayne (Mgr.) 1981
REIDY, Thomas (LHB)
Boston, Mass., 1907-08
REIER, Chris (CB)
Jacksonville, Fla., 1998
REILLY, Mike (DG)
Mobile, Ala, 1966-67-68
REITZ, John David (DE-OT)
Morristown, Tenn., 1965-66-67
REESE, Kenny (HB)
El Dorado, Ark., 1942
REYES, Marlon (CB)
Mexico City, MX., 1995-96
REYNOLDS, Mike (SS)
Centerville, Ala., 1995
RHOADS, Wayne R. (DE)
Jackson, Miss., 1969-70
RHODEN, Steve (K)
Red Bay, Ala., 1981
RHODES, D. Wayne, Jr. (DB)
Decatur, Ga., 1973-74-75
RICE, William J. "Bill" (E)
Troy, Ala., 1959-60-61
RICH, Jerry (HB)
Attalla, Ala., 1959

RICHARD, Arvin (TB)
Atlanta, Ga., 1997-98-99
RICHARDSON, Greg (WR)
Mobile, Ala., 1983-84-85-86
RICHARDSON, Jesse (G)
Philadelphia, Pa., 1950-51-52
RICHARDSON, Ron (DB)
Columbus, Ga., 1971
RICHARDSON, Todd (DB-WR)
Syracuse, N.Y., 1986-87-88
RICHARDSON, W. E. (HB)
Jasper, Ala., 1959-60-61
RICHESON, George (T)
Russellville, Ala., 1942
RICHESON, Ray (T)
Russellville, Ala., 1946-47-48
RIDDLE, Charles D. (C)
Talladega, Ala., 1912-13
RIDDLE, Dennis (TB)
Tuscaloosa, Ala., 1994-95-96-97
RIDGEWAY, Danny Howard (K)
Fyffe, Ala., 1973-74-75
RILEY, Joe (HB)
Dothan, Ala., 1934-35-36
RILEY, Mike (DB)
Corvallis, Ore., 1974
RIPPETOE, Benny (QB)
Greenville, Tenn., 1971
ROBBINS, Joe (C)
Opp, Ala., 1978-79-80
ROBBINS, Shelby (LB)
Mobile, Ala., 1994
ROBERTS, James "Babs" (E)
Blytheville, Ark., 1940-42
ROBERTS, Johnny (FB)
Birmingham, Ala.,1937
ROBERTS, Kenneth (C)
Anniston, Ala., 1956-57-58
ROBERTS, Larry (DT)
Dothan, Ala., 1982-83-84-85
ROBERTS, Rob (C)
Birmingham, Ala., 1984-85
ROBERTSON, James (HB)
Scottsboro, Ala., 1944-45-46
ROBERTSON, Ronald Dale (LB)
Signal Mtn., Tenn., 1973-74
ROBINETTE, Chris (OG)
Enterprise, Ala., 1988-89-90
ROBINSON, Carlos (FB)
Enterprise, Ala., 1986-87
ROBINSON, Freddie (DB)
Mobile, Ala., 1983-84-85-86
ROCKWELL, Bragg (OLB)
Daphne, Ala., 1989-90-91
ROCKWELL, Randy (OLB)
Daphne, Ala., 1984-85-86-87
RODDAM, J. D. (HB)
Pinson, Ala., 1949
RODDAM, Ronnie (C)
Birmingham, Ala., 1968-69
RODRIGUEZ, Mike (MG)
Melbourne, Fla., 1981-82-83
ROGERS, Eddie Bo (LB)
Bessemer, Ala., 1966-67
ROGERS, Isaac "Ike" (RT)
Vina, Ala., 1916-17-18-19
ROGERS, John David (OG)
Montgomery, Ala., 1972-73-74
ROGERS, Michael (LB)
Luverne, Ala., 1991-92-93-94

ROGERS, O'Neal (B)
Russellville, Ala., 1927
ROGERS, Richard (OG)
Boise, Idaho, 1973
ROHRDANZ, Clarence (FB)
Harvey, Ind., 1935
RONSONET, Norbie (E)
Biloxi, Miss., 1958-59-60
ROOT, Steve (LB)
Indio, Calif., 1971
ROPER, Todd (LB)
Snellville, Ga., 1981-83-84-85
ROSE, Larry (OT)
Gadsden, Ala., 1985-86-87-88
ROSENFELD, David (HB)
Ensley, Ala., 1925-26
ROSENFELD, Max (QB)
Birmingham, Ala., 1920-21
ROSSER, Jimmy Lynn (OT)
Birmingham, Ala., 1969-70-71
ROUZIE, Jefferson Carr (LB)
Jacksonville, Fla., 1970-71-73
ROWAN, Robert "Robby" (DB)
Huntsville, Ala., 1972
ROWE, Harry (RG)
Elba, Ala., 1919
ROWELL, Jeff (SS)
Northport, Ala., 1998
ROWELL, Terry (DT)
Heidelberg, Miss., 1969-70-71
ROYAL, Andre (LB)
Northport, Ala., 1991-92-93
RUDD, Dwayne (LB)
Batesville, Miss., 1994-95-96
RUDOLPH, Jonathan (LB)
Mobile, Ala., 1997
RUFFIN, Larry Joe (OG)
Fayette, Ala., 1973-74-75
RUMBLEY, Roy (OG)
Moss Point, Miss., 1981-82
RUSHTON, Derrick (DT)
Mobile, Ala., 1986-88-89
RUSSELL, Lamonde (TE-SE)
Oneonta, Ala., 1987-88-89-90
RUSTIN, Nathan (DT)
Phenix City, Ala., 1966-67
RUTLEDGE, Gary (QB)
Birmingham, Ala., 1972-73-74
RUTLEDGE, Jack (G)
Birmingham, Ala., 1959-60-61
RUTLEDGE, Jeffery R. (QB)
Birmingham, Ala., 1975-76-77-78
RUTLEDGE, Rod (TE)
Birmingham, Ala., 1994-95-96-97
RYBA, Jim (T)
Cicero, Ill., 1937
RYLES, Willie (DT)
Phenix City, Ala., 1985

S

SABO, Al (QB)
Los Angeles, Calif., 1940-41-42
SADLER, David A. (OG)
Cadiz, Ky., 1975-76-77
SALEM, Ed (HB)
Birmingham, Ala., 1947-48-49-50
SALEM, George (HB)
Birmingham, Ala., 1956
SALEM, George (OG)
Birmingham, Ala., 1986

SALEM, Jimbo (LB)
Birmingham, Ala., 1988
SALLS, Don (FB)
White Plains, N.Y., 1940-41-42
SAMFORD, Conner (RG)
Montgomery, Ala., 1916
SAMPLES, Alvin (OG)
Tarrant, Ala., 1967-68-69
SAMUEL, Cedric (CB)
Demopolis, Ala., 1993-94-95-96
SAMUELS, Chris (OT)
Mobile, Ala., 1996-97-98-99
SANDERS, Terry (K)
Birmingham, Ala.,
1981-82-83-84
SANDERSON, Craig (WR)
Hamilton, Ala., 1988-89
SANFORD, Donald (G)
Parrish, Ala., 1930-31-32
SANFORD, Hayward "Sandy"
(E-K) Adona, Ark., 1936-37
SANSING, Walter (FB)
West Blocton, Ala., 1958
SARTAIN, Harvey (T)
Tuscaloosa, Ala., 1904
SASSER, Mike (DB)
Brewton, Ala., 1966-69
SAUL, Calhoun "Sunbeam" (G)
Montgomery, Ala., 1916
SAVAGE, Frank (RT)
Centre, Ala., 1892-93
SAWYER, Bubba (SE)
Fairhope, Ala., 1969-71
SCALES, Lou (FB)
Gadsden, Ala., 1941-42-45
SCHAMUN, Russ (SE)
Napa, Calif., 1974-76
SCHMISSRAUTER, Kurt (OT)
Chattanooga, Tenn.,
1981-82-83
SCHUMANN, Eric (DB)
Blue Island, Ill., 1977
SCISSUM, Ed (FB)
Attalla, Ala., 1994-95-96-97
SCISSUM, Willard (OG)
Huntsville, Ala., 1981-82-83-84
SCOTT, Authur (T)
Jasper, Ala., 1957
SCOTT, James Alfred (E)
Thomasville, Ala., 1910
SCOTT, Randy (LB)
Decatur, Ga., 1978-79-80
SCROGGINS, Billy (SE)
Jacksonville, Fla., 1967-68
SEARCEY, Bill (OG)
Savannah, Ga., 1978-80
SEAY, Buddy (HB)
Dadeville, Ala., 1969-70
SEBASTIAN, Mike (DT)
Columbus, Ga., 1978
SECRIST, Troy (WR)
Pensacola, Fla., 1988
SEGREST, Rory (OT)
Waycross, Ga., 1995
SEIBERT, Chris (LB)
Union Hill, Ala., 1996
SELF, Hal (QB)
Decatur, Ala., 1944-45-46
SELMAN, Tom (T)
Rome, Ga., 1950

SESSIONS, Tram (C)
Birmingham, Ala., 1917-19-20
SEWELL, J. Luke (QB)
Titus, Ala., 1919-20
SEWELL, Joe (HB)
Titus, Ala., 1917-18-19
SEWELL, Junior (FB)
Abbeville, Ala., 1990
SEWELL, Ray (QB)
Bremen, Ga., 1976
SEWELL, Toxey
Titus, Ala., 1913-14
SHACKELFORD, James (FS)
Plant City, Fla., 1992
SHADE, Sam (CB)
Birmingham, Ala., 1991-92-93-94
SHANKLES, Don (E)
Fort Payne, Ala., 1967
SHARPE, Jimmy (OG)
Montgomery, Ala., 1960-61-62
SHARPE, Joe F. (C)
Mobile, Ala., 1929-30-31
SHARPE, Sam (E)
Birmingham, Ala., 1940-41-42
SHARPLESS, John W., Jr. (SE)
Elba, Ala., 1972-73
SHAW, Wayne (FB)
Tullahoma, Tenn., 1987-88-89
SHEALY, Steadman (QB)
Dothan, Ala., 1977-78-79
SHEILS, Tobie (C)
Fairhope, Ala., 1990-91-92-93
SHELBY, Willie (HB)
Purvis, Miss., 1973-74-75
SHEPHARD, Willie (LB)
Prichard, Ala., 1985-86-87-88
SHEPHERD, Joe Ruffus (G)
Tuscaloosa, Ala., 1935-36
SHERRER, Kevin (TE)
Cleveland, Ala., 1995
SHERRILL, Jackie (FB-LB)
Biloxi, Miss., 1963-64-65
SHERRILL, Wm. Swift (E)
Athens, Ala., 1901-02-03
SHINN, Richard (DT)
Columbiana, Ala., 1980-82
SHIPP, Billy (T)
Mobile, Ala., 1949-52-53
SHIRLEY, Patrick Kyle
Wetumpka, Ala., 1910
SHOEMAKER, Perron "Tex" (E)
Birmingham, Ala., 1937-38-39
SHORT, Andre (SS)
LaGrange, Ga., 1994-95-96-97
SHULA, Mike (QB)
Miami, Fla., 1984-85-86
SHULTZ, Roger (C)
Atlanta, Ga., 1987-88-89-90
SIDES, John "Brownie" (DT)
Tuskegee, Ala., 1966-67
SIGLER, Kelvin (SS)
Mobile, Ala., 1995-96-97-98
SIGN, Chris (OG)
Arlington, Tex., 1997
SIMON, Kenny (RB)
Montgomery, Ala., 1979-81
SIMMONS, Jim (T)
Piedmont, Ala., 1962-63-64
SIMMONS, Jim (TE)
Yazoo City, Miss., 1969-70-71

SIMMONS, Malcolm (P)
Montgomery, Ala., 1981-82-83
SIMPSON, L.W. (T), 1893
SIMS, T. S. (LG)
Birmingham, Ala., 1905-06
SIMS, Wayne (G)
Columbiana, Ala., 1958-59
SIMS, Williams Comer (G)
Searight, Ala., 1931-32
SINGTON, Dave (T)
Birmingham, Ala.,1956-57-58
SINGTON, Fred (T)
Birmingham, Ala., 1928-29-30
SINGTON, Fred, Jr. (T)
Birmingham, Ala., 1958-59
SISIA, Joseph (T)
Clark, N.J., 1960
SKELTON, Robert "Bobby"
(QB) Pell City, Ala., 1957-59-60
SKIDMORE, Jim (G)
Winchester, Tenn., 1928
SLAUGHTER, Derrick (DT)
Birmingham, Ala., 1985-86
SLAY, Marcus (CB)
Dunwoody, Ga., 1998
SLEMONS, Billy (HB)
Orlando, Fla., 1937-38
SLOAN, Steve (QB)
Cleveland, Tenn., 1963-64-65
SLONE, Samuel Byron (E)
Lebanon, Ala., 1893-94-95-96
SMALLEY, Jack (T)
Tuscaloosa, Ala., 1951-52-53
SMALLEY, Jack, Jr. (LB)
Douglasville, Ga., 1976-77
SMALLEY, Roy (G)
Birmingham, Ala., 1950
SMILEY, Anthony (DE)
Birmingham, Ala., 1981-82-83
SMITH, Anthony (DT)
Elizabeth City, N.C.,
1985-86-87
SMITH, Barry S. (C)
Anniston, Ala., 1977-78-79
SMITH, Ben (E)
Haleyville, Ala., 1929-30-31
SMITH, Bill (P)
Russellville, Ala., 1989
SMITH, Bobby (DB)
Fairhope, Ala., 1978-79
SMITH, Bobby (QB)
Brewton, Ala., 1956-57-58
SMITH, Dan (P)
Hayden, Ala., 1984
SMITH, Dan H. (LH)
Anniston, Ala., 1892-93
SMITH, Darrell (C)
Munford, Ala., 1994
SMITH, David (QB)
Gadsden, Ala., 1986-87-88
SMITH, Earl (E)
Haleyville, Ala., 1926-27-28
SMITH, Jack (G)
Hueytown, Ala., 1949
SMITH, James Sidney (C)
Warner Robins, Ga., 1974-75-76
SMITH, Joe (WR)
Mobile, Ala., 1983-84-85
SMITH, Kenny (DT)
Meridian, Miss., 1997-98-99

SMITH, Mike (S-SE)
Gainesville, Fla., 1987-88-89-90
SMITH, Molton (G-T)
Birmingham, Ala., 1928-29
SMITH, Riley H. (QB)
Columbus, Miss., 1933-34-35
SMITH, Sammy Wayne (G)
Talladega, Ala., 1957
SMITH, Tito (LB)
Birmingham, Ala., 1996-97-98
SMITH, Trevis (FB/LB)
Montgomery, Ala.,
1995-96-97-98
SMITH, Truman A. (HB)
University, Ala., 1903-04
SNEED, Byron (DE)
Alexandria, Va., 1988-89-90-91
SNODERLY, John M. (C)
Montgomery, Ala., 1952-53-56
SOMERVILLE, Tom (OG)
White Station, Tenn., 1965-66-67
SOWELL, Brent (DT)
Clearwater, Fla., 1983-84-85
SPEED, Elliott (C)
Selma, Ala., 1948-49-50
SPENCER, Marcus (FS)
York, Ala., 1997-98-99
SPENCER, Paul (FB)
Hampton, Va., 1939-40
SPENCER, Tom (DB)
Fairfax, Va., 1979
SPIKES, Irving (RB)
Ocean Springs, Miss., 1991
SPIVEY, Paul Randall (FB)
Montgomery, Ala., 1972-73
SPRAYBERRY, Steve (OT)
Sylacauga, Ala., 1972-73
SPREE, Sage (OT)
Boligee, Ala., 1995-96-98
SPRINKLE, Jerrill (DB)
Chamblee, Ga., 1980-81-82
SPRUIELL, Jerry (E)
Pell City, Ala., 1960
STABLER, Ken "Snake" (QB)
Foley, Ala., 1965-66-67
STACY, Siran (RB)
Geneva, Ala., 1989-91
STAFFORD, Angelo (TE)
Prichard, Ala., 1986-87
STANFORD, Robert "Bobby"
(OT) Albany, Ga., 1969-72
STANLEY, Steve (FS/LB)
Leighton, Ala., 1995-96-97-98
STAPP, Charlie (HB)
Birmingham, Ala., 1935
STAPP, Laurien "Goobie" (QB-K)
Birmingham, Ala., 1958-59-60
STAPLES, John (G)
Owensboro, Ky., 1942-46
STARLING, Hugh (E)
Troy, Ala. 1928-29
STARR, Bryan Bartlett (QB)
Montgomery, Ala.,
1952-53-54-55
STATEN, Ralph (LB)
Semmes, Ala., 1993-94-95-96
STEAKLEY, Rod (SE)
Huntsville, Ala., 1971
STEGER, Brian (TB)
New Market, Ala., 1993-94-95

STEINER, Rebel (E)
Ensley, Ala., 1945-47-48-49
STENNIS, Carlos (NT)
Meridian, Miss., 1998
STEPHENS, Bruce (G)
Thomasville, Ala., 1965-66-67
STEPHENS, Charles (E)
Thomasville, Ala., 1962-63-64
STEPHENS, Gerald (C)
Thomasville, Ala., 1962
STEPHENSON, Dwight (C)
Hampton, Va., 1977-78-79
STEPHENSON, Lovick Leonidas
(RE) Birmingham, Ala., 1915-16
STEPHENSON, Riggs (FB)
Akron, Ala., 1917-19-20
STEVENS, Wayne (E)
Gadsden, Ala., 1966
STEVENSON, Jon (OT)
Memphis, Tenn., 1991-92-93-94
STEWART, Arthur Walter (HB)
Marion, Ala., 1901
STEWART, Robert (LB-FB-NG)
Ashford, Ala., 1987-88-90-91
STEWART, Vaughn (C)
Anniston, Ala., 1941
STICKNEY, Enoch Morgan (B)
University, Ala., 1912
STICKNEY, Frederick Grist (E)
Tuscaloosa, Ala., 1901-02
STICKNEY, Ravis "Red" (FB)
Key West, Fla., 1957-59
STOCK, Mike (HB)
Elkhart, Ind., 1973-74-75
STOCKTON, Hayden (P)
Double Springs, Ala., 1994-95-96
STOKES, Ralph Anthony (HB)
Montgomery, Ala., 1972-74
STONE, G. E. (C)
Mobile, Ala., 1894
STONE, Rocky (G)
Birmingham, Ala., 1969
STONE, William J. (FB)
Yukon, W.Va., 1953-54-55
STOWERS, Max Frederick (QB)
Attalla, Ala., 1916-17
STRICKLAND, Charles "Chuck"
(LB) East Ridge, Tenn.,
1971-72-73
STRICKLAND, Lynwood (DE)
Alexander City, Ala., 1965
STRICKLAND, Vince (OT)
College Park, Ga., 1989
STRICKLAND, William Ross (T)
Birmingham, Ala., 1970
STRUM, Richard (HB)
Biloxi, Miss., 1957
STUBBS, Jay (FL)
Tuscaloosa, Ala., 1999
STURDIVANT, Raymond (B)
Dadeville, Ala., 1906-07
STUTSON, Brian (DB)
Birmingham, Ala.,
1988-89-90-91
SUGG, Joseph Cullen (G)
Russellville, Ala., 1938-39
SULLEN, James, Jr., (FL)
Tuskegee, Ala. 1999
SULLINS, John (LB)
Oxford, Miss., 1988-89-90-91

SULLIVAN, Johnny (DT)
Nashville, Tenn., 1964-65-66
SURLAS, Tom (LB)
Mt. Pleasant, Pa., 1970-71
SUTHER, John Henry (HB)
Tuscaloosa, Ala., 1928-29-30
SUTTON, Donnie (SE)
Blountsville, Ala., 1966-67-68
SUTTON, Mike (DB)
Brewton, Ala., 1978
SUTTON, Vince (QB)
LaGrange, Ga., 1984-87-88
SWAFFORD, Bobby "Hawk"
(SE) Heflin, Ala., 1967-68
SWAIM, M. M. (G)
Tuscaloosa, Ala., 1931-32
SWAIN, Manuel (TE)
Alabaster, Ala., 1989
SWANN, Gerald (DB)
Ashville, Ala., 1982
SWINNEY, Dabo (WR)
Pelham, Ala., 1990-91-92
SWOPES, Herold, (FB)
Decatur, Ala., 1993
SWORDS, Josh, (OG)
Brentwood, Tenn., 1997

T
TANKS, John (LB)
Butler, Ala., 1993-94-95-96
TAYLOR, Archie (B)
Savannah, Ga., 1926-27
TAYLOR, J. K. (RH)
Adkinville, N.C., 1914-15
TAYLOR, James E. (HB)
Citronelle, Ala., 1973-74-75
TAYLOR, Paul (FB)
Hartford, Ala., 1948
TEAGUE, George (CB)
Montgomery, Ala.,
1989-90-91-92
TEAGUE, Matt (FB)
Montgomery, Ala., 1998
TERLIZZI, Nicholas (T)
Upper Montclair, N.J., 1945
TEW, Lowell (FB)
Waynesboro, Miss.,
1944-45-46-47
THARP, Thomas "Corky" (HB)
Birmingham, Ala.,
1951-52-53-54
THERIS, Bill (T)
Mobile, Ala., 1948-49
THOMAS, Cliff (NG)
Pearl, Miss., 1984-86
THOMAS, Daniel Martin (C)
Clinton, Tenn., 1970
THOMAS, Derrick (LB)
Miami, Fla., 1985-86-87-88
THOMAS, Efrum (CB-S)
Long Beach, Calif., 1989-90
THOMAS, Lester (FB)
Birmingham, Ala., 1921
THOMAS, Ricky (S)
Eglin AFB, Fla.,
1983-84-85-86
THOMASON, Frank Boyd (E)
Albertville, Ala., 1919
THOMPSON, Louis (DT)
Lebanon, Tenn., 1965-66

THOMPSON, Richard "Dickey"
(DHB) Thomasville, Ga.,
1965-66-67
THOMPSON, Wesley (T)
Decatur, Ala., 1951-55-56
THORNTON, Bryan (DE)
Mobile, Ala., 1992-93-94-95
THORNTON, George (DT)
Montgomery, Ala., 1988-89-90
TIDWELL, Robert Earl (C)
Blountsville, Ala., 1903-04
TIFFIN, Van (PK)
Red Bay, Ala., 1983-84-85-86
TILLMANN, Homer Newton
"Chip" (OT) Panama City, Fla.,
1976-77
TILLMAN, Tommy (E)
Haleyville, Ala., 1952-53-54
TIPTON, Jim (T)
Blytheville, Ark., 1936-37
TODD, Richard (QB)
Mobile, Ala., 1973-74-75
TOLLESON, Tommy (SE)
Talladega, Ala., 1963-64-65
TORRENCE, Jeff (LB)
Atmore, Ala., 1992-93-95
TOWNSEND, Deshea (CB)
Batesville, Miss., 1994-95-96-97
TRAMMELL, Pat (QB)
Scottsboro, Ala., 1959-60-61
TRAVIS, Timothy Lee "Tim" (TE)
Bessemer, Ala., 1976-77-78-79
TRIMBLE, Delan (LB)
Cullman, Ala., 1993
TRIMBLE, Wayne (QB)
Cullman, Ala., 1964-65-66
TRIPOLI, Paul (DB)
Liverpool, N.Y., 1983-84
TRODD, Paul (PK)
Eufaula, Ala., 1981-83
TUCK, Ed (SE)
Sacramento, Calif., 1984
TUCK, Floyd (B)
Decatur, Ala., 1927
TUCKER, John (QB)
Russellville, Ark., 1930-31
TUCKER, Lance (QB)
Fayette, Ala., 1994-95-96-97
TUCKER, Michael V. (DB)
Alexandria, Ala., 1975-76-77
TUCKER, Richard "Ricky" (DB)
Florence, Ala., 1977-78-79-80
TULEY, James (PK)
Montgomery, Ala., 1992
TURNER, Craig (FB)
Gaithersburg, Md., 1982-83-85
TURNER, Eric (SS)
Fort Payne, Ala., 1992-93-94
TURNER, Kevin (FB)
Prattville, Ala., 1988-89-90-91
TURNER, Rory (DB)
Decatur, Ga., 1984-85-87
TURNER, Steve (DT)
Bessemer, Ala., 1987-88
TURNER, Tarus (FB)
Fort Payne, Ala., 1993-94
TURNIPSEED, Thad (LB)
Montgomery, Ala., 1993
TURPIN, John R. (FB)
Birmingham, Ala., 1977-78

TURPIN, Richard "Dick" (DE)
Birmingham, Ala., 1973-74-75
TUTWILER, Edward McGruder
(B) Birmingham, Ala., 1898
TYSON, Adrian (NG)
Mobile, Ala., 1983

U
UMPHREY, Woody (P)
Bourbonnais, Ill., 1978-79-80

V
VAGOTIS, Chris (OG)
Canton, Ohio, 1966
VALLETTO, Carl (E)
Oakmont, Pa., 1957-58
VALLETTO, David (DB)
Gulf Breeze, Fla., 1983-84
VANDEGRAAFF, Adrian V. (B)
Tuscaloosa, Ala., 1911-12
VANDEGRAAFF, Hargrove
(LHB) Tuscaloosa, Ala.,
1913
VANDEGRAAFF, W. T. "Bully"
(T-FB) Tuscaloosa, Ala.,
1912-13-14-15
VARNADO, Carey Reid (C)
Hattiesburg, Miss., 1970
VAUGHN, Michael (FL)
Clarksdale, Miss., 1995-96-98
VAUGHANS, Cedric (SE)
Montgomery, Ala., 1984
VEAZY, Louis (G)
Alexander City, Ala., 1955
VERSPRILLE, Eddie (FB)
Norfolk, Va., 1961-62-63
VERSPRILLE, Steve (LB)
Norfolk, Va., 1991
VICKERS, Doug (OG)
Enterprise, Ala., 1981-82-83
VICKERY, Michael FL)
Mobile, Ala., 1999
VICKERY, Roy Leon (T)
Charlotte, N.C., 1956
VINES, Jay (OG)
Birmingham, Ala., 1978
VINES, Melvin (E)
Bessemer, Ala., 1926-28-29

W
WADE, Steve (DB)
Dothan, Ala., 1971-72
WADE, Tommy (DB)
Dothan, Ala., 1967-68-70
WAGGONER, Clint (TE/DE)
Fairburn, Ga., 1996-97-98
WAGNER, Richard (OLB)
Ft. Payne, Ala., 1983
WAGSTAFF, Granison (LB)
Enterprise, Ala., 1995-96-98
WAITES, W. L. (HB)
Tuscaloosa, Ala., 1938
WALKER, Bland, Jr. (C)
Eutaw, Ala., 1957
WALKER, Edgar (DE)
Dothan, Ala., 1995-96-97
WALKER, Erskine "Bubba" (HB)
Ensley, Ala., 1931-32-33
WALKER, Hardy (OT)
Huntsville, Ala., 1981-83-85

WALKER, Hilmon (E)
Hattiesburg, Miss., 1936
WALKER, James E. (E)
Holt, Ala., 1935
WALKER, Jeremy (FB)
Prattville, Ala., 1999
WALKER, M. P. (E)
Birmingham, Ala., 1892
WALKER, Noojin (FB)
Falkville, Ala., 1955
WALKER, Wayne D. (T)
Martha, Tenn., 1944
WALKER, William Mudd (QB)
Birmingham, Ala., 1892-94
WALL, Jeff (H)
Birmingham, Ala.,
1989-90-91-92
WALL, Larry "Dink" (FB)
Fairfax, Ala., 1961-62-64
WALLS, Clay (HB)
Bessemer, Ala., 1955-56-57
WALTERS, John (LB)
Richardson, Tex., 1992-93-94-95
WARD, Alan (PK)
Pensacola, Fla., 1987-89-90
WARD, Lorenzo (S)
Greensboro, Ala., 1987-88-89-90
WARD, Wm. LaFayette (HB)
Greensboro, Ala., 1904-05
WARNOCK, Robert (SE)
Birmingham, Ala., 1997
WARREN, Derrick (TE)
Pensacola, Fla., 1989-90-91
WARREN, Erin "Tut" (E)
Montgomery, Ala., 1937-38-39
WARREN, Jarrod (FS)
Birmingham, Ala., 1998
WASHCO, Gerard George (DT)
West Orange, N.J., 1973-74-75
WASHINGTON, Eric (DB)
Miami, Fla., 1990-91
WASHINGTON, Mike (DB)
Montgomery, Ala., 1972-73-74
WATFORD, Jerry (G)
Gadsden, Ala., 1950-51-52
WATKINS, David (DE)
Rome, Ga., 1971-72-73
WATSON, Rick, (FB)
Birmingham, Ala., 1974-75-76
WATSON, William C. (E)
New Decatur, Ala., 1908
WATTS, Jimmy (DE)
Gulf Breeze, Fla., 1981-82-83
WATTS, Tyler (QB)
Pelham, Ala., 1999
WATTS, William (PK)
Pleasant Grove, Ala.,
1993-94-95-96
WEAVER, Sam (E)
Birmingham, Ala., 1928-29
WEBB, Steve (DE)
Holt, Ala., 1988-89-90-91
WEEKS, George (E)
Dothan, Ala., 1940-41-42
WEEKS, Phillip (SS)
Lake Butler, Fla., 1999
WEIGAND, Tommy (HB)
Enterprise, Ala., 1968
WEIST, T. J. (WR)
Bay City, Mich., 1987

WELSH, Clem (HB)
Winchester, Ill., 1948
WERT, Thomas William (RT-FB)
Birmingham, Ala., 1899
WESLEY, L. O. (QB)
Guin, Ala., 1922-23
WESLEY, Wm. Earl "Buddy"
(FB) Talladega, Ala.,
1958-59-60
WEST, Marcell (FL)
Niceville, Fla., 1993-94-95-96
WETHINGTON, Matt (PK)
Titusville, Fla., 1991-94
WHALEY, Frank (DE)
Lineville, Ala., 1965-66
WHATLEY, James W. (T)
Alexander City, Ala.,
1933-34-35
WHATLEY, Seaborn Thornton
(B) Havana, Ala., 1906
WHEELER, Wayne (SE)
Orlando, Fla., 1971-72-73
WHETSTONE, Darryl (DT)
Montgomery, Ala., 1987
WHISENHUNT, Tab (LB)
Bessemer, Ala., 1992
WHITAKER, Hulet (E)
Guntersville, Ala., 1925
WHITE, Arthur P. "Tarzan" (G)
Atmore, Ala., 1934-35-36
WHITE, Brent (QB)
Colorado Springs, Col., 1991
WHITE, Chris (SE)
South Easton, Ma., 1987
WHITE, Darryl (SE)
Tuscaloosa, Ala., 1981-82
WHITE, Ed (E)
Anniston, Ala., 1947-48-49
WHITE, Frank S., Jr. (FB)
Birmingham, Ala., 1897-98-99
WHITE, Gus (MG)
Dothan, Ala., 1974-75-76
WHITE, Jack (OG)
Louisville, Miss., 1971
WHITE, Kelvis (DT)
Courtland, Ala., 1998-99
WHITE, Laron (NT-C)
Courtland, Ala., 1993-94-95-96

WHITE, Mike (OG)
Decatur, Ga., 1983-84
WHITE, Tommy (FB)
West Blocton, Ala.,
1958-59-60
WHITEHURST, Clay (SE)
Nashville, Tenn, 1984-85-86-87
WHITLEY, Tom (T)
Birmingham, Ala.,
1944-45-46-47
WHITLOCK, Darin (C)
Orlando, Fla., 1985-86
WHITMAN, Steven K. (FB)
Birmingham, Ala., 1977-78-79
WHITMIRE, Don (G)
Decatur, Ala., 1941-42
WHITTLESLEY, C. S. (LG)
Opelika, Ala., 1916-17
WHITWORTH, J. B. "Ears" (T)
Blytheville, Ark., 1930-31
WICKE, Dallas (QB)
Pensacola, Fla., 1938-39
WIESEMAN, Bill (G)
Louisville, Ky., 1962-63
WILBANKS, Danny (FB)
Tallassee, Ala., 1957
WILCOX, George Spigener (E)
Montgomery, Ala., 1903-04
WILCOX, Tommy (DB)
Harahan, La., 1979-80-81-82
WILDER, Ken (OT)
Columbiana, Ala., 1968-69
WILDER, Roosevelt (FB)
Macon, Ga., 1982
WILGA, Bob (G)
Webster, Mass., 1951-52-53
WILHITE, Al (T)
Tuscumbia, Ala., 1949-50-51
WILKINS, Red (E)
Bay Minette, Ala., 1961
WILKINSON, Everett (B-K)
Prattville, Ala., 1909-10-12-13
WILKINSON, Vernon (DB)
Enterprise, Ala., 1984-85-87
WILLIAMS, Billy (T)
Lincoln, Ala., 1951-52
WILLIAMS, Charlie (FB)
Bessemer, Ala., 1980

WILLIAMS, John Byrd (G)
Decatur, Ala., 1965-66
WILLIAMS, Sherman (TB)
Mobile, Ala., 1991-92-93-94
WILLIAMS, Steven Edward
(DB) Moline, Ill., 1969-70-71
WILLIAMSON, Richard (SE)
Fort Deposit, Ala., 1961-62
WILLIAMSON, Tank (P)
Orrville, Ala., 1990-91
WILLIAMSON, Temple (QB)
Tuscaloosa, Ala., 1935
WILLIS, Perry (SE)
Dadeville, Ala., 1967
WILLIS, Virgil "Bud" (E)
Tifton, Ga., 1951-52
WILSON, Bobby (QB)
Bay Minette, Ala.,
1950-51-52
WILSON, George (OG)
Bessemer, Ala., 1990-91-92
WILSON, George "Butch" (HB)
Hueytown, Ala., 1960-61-62
WILSON, Jimmy (OG)
Haleyville, Ala., 1961-62
WILSON, Steve (DB)
Brundidge, Ala., 1985-86-87
WILSON, Woody (LB)
Shawnee, Okla., 1987-88-89
WIMBLEY, Prince (SE)
Miami, Fla., 1988-89-91-92
WINDHAM, Edward Price (B)
Stone, Ala., 1897
WINGO, Richard "Rich" (LB)
Elkhart, Ind., 1976-77-78
WINSLETT, Hoyt "Wu" (E)
Dadeville, Ala., 1924-25-26
WINSTON, Owen (CB)
Montgomery, Ala.,
1995-96-98
WISE, Mack (HB)
Elba, Ala., 1958
WISNIEWSKI, Mark (PK)
Jacksonville, Fla., 1998
WOFFORD, Curtis (DB)
Atlanta, Ga., 1984
WOFFORD, Lloyd (DT)
Atlanta, Ga., 1984

WOOD, Bobby (DT)
McComb, Miss., 1937-38
WOOD, Russ (DE)
Elba, Ala., 1980-81-82
WOOD, William B (E)
Guntersville, Ala., 1957
WOOD, William Dexter (SE)
Ozark, Ala., 1970-71-72
WOODRUFF, Glen (TE)
Aliceville, Ala., 1971
WOODSON, Danny (QB)
Mobile, Ala., 1990-91
WOODY, Rock (CB)
Springville, Ala., 1991
WORLEY, Butch (PK)
Huntsville, Ala., 1986
WOZNIAK, John (G)
Fairhope, Pa., 1944-45-46-47
WRIGHT, Bo (FB)
Prichard, Ala., 1985-86-87
WRIGHT, Steve (T)
Louisville, Ky., 1962-63
WYATT, Willie (NG)
Gardendale, Ala., 1986-87-88-89
WYATT, W. S. (QB)
New Decatur, Ala., 1903-04
WYHONIC, John (G)
Connorville, Ohio 1939-40-41

Y
YATES, Ollie Porter (QB)
Hattiesburg, Miss., 1954
YELVINGTON, Gary (DB)
Daytona Beach, Fla., 1973-74
YOUNG, Cecil Hugh (HB)
Anniston, Ala., 1902-03
YOUNG, William A. (T)
Pine Bluff, Ark., 1936
YOUNGLEMAN, Sid (T)
Brooklyn, N.Y., 1952-53-54

Z
ZIVICH, George (HB)
East Chicago, Ind., 1937-38
ZOW, Andrew (QB)
Lake Butler, Fla,. 1998-99
ZUGA, Mike (C)
Newnan, Ga., 1987-88-89

ALL-TIME GAME RECORD

1892 ~ 1999

Courtesy UA Athletics Media Relations

1892 — Won 2, Lost 2
Coach E.B. Beaumont

56	B'ham H. Sch.	0	Birmingham	Nov. 11
4	B'ham A.C.	5	Birmingham	Nov. 12
14	B'ham A.C.	0	Birmingham	Dec. 10
22	Auburn	32	Birmingham	Feb. 22, 1893
96		37		

1893 — Won 0, Lost 4
Coach Eli Abbott

0	B'ham A.C.	4	Tuscaloosa	Oct. 14
8	B'ham A.C.	10	Birmingham	Nov. 4
0	Sewanee	20	Birmingham	Nov. 11
16	Auburn	40	Montgomery	Nov. 30
24		74		

1894 — Won 3, Lost 1
Coach Eli Abbott

0	Mississippi	6	Jackson	Oct. 27
18	Tulane	6	New Orleans	Nov. 3
24	Sewanee	4	Birmingham	Nov. 15
18	Auburn	0	Montgomery	Nov. 29
60		16		

1895 — Won 0, Lost 4
Coach Eli Abbott

6	Georgia	30	Columbus, Ga.	Nov. 2
0	Tulane	22	New Orleans	Nov. 16
6	LSU	12	Baton Rouge	Nov. 18
0	Auburn	48	Tuscaloosa	Nov. 23
12		112		

1896 — Won 2, Lost 1
Coach Otto Wagonhurst

30	B'ham A.C.	0	Tuscaloosa	Oct. 24
6	Sewanee	10	Tuscaloosa	Oct. 31
20	Miss. State	0	Tuscaloosa	Nov. 14
56		10		

1897 — Won 1, Lost 0
Coach Allen McCants

6	Tuscaloosa A.C.	0	Tuscaloosa	Nov. 13

1898 — NO TEAM

1899 — Won 3, Lost 1
Coach W.A. Martin

16	Tuscaloosa A.C.	5	Tuscaloosa	Oct. 21
16	Montgomery A.C.	0	Tuscaloosa	Nov. 11
7	Mississippi	5	Jackson	Nov. 24
0	N. Orleans A.C.	21	New Orleans	Nov. 25
39		31		

1900 — Won 2, Lost 3
Coach M. Griffin

35	Taylor School	0	Tuscaloosa	Oct. 21
12	Mississippi	5	Tuscaloosa	Oct. 26
0	Tulane	6	Tuscaloosa	Nov. 3
5	Auburn	53	Montgomery	Nov. 17
0	Clemson	35	Birmingham	Nov. 29
52		99		

1901 — Won 2, Lost 1, Tied 2
Coach M.H. Harvey

41	Mississippi	0	Tuscaloosa	Oct. 19
0	Georgia	0	Montgomery	Nov. 9
0	Auburn	17	Tuscaloosa	Nov. 15
45	Miss. State	0	Tuscaloosa	Nov. 16
6	Tennessee	6	Birmingham	Nov. 28
92		23		

1902 — Won 4, Lost 4
Coach Eli Abbott

57	B'ham H.S.	0	Tuscaloosa	Oct. 10
81	Marion Inst.	0	Tuscaloosa	Oct. 13
0	Auburn	23	Birmingham	Oct. 18
0	Georgia	5	Birmingham	Nov. 1
27	Miss. State	0	Tuscaloosa	Nov. 8
0	Texas	10	Tuscaloosa	Nov. 11
26	Georgia Tech	0	Birmingham	Nov. 27
0	LSU	11	Tuscaloosa	Nov. 29
191		49		

1903 — Won 3, Lost 4
Coach W.B. Blount

0	Vanderbilt	30	Nashville	Oct. 10
0	Miss. State	11	Columbus, Miss.	Oct. 16
18	Auburn	6	Montgomery	Oct. 23
0	Sewanee	23	Birmingham	Nov. 2
18	LSU	0	Tuscaloosa	Nov. 9
0	Cumberland U.	44	Tuscaloosa	Nov. 14
24	Tennessee	0	Birmingham	Nov. 26
60		114		

1904 — Won 7, Lost 3
Coach W.B. Blount

29	Florida	0	Tuscaloosa	Oct. 3
0	Clemson	18	Birmingham	Oct. 8
6	Miss. State	0	Columbus, Miss.	Oct. 15
17	Nashville U.	0	Tuscaloosa	Oct. 24
16	Georgia	5	Tuscaloosa	Nov. 5
5	Auburn	29	Birmingham	Nov. 12
0	Tennessee	5	Birmingham	Nov. 24
11	LSU	0	Baton Rouge	Dec. 2
6	Tulane	0	New Orleans	Dec. 3
10	Pensacola A.C.	5	Pensacola, Fla.	Dec. 4
100		62		

1905 — Won 6, Lost 4
Coach Jack Leavenworth

17	Maryville	0	Tuscaloosa	Oct. 3
0	Vanderbilt	34	Nashville	Oct. 7
34	Miss. State	0	Tuscaloosa	Oct. 14
5	Georgia Tech	12	Atlanta	Oct. 21
0	Clemson	25	Columbia, S.C.	Oct. 25
36	Georgia	0	Birmingham	Nov. 4
21	Centre	0	Tuscaloosa	Nov. 9
30	Auburn	0	Birmingham	Nov. 18
6	Sewanee	42	Birmingham	Nov. 23
29	Tennessee	0	Birmingham	Nov. 30
178		113		

1906 — Won 5, Lost 1
Coach J.W.H. Pollard

6	Maryville	0	Tuscaloosa	Oct. 6
14	Howard	0	Tuscaloosa	Oct. 13
0	Vanderbilt	78	Nashville	Oct. 20
16	Miss. State	4	Starkville	Nov. 3
10	Auburn	0	Birmingham	Nov. 17
51	Tennessee	0	Birmingham	Nov. 29
97		82		

1907 — Won 5, Lost 1, Tied 2
Coach J.W.H. Pollard

17	Maryville	0	Tuscaloosa	Oct. 5
20	Mississippi	0	Columbus, Miss.	Oct. 12
4	Sewanee	54	Tuscaloosa	Oct. 21
0	Georgia	0	Montgomery	Oct. 25
12	Centre	0	Birmingham	Nov. 2
6	Auburn	6	Birmingham	Nov. 16
6	LSU	4	Mobile	Nov. 23
5	Tennessee	0	Birmingham	Nov. 28
70		64		

1908 — Won 6, Lost 1, Tied 1
Coach J.W.H. Pollard

27	Wetumpka	0	Tuscaloosa	Oct. 3
17	Howard	0	Birmingham	Oct. 10
16	Cincinnati	0	Birmingham	Oct. 17
6	Georgia Tech	11	Atlanta	Oct. 24
23	Chattanooga	6	Tuscaloosa	Oct. 31
6	Georgia	6	Birmingham	Nov. 14
9	Haskell Institute	8	Tuscaloosa	Nov. 20
4	Tennessee	0	Birmingham	Nov. 26
108		31		

1909 — Won 5, Lost 1, Tied 2
Coach J.W.H. Pollard

16	Union	0	Tuscaloosa	Oct. 2
14	Howard	0	Tuscaloosa	Oct. 9
3	Clemson	0	Birmingham	Oct. 16
0	Mississippi	0	Jackson	Oct. 23
14	Georgia	0	Atlanta	Oct. 30
10	Tennessee	0	Knoxville	Nov. 13
5	Tulane	5	New Orleans	Nov. 20
6	LSU	12	Birmingham	Nov. 25
68		17		

1910 — Won 4, Lost 4
Coach Guy Lowman

25	B'ham Southern	0	Tuscaloosa	Oct. 1
26	Marion Inst.	0	Tuscaloosa	Oct. 8
0	Georgia	22	Birmingham	Oct. 15
0	Georgia Tech	36	Tuscaloosa	Oct. 22
0	Mississippi	16	Greenville, Miss.	Nov. 5
0	Sewanee	30	Birmingham	Nov. 12
5	Tulane	3	New Orleans	Nov. 19
9	Washington & Lee	0	Birmingham	Nov. 24
65		107		

1911 — Won 5, Lost 2, Tied 2
Coach D.V. Graves

24	Howard	0	Tuscaloosa	Sept. 30
3	Georgia	11	Birmingham	Oct. 7
47	B'ham Southern	5	Birmingham	Oct. 14
6	Miss. State	6	Columbus, Miss.	Oct. 21
0	Georgia Tech	0	Atlanta	Oct. 29
35	Marion Inst.	0	Marion, Ala.	Nov. 4
0	Sewanee	3	Tuscaloosa	Nov. 11
22	Tulane	0	Tuscaloosa	Nov. 18
16	Davidson	6	Birmingham	Nov. 30
153		31		

1912 — Won 5, Lost 3, Tied 1
Coach D.V. Graves

52	Marion Inst.	0	Tuscaloosa	Sept. 28
62	B'ham Southern	0	Tuscaloosa	Oct. 5
3	Ga. Tech	20	Atlanta	Oct. 12
0	Miss. State	7	Aberdeen, Miss.	Oct. 18
9	Georgia	13	Columbus, Ga.	Oct. 26
7	Tulane	0	New Orleans	Nov. 2
10	Mississippi	9	Tuscaloosa	Nov. 9
6	Sewanee	6	Birmingham	Nov. 16
7	Tennessee	0	Birmingham	Nov. 28
156		55		

1913 — Won 6, Lost 3
Coach D.V. Graves

27	Howard	0	Tuscaloosa	Sept. 27
81	B'ham Southern	0	Tuscaloosa	Oct. 4
20	Clemson	0	Tuscaloosa	Oct. 11
0	Georgia	20	Birmingham	Oct. 18
26	Tulane	0	New Orleans	Oct. 25
21	Miss. College	3	Jackson	Nov. 1
7	Sewanee	10	Birmingham	Nov. 9
6	Tennessee	0	Tuscaloosa	Nov. 14
0	Miss. State	7	Birmingham	Nov. 27
188		40		

1914 — Won 5, Lost 4
Coach D.V. Graves

13	Howard	0	Tuscaloosa	Oct. 3
54	B'ham Southern	0	Tuscaloosa	Oct. 10
13	Georgia Tech	0	Birmingham	Oct. 17
7	Tennessee	17	Knoxville	Oct. 24
58	Tulane	0	Tuscaloosa	Oct. 31
0	Sewanee	18	Birmingham	Nov. 7
63	Chattanooga	0	Tuscaloosa	Nov. 13
0	Miss. State	9	Birmingham	Nov. 26
3	Carlisle	20	Birmingham	Dec. 2
211		64		

1915 — Won 6, Lost 2
Coach Thomas Kelley

44	Howard	0	Tuscaloosa	Oct. 2
67	B'ham Southern	0	Tuscaloosa	Oct. 9
40	Miss. College	0	Tuscaloosa	Oct. 16
16	Tulane	0	Tuscaloosa	Oct. 23
23	Sewanee	10	Birmingham	Oct. 30
7	Georgia Tech	21	Atlanta	Nov. 6
0	Texas	20	Austin, Tex.	Nov. 13
53	Mississippi	0	Birmingham	Nov. 25
250		51		

1916 — Won 6, Lost 3
Coach Thomas Kelley

13	B'ham Southern	0	Tuscaloosa	Sept. 30
80	Sou. Univ.	0	Tuscaloosa	Oct. 7
13	Miss. College	7	Tuscaloosa	Oct. 14
16	Florida	0	Jacksonville, Fla.	Oct. 21
27	Mississippi	0	Tuscaloosa	Oct. 28
7	Sewanee	6	Birmingham	Nov. 4
0	Georgia Tech	13	Atlanta	Nov. 11
0	Tulane	33	New Orleans	Nov. 18
0	Georgia	3	Birmingham	Nov. 30
156		62		

1917 — Won 5, Lost 2, Tied 1
Coach Thomas Kelley

7	Ohio Am. Corp.	0	Montgomery	Oct. 3
13	Marion Inst.	0	Tuscaloosa	Oct. 12
46	Miss. College	0	Tuscaloosa	Oct. 20
64	Mississippi	0	Tuscaloosa	Oct. 26
3	Sewanee	3	Birmingham	Nov. 3
2	Vanderbilt	7	Birmingham	Nov. 10
27	Kentucky	0	Lexington	Nov. 17
6	Camp Gordon	19	Birmingham	Nov. 29
168		29		

1918 — NO TEAM

1919 — Won 8, Lost 1
Coach Xen Scott

27	B'ham Southern	0	Tuscaloosa	Oct. 4
49	Mississippi	0	Tuscaloosa	Oct. 11
48	Howard	0	Tuscaloosa	Oct. 18
61	Marion Inst.	0	Tuscaloosa	Oct. 24
40	Sewanee	0	Birmingham	Nov. 1
12	Vanderbilt	16	Nashville	Nov. 8
23	LSU	0	Baton Rouge	Nov. 15
6	Georgia	0	Atlanta	Nov. 22
14	Miss. State	6	Birmingham	Nov. 27
280		22		

1920 — Won 10, Lost 1
Coach Xen Scott

59	Southern Mil. Aca.	0	Tuscaloosa	Sept. 25
49	Marion Inst.	0	Tuscaloosa	Oct. 2
45	B'ham Southern	0	Tuscaloosa	Oct. 9
57	Miss. College	0	Tuscaloosa	Oct. 16
33	Howard	0	Tuscaloosa	Oct. 23
21	Sewanee	0	Birmingham	Oct. 30
14	Vanderbilt	7	Birmingham	Nov. 6
21	LSU	0	Tuscaloosa	Nov. 11
14	Georgia	21	Atlanta	Nov. 20
24	Miss. State	7	Birmingham	Nov. 25
40	Case College	0	Cleveland, Ohio	Nov. 27
377		35		

1921 — Won 5, Lost 4, Tied 2
Coach Xen Scott

34	Howard	14	Tuscaloosa	Sept. 24
27	Spring Hill	7	Tuscaloosa	Oct. 1
55	Marion Inst.	0	Tuscaloosa	Oct. 8
95	Bryson Tenn.	0	Tuscaloosa	Oct. 15
0	Sewanee	17	Birmingham	Oct. 22
7	LSU	7	New Orleans	Oct. 29
0	Vanderbilt	14	Birmingham	Nov. 5
2	Florida	9	Tuscaloosa	Nov. 11
0	Georgia	22	Atlanta	Nov. 19
7	Miss. State	7	Birmingham	Nov. 24
14	Tulane	7	New Orleans	Dec. 3
241		104		

1922 — Won 6, Lost 3, Tied 1
Coach Xen Scott

110	Marion Institute	0	Tuscaloosa	Sept. 30
41	Oglethorpe	0	Tuscaloosa	Oct. 7
7	Georgia Tech	33	Atlanta	Oct. 14
7	Sewanee	7	Birmingham	Oct. 21
10	Texas	19	Austin, Tex.	Oct. 28
9	Pennsylvania	7	Philadelphia	Nov. 4
47	LSU	3	Tuscaloosa	Nov. 10
0	Kentucky	6	Lexington	Nov. 18
10	Georgia	6	Montgomery	Nov. 25
59	Miss. State	0	Birmingham	Nov. 30
300		81		

COACH WALLACE WADE
1923-1930 — Won 61, Lost 13, Tied 3

1923 — Won 7, Lost 2, Tied 1

12	Union	0	Tuscaloosa	Sept. 29
56	Mississippi	0	Tuscaloosa	Oct. 6
0	Syracuse	23	Syracuse, N.Y.	Oct. 13
7	Sewanee	0	Birmingham	Oct. 20
59	Spring Hill	0	Mobile	Oct. 27
0	Georgia Tech	0	Atlanta	Nov. 3
16	Kentucky	8	Tuscaloosa	Nov. 10
30	LSU	3	Montgomery	Nov. 16
36	Georgia	0	Montgomery	Nov. 24
6	Florida	16	Birmingham	Nov. 29
222		50		

1924 — Won 8, Lost 1
Southern Conference Champions

55	Union	0	Tuscaloosa	Sept. 27
20	Furman	0	Greenville, S.C.	Oct. 4
55	Miss. College	0	Tuscaloosa	Oct. 11
14	Sewanee	0	Birmingham	Oct. 18
14	Georgia Tech	0	Atlanta	Oct. 25
61	Mississippi	0	Montgomery	Nov. 1
42	Kentucky	7	Tuscaloosa	Nov. 8
0	Centre College	17	Birmingham	Nov. 15
33	Georgia	0	Birmingham	Nov. 27
294		24		

1925 — Won 10, Lost 0
National Champions
Southern Conference Champions

53	Union College	0	Tuscaloosa	Sept. 26
50	B'ham Southern	7	Tuscaloosa	Oct. 2
42	LSU	0	Baton Rouge	Oct. 10
27	Sewanee	0	Birmingham	Oct. 17
7	Georgia Tech	0	Atlanta	Oct. 24
6	Miss. State	0	Tuscaloosa	Oct. 31
31	Kentucky	0	Birmingham	Nov. 7
34	Florida	0	Montgomery	Nov. 14
27	Georgia	0	Birmingham	Nov. 26
*20	Washington	19	Rose Bowl	Jan. 1, 1926
297		26		

1926 — Won 9, Lost 0, Tied 1
National Champions
Southern Conference Champions

54	Millsaps	0	Tuscaloosa	Sept. 24
19	Vanderbilt	7	Nashville	Oct. 2
26	Miss. State	7	Meridian, Miss.	Oct. 9
21	Georgia Tech	0	Atlanta	Oct. 16
2	Sewanee	0	Birmingham	Oct. 23
24	LSU	0	Tuscaloosa	Oct. 30
14	Kentucky	0	Birmingham	Nov. 6
49	Florida	0	Montgomery	Nov. 13
33	Georgia	6	Birmingham	Nov. 25
*7	Stanford	7	Rose Bowl	Jan. 1, 1927
249		27		

*Bowl Game

1927 — Won 5, Lost 4, Tied 1

46	Millsaps	0	Tuscaloosa	Sept. 24
31	So. Pres. U.	0	Tuscaloosa	Sept. 30
0	LSU	0	Birmingham	Oct. 8
0	Georgia Tech	13	Atlanta	Oct. 15
24	Sewanee	0	Birmingham	Oct. 22
13	Miss. State	7	Tuscaloosa	Oct. 29
21	Kentucky	6	Birmingham	Nov. 5
6	Florida	13	Montgomery	Nov. 12
6	Georgia	20	Birmingham	Nov. 27
7	Vanderbilt	14	Birmingham	Dec. 3
154		73		

1928 — Won 6, Lost 3

27	Mississippi	0	Tuscaloosa	Oct. 6
46	Miss. State	0	Starkville	Oct. 13
13	Tennessee	15	Tuscaloosa	Oct. 20
42	Sewanee	12	Birmingham	Oct. 27
0	Wisconsin	15	Madison	Nov. 3
14	Kentucky	0	Montgomery	Nov. 10
13	Georgia Tech	33	Atlanta	Nov. 17
19	Georgia	0	Birmingham	Nov. 29
13	LSU	0	Birmingham	Dec. 8
187		75		

1929 — Won 6, Lost 3

55	Miss. College	0	Tuscaloosa	Sept. 28
22	Mississippi	7	Tuscaloosa	Oct. 5
46	Chattanooga	0	Tuscaloosa	Oct. 12
0	Tennessee	6	Knoxville	Oct. 19
35	Sewanee	7	Birmingham	Oct. 26
0	Vanderbilt	13	Nashville	Nov. 2
24	Kentucky	13	Montgomery	Nov. 9
13	Georgia Tech	0	Atlanta	Nov. 16
0	Georgia	12	Birmingham	Nov. 28
196		58		

1930 — Won 10, Lost 0
National Champions
Southern Conference Champions

43	Howard	0	Tuscaloosa	Sept. 27
64	Mississippi	0	Tuscaloosa	Oct. 4
25	Sewanee	0	Birmingham	Oct. 11
18	Tennessee	6	Tuscaloosa	Oct. 18
12	Vanderbilt	7	Birmingham	Oct. 25
19	Kentucky	0	Lexington	Nov. 1
20	Florida	0	Gainesville	Nov. 8
33	LSU	0	Montgomery	Nov. 15
13	Georgia	0	Birmingham	Nov. 27
*24	Washington State	0	Rose Bowl	Jan. 1, 1931
271		13		

COACH FRANK THOMAS
1931-1946 — Won 115, Lost 24, Tied 7

1931 — Won 9, Lost 1

42	Howard	0	Tuscaloosa	Sept. 26
55	Mississippi	6	Tuscaloosa	Oct. 3
53	Miss. State	0	Meridian, Miss.	Oct. 10
0	Tennessee	25	Knoxville	Oct. 17
33	Sewanee	0	Birmingham	Oct. 24
9	Kentucky	7	Tuscaloosa	Oct. 31
41	Florida	0	Birmingham	Nov. 7
74	Clemson	7	Montgomery	Nov. 14
14	Vanderbilt	6	Nashville	Nov. 26
39	Chattanooga	0	Chattanooga	Dec. 2
360		57		

1932 — Won 8, Lost 2

45	Southwestern	6	Tuscaloosa	Sept. 24
43	Miss. State	0	Montgomery	Oct. 1
28	George Wash.	6	Washington, D.C.	Oct. 8
3	Tennessee	7	Birmingham	Oct. 15
24	Mississippi	13	Tuscaloosa	Oct. 22
12	Kentucky	7	Lexington	Oct. 29
9	Virginia Tech	6	Tuscaloosa	Nov. 5
0	Georgia Tech	6	Atlanta	Nov. 12
20	Vanderbilt	0	Birmingham	Nov. 24
6	St. Mary's	0	San Francisco	Dec. 5
200		51		

1933 — Won 7, Lost 1, Tied 1
SEC Champions

34	Oglethorpe	0	Tuscaloosa	Sept. 30
0	Mississippi	0	Birmingham	Oct. 7
18	Miss. State	0	Tuscaloosa	Oct. 14
12	Tennessee	6	Knoxville	Oct. 21
0	Fordham	2	New York	Oct. 28
20	Kentucky	0	Birmingham	Nov. 4
27	Virginia Tech	0	Tuscaloosa	Nov. 11
12	Georgia Tech	9	Atlanta	Nov. 18
7	Vanderbilt	0	Nashville	Nov. 30
130		17		

1934 — Won 10, Lost 0
National Champions
SEC Champions

24	Howard	0	Tuscaloosa	Sept. 29
35	Sewanee	6	Montgomery	Oct. 5
41	Miss. State	0	Tuscaloosa	Oct. 13
13	Tennessee	6	Birmingham	Oct. 20
26	Georgia	6	Birmingham	Oct. 27
34	Kentucky	14	Lexington	Nov. 3
40	Clemson	0	Tuscaloosa	Nov. 10
40	Georgia Tech	0	Atlanta	Nov. 17
34	Vanderbilt	0	Birmingham	Nov. 29
*29	Stanford	13	Rose Bowl	Jan. 1, 1935
316		45		

1935 — Won 6, Lost 2, Tied 1

7	Howard	7	Tuscaloosa	Sept. 28
39	Geo. Wash.	0	Washington, D.C.	Oct. 5
7	Miss. State	20	Tuscaloosa	Oct. 12
25	Tennessee	0	Knoxville	Oct. 19
17	Georgia	7	Athens	Oct. 26
13	Kentucky	0	Birmingham	Nov. 2
33	Clemson	0	Tuscaloosa	Nov. 9
38	Georgia Tech	7	Birmingham	Nov. 16
6	Vanderbilt	14	Nashville	Nov. 28
185		55		

1936 — Won 8, Lost 0, Tied 1

34	Howard	0	Tuscaloosa	Sept. 26
32	Clemson	0	Tuscaloosa	Oct. 3
7	Miss. State	0	Tuscaloosa	Oct. 10
0	Tennessee	0	Birmingham	Oct. 17
13	Loyola, N.O.	6	New Orleans	Oct. 24
14	Kentucky	0	Lexington	Oct. 31
34	Tulane	7	Birmingham	Nov. 7
20	Georgia Tech	16	Atlanta	Nov. 14
14	Vanderbilt	6	Birmingham	Nov. 25
168		35		

1937 — Won 9, Lost 1*
SEC Champions

41	Howard	0	Tuscaloosa	Sept. 25
65	Sewanee	0	Birmingham	Oct. 2
20	South Carolina	0	Tuscaloosa	Oct. 9
14	Tennessee	7	Knoxville	Oct. 16
19	George Wash.	0	Washington, D.C.	Oct. 23
41	Kentucky	0	Tuscaloosa	Oct. 30
9	Tulane	6	N. Orleans	Nov. 6
7	Georgia Tech	0	Birmingham	Nov. 13
9	Vanderbilt	7	Nashville	Nov. 25
*0	California	13	Rose Bose	Jan. 1, 1938
225		33		

1938 — Won 7, Lost 1, Tied 1

19	Southern Cal.	7	Los Angeles	Sept. 24
34	Howard	0	Tuscaloosa	Oct. 1
14	NC State	0	Tuscaloosa	Oct. 8
0	Tennessee	13	Birmingham	Oct. 15
32	Sewanee	0	Tuscaloosa	Oct. 22
26	Kentucky	6	Lexington	Oct. 29
3	Tulane	0	Birmingham	Nov. 5
14	Georgia Tech	14	Atlanta	Nov. 12
7	Vanderbilt	0	Birmingham	Nov. 24
149		40		

1939 — Won 5, Lost 3, Tied 1

21	Howard	0	Tuscaloosa	Sept. 30
7	Fordham	6	New York	Oct. 7
20	Mercer	0	Tuscaloosa	Oct. 14
0	Tennessee	21	Knoxville	Oct. 21
7	Miss. State	0	Tuscaloosa	Oct. 28
7	Kentucky	7	Tuscaloosa	Nov. 4
0	Tulane	13	New Orleans	Nov. 11
0	Georgia Tech	6	Birmingham	Nov. 18
39	Vanderbilt	0	Nashville	Nov. 30
101		53		

1940 — Won 7, Lost 2

26	Spring Hill	0	Mobile (N)	Sept. 27
20	Mercer	0	Tuscaloosa	Oct. 5
31	Howard	0	Tuscaloosa	Oct. 12
12	Tennessee	27	Birmingham	Oct. 19
25	Kentucky	0	Lexington	Nov. 2
13	Tulane	6	Birmingham	Nov. 9
14	Georgia Tech	13	Atlanta	Nov. 16
25	Vanderbilt	21	Birmingham	Nov. 23
0	Miss. State	13	Tuscaloosa	Nov. 30
166		80		

1941 — Won 9, Lost 2
National Champions

47	SW Louisiana	6	Tuscaloosa	Sept. 27
0	Miss. State	14	Tuscaloosa	Oct. 4
61	Howard	0	Birmingham	Oct. 11
9	Tennessee	2	Knoxville	Oct. 18
27	Georgia	14	Birmingham	Oct. 25
30	Kentucky	0	Tuscaloosa	Nov. 1
19	Tulane	14	New Orleans	Nov. 8
20	Georgia Tech	0	Birmingham	Nov. 15
0	Vanderbilt	7	Nashville	Nov. 22
21	Miami (Fla.)	7	Miami (N)	Nov. 28
*29	Texas A&M	21	Cotton Bowl	Jan. 1, 1942
263		85		

*Bowl Game
(N)=Night Game
(TV)=Television Game

1942 — Won 8, Lost 3

54	SW Louisiana	0	Montgomery (N)	Sept. 25
21	Miss. State	6	Tuscaloosa	Oct. 3
27	Pensacola N.A.S.	0	Mobile	Oct. 10
8	Tennessee	0	Birmingham	Oct. 17
14	Kentucky	0	Lexington	Oct. 24
10	Georgia	21	Atlanta	Oct. 31
29	South Carolina	0	Tuscaloosa	Nov. 7
0	Georgia Tech	7	Atlanta	Nov. 14
27	Vanderbilt	7	Birmingham	Nov. 21
19	Ga. N. Pre-Fit	35	Birmingham	Nov. 28
*37	Boston College	21	Orange Bowl	Jan. 1, 1943
246		97		

1943 — NO TEAM

1944 — Won 5, Lost 2, Tied 2

27	LSU	27	Baton Rouge (N)	Sept. 30
63	Howard	7	Birmingham	Oct. 7
55	Millsaps	0	Tuscaloosa	Oct. 14
0	Tennessee	0	Knoxville	Oct. 21
41	Kentucky	0	Montgomery (N)	Oct. 27
7	Georgia	14	Birmingham	Nov. 4
34	Mississippi	6	Mobile	Nov. 11
19	Miss. State	0	Tuscaloosa	Nov. 18
*26	Duke	29	Sugar Bowl	Jan. 1, 1945
272		83		

1945 — Won 10, Lost 0
SEC Champions

21	Keesler A.A.F.	0	Biloxi, Miss.	Sept. 29
26	LSU	7	Baton Rouge (N)	Oct. 6
55	South Carolina	0	Montgomery	Oct. 13
25	Tennessee	7	Birmingham	Oct. 20
28	Georgia	14	Birmingham	Oct. 27
60	Kentucky	19	Louisville	Nov. 3
71	Vanderbilt	0	Nashville	Nov. 17
55	Pensacola N.A.S.	6	Tuscaloosa	Nov. 24
55	Miss. State	13	Tuscaloosa	Dec. 1
*34	Southern Cal.	14	Rose Bowl	Jan. 1, 1946
430		80		

1946 — Won 7, Lost 4

26	Furman	7	Birmingham	Sept. 20
7	Tulane	6	New Orleans	Sept. 28
14	South Carolina	6	Columbia	Oct. 5
54	SW Louisiana	0	Tuscaloosa	Oct. 12
0	Tennessee	12	Knoxville	Oct. 19
21	Kentucky	7	Montgomery	Oct. 26
0	Georgia	14	Athens	Nov. 2
21	LSU	31	Baton Rouge	Nov. 9
12	Vanderbilt	7	Birmingham	Nov. 16
7	Boston College	13	Boston	Nov. 23
24	Miss. State	7	Tuscaloosa	Nov. 30
186		110		

COACH HAROLD "RED" DREW
1947-1954 — Won 54, Lost 28, Tied 7

1947 — Won 8, Lost 3

34	Miss. Southern	7	Birmingham (N)	Sept. 20
20	Tulane	21	New Orleans	Sept. 27
7	Vanderbilt	14	Nashville	Oct. 4
26	Duquesne	0	Tuscaloosa	Oct. 11
10	Tennessee	0	Birmingham	Oct. 18
17	Georgia	7	Athens	Oct. 25
13	Kentucky	0	Lexington	Nov. 1
14	Georgia Tech	7	Birmingham	Nov. 15
41	LSU	12	Tuscaloosa	Nov. 22
21	Miami (Fla.)	6	Miami	Nov. 29
*7	Texas	27	Sugar Bowl	Jan. 1, 1948
210		101		

1948 — Won 6, Lost 4, Tied 1

14	Tulane	21	New Orleans	Sept. 25
14	Vanderbilt	14	Mobile	Oct. 2
48	Duquesne	6	Tuscaloosa (N)	Oct. 8
6	Tennessee	21	Knoxville	Oct. 16
10	Miss. State	7	Starkville	Oct. 23
0	Georgia	35	Birmingham	Oct. 30
27	Miss. Southern	0	Tuscaloosa	Nov. 6
14	Georgia Tech	12	Atlanta	Nov. 13
6	LSU	26	Baton Rouge	Nov. 20
34	Florida	28	Tuscaloosa	Nov. 27
55	Auburn	0	Birmingham	Dec. 4
228		170		

1949 — Won 6, Lost 3, Tied 1

14	Tulane	28	Mobile	Sept. 24
7	Vanderbilt	14	Nashville	Oct. 1
48	Duquesne	8	Tuscaloosa (N)	Oct. 7
7	Tennessee	7	Birmingham	Oct. 15
35	Miss. State	6	Tuscaloosa	Oct. 22
14	Georgia	7	Athens	Oct. 29
20	Georgia Tech	7	Birmingham	Nov. 12
34	Miss. Southern	26	Tuscaloosa	Nov. 19
35	Florida	13	Gainesville	Nov. 26
13	Auburn	14	Birmingham	Dec. 3
227		130		

1950 — Won 9, Lost 2

27	Chattanooga	0	Birmingham	Sept. 23
26	Tulane	14	New Orleans	Sept. 30
22	Vanderbilt	27	Mobile	Oct. 7
34	Furman	6	Tuscaloosa (N)	Oct. 13
9	Tennessee	14	Knoxville	Oct. 21
14	Miss. State	7	Tuscaloosa	Oct. 28
14	Georgia	7	Birmingham	Nov. 4
53	Miss. Southern	0	Tuscaloosa	Nov. 11
54	Georgia Tech	19	Atlanta	Nov. 18
41	Florida	13	Jacksonville	Nov. 25
34	Auburn	0	Birmingham	Dec. 2
328		107		

1951 — Won 5, Lost 6

89	Delta State	0	Montgomery (N)	Sept. 21
7	LSU	13	Mobile (N)	Sept. 29
20	Vanderbilt	22	Nashville (N)	Oct. 6
18	Villanova	41	Tuscaloosa (N)	Oct. 12
13	Tennessee	27	Birmingham (TV)	Oct. 20
7	Miss. State	0	Starkville	Oct. 27
16	Georgia	14	Athens	Nov. 3
40	Miss. Southern	7	Tuscaloosa	Nov. 10
7	Georgia Tech	27	Birmingham	Nov. 17
21	Florida	30	Tuscaloosa	Nov. 24
25	Auburn	7	Birmingham	Dec. 2
263		188		

1952 — Won 10, Lost 2

20	Miss. Southern	6	Montgomery (N)	Sept. 19
21	LSU	20	Baton Rouge (N)	Sept. 27
21	Miami	7	Miami (N)	Oct. 3
33	Virginia Tech	0	Tuscaloosa	Oct. 11
0	Tennessee	20	Knoxville	Oct. 18
42	Miss. State	19	Tuscaloosa	Oct. 25
34	Georgia	19	Birmingham	Nov. 1
42	Chattanooga	28	Tuscaloosa	Nov. 8
3	Georgia Tech	7	Atlanta (TV)	Nov. 15
27	Maryland	7	Mobile	Nov. 22
21	Auburn	0	Birmingham	Nov. 29
*61	Syracuse	6	Orange Bowl	Jan. 1, 1953
325		139		

1953 — Won 6, Lost 3, Tied 3
SEC Champions

19	Miss. Southern	25	Montgomery (N)	Sept. 18
7	LSU	7	Mobile (N)	Sept. 26
21	Vanderbilt	12	Nashville (N)	Oct. 3
41	Tulsa	13	Tuscaloosa	Oct. 10
0	Tennessee	0	Birmingham (TV)	Oct. 17
7	Miss. State	7	Tuscaloosa	Oct. 24
33	Georgia	12	Athens	Oct. 31
21	Chattanooga	14	Tuscaloosa	Nov. 7
13	Georgia Tech	6	Birmingham	Nov. 14
0	Maryland	21	College Park	Nov. 21
10	Auburn	7	Birmingham	Nov. 28
*6	Rice	28	Cotton Bowl	Jan. 1, 1954
178		152		

1954 — Won 4, Lost 5, Tied 2

2	Miss. Southern	7	Montgomery (N)	Sept. 17
12	LSU	0	Baton Rouge (N)	Sept. 25
28	Vanderbilt	14	Mobile (N)	Oct. 2
40	Tulsa	0	Tuscaloosa	Oct. 9
27	Tennessee	0	Knoxville	Oct. 16
7	Miss. State	12	Tuscaloosa	Oct. 23
0	Georgia	0	Birmingham	Oct. 30
0	Tulane	0	New Orleans	Nov. 6
0	Georgia Tech	20	Atlanta (TV)	Nov. 13
7	Miami	23	Miami (N)	Nov. 19
0	Auburn	28	Birmingham	Nov. 27
123		104		

COACH J.B. "EARS" WHITWORTH
1955-1957 — Won 4, Lost 24, Tied 4

1955 — Won 0, Lost 10

0	Rice	20	Houston (N)	Sept. 24
6	Vanderbilt	21	Nashville (N)	Oct. 1
0	TCU	21	Tuscaloosa	Oct. 8
0	Tennessee	20	Birmingham	Oct. 15
7	Miss. State	26	Tuscaloosa	Oct. 22
14	Georgia	35	Athens	Oct. 29
7	Tulane	27	Mobile	Nov. 5
2	Georgia Tech	26	Birmingham	Nov. 12
12	Miami	34	Miami (N)	Nov. 18
0	Auburn	26	Birmingham	Nov. 26
48		256		

1956 — Won 2, Lost 7, Tied 1

13	Rice	20	Houston (N)	Sept. 22
7	Vanderbilt	32	Mobile (N)	Oct. 6
6	TCU	23	Tuscaloosa	Oct. 13
0	Tennessee	24	Knoxville	Oct. 20
13	Miss. State	12	Tuscaloosa	Oct. 27
13	Georgia	16	Birmingham	Nov. 3
13	Tulane	7	New Orleans	Nov. 10
0	Georgia Tech	27	Atlanta	Nov. 17
13	Miss. Southern	13	Tuscaloosa	Nov. 24
7	Auburn	34	Birmingham	Dec. 1
85		208		

1957 — Won 2, Lost 7, Tied 1

0	LSU	28	Baton Rouge (N)	Sept. 28
6	Vanderbilt	6	Nashville (N)	Oct. 5
0	TCU	28	Ft. Worth (N)	Oct. 12
0	Tennessee	14	Birmingham	Oct. 19
13	Miss. State	25	Tuscaloosa	Oct. 26
14	Georgia	13	Athens	Nov. 2
0	Tulane	7	Mobile	Nov. 9
7	Georgia Tech	10	Birmingham	Nov. 16
29	Miss. Southern	2	Tuscaloosa	Nov. 23
0	Auburn	40	Birmingham	Nov. 30
69		173		

COACH PAUL W. "BEAR" BRYANT
1947-1954 — Won 232, Lost 46, Tied 9

1958 — Won 5, Lost 4, Tied 1

3	LSU	13	Mobile (N)	Sept. 27
0	Vanderbilt	0	Birmingham (N)	Oct. 4
29	Furman	6	Tuscaloosa (N)	Oct. 11
7	Tennessee	14	Knoxville	Oct. 18
9	Miss. State	7	Starkville	Oct. 25
12	Georgia	0	Tuscaloosa	Nov. 1
7	Tulane	13	New Orleans (N)	Nov. 8
17	Georgia Tech	8	Atlanta	Nov. 15
14	Memphis State	0	Tuscaloosa	Nov. 22
8	Auburn	14	Birmingham	Nov. 29
106		75		

1959 — Won 7, Lost 2, Tied 2

3	Georgia	17	Athens	Sept. 19
3	Houston	0	Houston (N)	Sept. 26
7	Vanderbilt	0	Nashville (N)	Oct. 3
13	Chattanooga	0	Tuscaloosa	Oct. 10
7	Tennessee	7	Birmingham	Oct. 17
10	Miss. State	0	Tuscaloosa	Oct. 31
19	Tulane	7	Mobile (N)	Nov. 7
9	Georgia Tech	7	Birmingham	Nov. 14
14	Memphis State	7	Tuscaloosa	Nov. 21
10	Auburn	0	Birmingham	Nov. 28
*0	Penn State	7	Liberty Bowl	Dec. 19
95		59		

1960 — Won 8, Lost 1, Tied 2

21	Georgia	6	Birmingham (TV)	Sept. 17
6	Tulane	6	New Orleans (N)	Sept. 24
21	Vanderbilt	0	Birmingham (N)	Oct. 1
7	Tennessee	20	Knoxville	Oct. 15
14	Houston	0	Tuscaloosa	Oct. 22
7	Miss. State	0	Starkville	Oct. 29
51	Furman	0	Tuscaloosa	Nov. 5
16	Georgia Tech	15	Atlanta	Nov. 12
34	Tampa	6	Tuscaloosa	Nov. 19
3	Auburn	0	Birmingham	Nov. 26
*3	Texas	3	Bluebonnet Bowl	Dec. 17
183		56		

1961 — Won 11, Lost 0
National Champions
SEC Champions

32	Georgia	6	Athens	Sept. 23
9	Tulane	0	Mobile (N)	Sept. 30
35	Vanderbilt	6	Nashville (N)	Oct. 7
26	N.C. State	7	Tuscaloosa	Oct. 14
34	Tennessee	3	Birmingham (TV)	Oct. 21
17	Houston	0	Houston (N)	Oct. 28
24	Miss. State	0	Tuscaloosa	Nov. 4
66	Richmond	0	Tuscaloosa	Nov. 11
10	Georgia Tech	0	Birmingham	Nov. 18
34	Auburn	0	Birmingham	Dec. 2
*10	Arkansas	3	Sugar Bowl	Jan. 1, 1962
297		25		

1962 — Won 10, Lost 1

35	Georgia	0	Birmingham (N)	Sept. 22
44	Tulane	6	New Orleans (N)	Sept. 28
17	Vanderbilt	7	Birmingham (N)	Oct. 6
14	Houston	3	Tuscaloosa	Oct. 13
27	Tennessee	7	Knoxville (TV)	Oct. 20
35	Tulsa	6	Tuscaloosa	Oct. 27
20	Miss. State	0	Starkville	Nov. 3
36	Miami	3	Tuscaloosa	Nov. 10
6	Georgia Tech	7	Atlanta	Nov. 17
38	Auburn	0	Birmingham	Dec. 1
*17	Oklahoma	0	Orange Bowl	Jan. 1, 1963
289		39		

1963 — Won 9, Lost 2

32	Georgia	7	Athens	Sept. 21
28	Tulane	0	Mobile (N)	Sept. 28
21	Vanderbilt	6	Nashville (N)	Oct. 5
6	Florida	10	Tuscaloosa	Oct. 12
35	Tennessee	0	Birmingham	Oct. 19
21	Houston	13	Tuscaloosa	Oct. 26
20	Miss. State	19	Tuscaloosa	Nov. 2
27	Georgia Tech	11	Birmingham	Nov. 16
8	Auburn	10	Birmingham	Nov. 30
17	Miami	12	Miami (TV)	Dec. 14
*12	Mississippi	7	Sugar Bowl	Jan. 1, 1964
227		95		

1964 — Won 10, Lost 1
National Champions
SEC Champions

31	Georgia	3	Tuscaloosa (N)	Sept. 19
36	Tulane	6	Mobile (N)	Sept. 26
24	Vanderbilt	0	Birmingham (N)	Oct. 3
21	N.C. State	0	Tuscaloosa	Oct. 10
19	Tennessee	8	Knoxville	Oct. 17
17	Florida	14	Tuscaloosa	Oct. 24
23	Miss. State	6	Jackson (N)	Oct. 31
17	LSU	9	Birmingham	Nov. 7
24	Georgia Tech	7	Atlanta	Nov. 14
21	Auburn	14	Birmingham (TV)	Nov. 26
*17	Texas	21	Orange Bowl (N)	Jan. 1
250		88		

<table>
<tr><td colspan="5">1965 — Won 9, Lost 1, Tied 1
AP National Champions
SEC Champions</td></tr>
</table>

1965 — Won 9, Lost 1, Tied 1
AP National Champions
SEC Champions

17	Georgia 18	Athens (TV)	Sept. 18
27	Tulane 0	Mobile (N)	Sept. 25
17	Mississippi 16	Birmingham (N)	Oct. 2
22	Vanderbilt 7	Nashville (N)	Oct. 9
7	Tennessee 7	Birmingham	Oct. 16
21	Florida State 0	Tuscaloosa	Oct. 23
10	Miss. State 7	Jackson (N)	Oct. 30
31	LSU 7	Baton Rouge (TV)	Nov. 6
35	South Carolina 14	Tuscaloosa	Nov. 13
30	Auburn 3	Birmingham	Nov. 27
*39	Nebraska 28	Orange Bowl (N)	Jan. 1
256	107		

1966 — Won 11, Lost 0
SEC Champions

34	La. Tech 0	Birmingham (N)	Sept. 24
17	Mississippi 7	Jackson (N)	Oct. 1
26	Clemson 0	Tuscaloosa	Oct. 8
11	Tennessee 10	Knoxville	Oct. 15
42	Vanderbilt 6	Birmingham	Oct. 22
27	Miss. State 14	Tuscaloosa	Oct. 29
21	LSU 0	Birmingham	Nov. 5
24	South Carolina 0	Tuscaloosa	Nov. 12
34	Southern Miss 0	Mobile	Nov. 26
34	Auburn 0	Birmingham (TV)	Dec. 3
*34	Nebraska 7	Sugar Bowl	Jan. 2, 1967
301	44		

1967 — Won 8, Lost 2, Tied 1

37	Florida State 37	Birmingham (N)	Sept. 23
25	Southern Miss. 3	Mobile (N)	Sept. 30
21	Mississippi 7	Birmingham (TV)	Oct. 7
35	Vanderbilt 21	Nashville (N)	Oct. 14
13	Tennessee 24	Birmingham	Oct. 21
13	Clemson 10	Clemson	Oct. 28
13	Miss. State 0	Tuscaloosa	Nov. 4
7	LSU 6	Baton Rouge (N)	Nov. 11
17	South Carolina 0	Tuscaloosa	Nov. 18
7	Auburn 3	Birmingham	Dec. 2
*16	Texas A&M 20	Cotton Bowl	Jan. 1, 1968
204	131		

1968 — Won 8, Lost 3

14	Virginia Tech 7	Birmingham (N)	Sept. 21
17	Southern Miss. 14	Mobile	Sept. 28
8	Mississippi 10	Jackson	Oct. 5
31	Vanderbilt 7	Tuscaloosa	Oct. 13
9	Tennessee 10	Knoxville (TV)	Oct. 19
21	Clemson 14	Tuscaloosa	Oct. 26
20	Miss. State 13	Tuscaloosa	Nov. 2
16	LSU 7	Birmingham	Nov. 9
14	Miami 6	Miami (N) (TV)	Nov. 16
24	Auburn 16	Birmingham	Nov. 30
*10	Missouri 35	Gator Bowl	Dec. 28
184	139		

1969 — Won 6, Lost 5

17	Virginia Tech 13	Blacksburg	Sept. 20
63	Southern Miss. 14	Tuscaloosa (N)	Sept. 27
33	Mississippi 32	Birmingham (N)	Oct. 4
10	Vanderbilt 14	Nashville (N)	Oct. 11
14	Tennessee 41	Birmingham	Oct. 18
38	Clemson 13	Clemson	Oct. 25
23	Miss. State 19	Jackson (N)	Nov. 1
15	LSU 20	Baton Rouge (N)	Nov. 8
42	Miami 6	Tuscaloosa	Nov. 15
26	Auburn 49	Birmingham	Nov. 29
*33	Colorado 47	Liberty Bowl	Dec. 13
314	268		

1970 — Won 6, Lost 5, Tied 1

21	Southern Cal. 42	Birmingham (N)	Sept. 12
51	Virginia Tech 18	Birmingham (N)	Sept. 19
46	Florida 15	Tuscaloosa	Sept. 26
23	Mississippi 48	Jackson (N) (TV)	Oct. 3
35	Vanderbilt 11	Tuscaloosa	Oct. 10
0	Tennessee 24	Knoxville	Oct. 17
30	Houston 21	Houston	Oct. 24
35	Miss. State 6	Tuscaloosa	Oct. 31
9	LSU 14	Birmingham (TV)	Nov. 7
32	Miami 8	Miami (N)	Nov. 14
28	Auburn 33	Birmingham (TV)	Nov. 28
*24	Oklahoma 24	Bluebonnet Bowl (N)	Dec. 31
334	264		

1971 — Won 11, Lost 1
SEC Champions

17	Southern Cal 10	Los Angeles (N)	Sept. 10
42	Southern Miss. 6	Tuscaloosa	Sept. 18
38	Florida 0	Gainesville	Sept. 25
40	Mississippi 6	Birmingham	Oct. 2
42	Vanderbilt 0	Nashville (N)	Oct. 9
32	Tennessee 15	Birmingham	Oct. 16
34	Houston 20	Tuscaloosa	Oct. 23
41	Miss. State 10	Jackson (N)	Oct. 30
14	LSU 7	Baton Rouge (N) (TV)	Nov. 6
31	Miami 3	Tuscaloosa	Nov. 13
31	Auburn 7	Birmingham (TV)	Nov. 27
*6	Nebraska 38	Orange Bowl (N)	Jan. 1, 1972
368	122		

1972 — Won 10, Lost 2
SEC Champions

35	Duke 12	Birmingham (N)	Sept. 9
35	Kentucky 0	Birmingham (N)	Sept. 23
48	Vanderbilt 21	Tuscaloosa (N)	Sept. 30
25	Georgia 7	Athens	Oct. 7
24	Florida 7	Tuscaloosa	Oct. 14
17	Tennessee 10	Knoxville	Oct. 21
48	Southern Miss. 11	Birmingham (N)	Oct. 28
58	Miss. State 14	Tuscaloosa	Nov. 4
35	LSU 21	Birmingham (TV)	Nov. 11
52	Virginia Tech 13	Tuscaloosa	Nov. 18
16	Auburn 17	Birmingham	Dec. 2
*13	Texas 17	Cotton Bowl	Jan. 1, 1973
406	150		

1973 — Won 11, Lost 1
UPI National Champions
SEC Champions

66	California 0	Birmingham (N)	Sept. 15
28	Kentucky 14	Lexington	Sept. 22
44	Vanderbilt 0	Nashville (N)	Sept. 29
28	Georgia 14	Tuscaloosa	Oct. 6
35	Florida 14	Gainesville	Oct. 13
42	Tennessee 21	Birmingham (TV)	Oct. 20
77	Virginia Tech 6	Tuscaloosa (N)	Oct. 27
35	Miss. State 0	Jackson (N)	Nov. 3
43	Miami 13	Tuscaloosa	Nov. 17
21	LSU 7	Baton Rouge (N) (TV)	Nov. 22
35	Auburn 0	Birmingham (N)	Dec. 1
*23	Notre Dame 24	Sugar Bowl (N)	Dec. 31
477	113		

1974 — Won 11, Lost 1
SEC Champions

21	Maryland 16	College Park	Sept. 14
52	Southern Miss. 0	Birmingham (N)	Sept. 21
23	Vanderbilt 10	Tuscaloosa	Sept. 28
35	Mississippi 21	Jackson (TV)	Oct. 5
8	Florida State 7	Tuscaloosa	Oct. 12
28	Tennessee 6	Knoxville	Oct. 19
41	TCU 3	Birmingham	Oct. 26
35	Miss. State 0	Tuscaloosa	Nov. 2
30	LSU 0	Birmingham (TV)	Nov. 9
28	Miami 7	Miami (N)	Nov. 16
17	Auburn 13	Birmingham (TV)	Nov. 29
*11	Notre Dame 13	Orange Bowl (N)	Jan. 1, 1975
329	96		

1975 — Won 11, Lost 1
SEC Champions

7	Missouri 20	Birmingham (N)	Sept. 8
56	Clemson 0	Tuscaloosa (N)	Sept. 20
40	Vanderbilt 7	Nashville	Sept. 27
32	Mississippi 6	Birmingham	Oct. 4
52	Washington 0	Tuscaloosa	Oct. 11
30	Tennessee 7	Birmingham	Oct. 18
45	TCU 0	Birmingham	Oct. 25
21	Miss. State 10	Jackson (N)	Nov. 1
23	LSU 10	Baton Rouge (N)	Nov. 8
27	Southern Miss. 6	Tuscaloosa	Nov. 15
28	Auburn 0	Birmingham (TV)	Nov. 29
*13	Penn State 6	Sugar Bowl (N)	Dec. 31
374	72		

1976 — Won 9, Lost 3

7	Mississippi 10	Jackson (N)	Sept. 11
56	SMU 3	Birmingham	Sept. 18
42	Vanderbilt 14	Tuscaloosa	Sept. 25
0	Georgia 21	Athens	Oct. 2
24	Southern Miss. 8	Birmingham	Oct. 9
20	Tennessee 13	Knoxville (TV)	Oct. 16
24	Louisville 3	Tuscaloosa	Oct. 23
34	Miss. State 17	Tuscaloosa	Oct. 30
28	LSU 17	Birmingham	Nov. 6
18	Notre Dame 21	South Bend (TV)	Nov. 13
38	Auburn 7	Birmingham	Nov. 27
*36	UCLA 6	Liberty Bowl (N)	Dec. 20
326	140		

1977 — Won 11, Lost 1
SEC Champions

34	Mississippi 13	Birmingham (N)	Sept. 10
24	Nebraska 31	Lincoln (TV)	Sept. 17
24	Vanderbilt 12	Nashville	Sept. 24
18	Georgia 10	Tuscaloosa	Oct. 1
21	Southern Cal 20	Los Angeles (TV)	Oct. 8
24	Tennessee 10	Birmingham	Oct. 15
55	Louisville 6	Tuscaloosa	Oct. 22
37	Miss. State 7	Jackson (N)	Oct. 29
24	LSU 3	Baton Rouge (TV)	Nov. 5
36	Miami 0	Tuscaloosa	Nov. 12
48	Auburn 21	Birmingham	Nov. 26
*35	Ohio State 6	Sugar Bowl	Jan. 2, 1978
380	139		

1978 — Won 11, Lost 1
AP National Champions
SEC Champions

20	Nebraska 3	Birmingham (N)	Sept. 2
38	Missouri 20	Columbia	Sept. 16
14	Southern Cal 24	Birmingham (TV)	Sept. 23
51	Vanderbilt 28	Tuscaloosa	Sept. 30
20	Washington 17	Seattle	Oct. 7
23	Florida 12	Tuscaloosa	Oct. 14
30	Tennessee 17	Knoxville	Oct. 21
35	Virginia Tech 0	Tuscaloosa	Oct. 28
35	Miss. State 14	Birmingham	Nov. 4
31	LSU 10	Birmingham (TV)	Nov. 11
34	Auburn 16	Birmingham	Dec. 2
*14	Penn State 7	Sugar Bowl	Jan. 1, 1979
345	168		

1979 — Won 12, Lost 0
AP & UPI National Champions
SEC Champions

30	Georgia Tech 6	Atlanta (TV)	Sept. 8
45	Baylor 0	Birmingham (N)	Sept. 22
66	Vanderbilt 3	Nashville	Sept. 29
38	Wichita State 0	Tuscaloosa	Oct. 6
40	Florida 0	Gainesville	Oct. 13
27	Tennessee 17	Birmingham	Oct. 20
31	Virginia Tech 7	Tuscaloosa	Oct. 27
24	Miss. State 7	Tuscaloosa	Nov. 3
3	LSU 0	Baton Rouge (N)	Nov. 10
30	Miami (Fla.) 0	Tuscaloosa (TV)	Nov. 17
25	Auburn 18	Birmingham	Dec. 1
*24	Arkansas 9	Sugar Bowl	Jan. 1, 1980
383	67		

1980 — Won 10, Lost 2

26	Georgia Tech 3	Birmingham	Sept. 6
59	Mississippi 35	Jackson	Sept. 20
41	Vanderbilt 0	Tuscaloosa	Sept. 27
45	Kentucky 0	Birmingham	Oct. 3
17	Rutgers 13	Meadowlands	Oct. 11
27	Tennessee 0	Knoxville (TV)	Oct. 18
42	Southern Miss. 7	Tuscaloosa	Oct. 25
3	Miss. State 6	Jackson	Nov. 1
28	LSU 7	Tuscaloosa	Nov. 8
0	Notre Dame 7	Birmingham (TV)	Nov. 15
34	Auburn 18	Birmingham	Nov. 29
*30	Baylor 2	Cotton Bowl	Jan. 1, 1981
352	98		

1981 — Won 9, Lost 2, Tied 1
SEC Champions

24	LSU 7	Baton Rouge (TV)	Sept. 5
21	Georgia Tech 24	Birmingham	Sept. 12
19	Kentucky 10	Lexington	Sept. 19
28	Vanderbilt 7	Nashville	Sept. 26
38	Mississippi 7	Tuscaloosa	Oct. 3
13	Southern Miss. 13	Birmingham	Oct. 10
38	Tennessee 19	Birmingham	Oct. 17
31	Rutgers 7	Tuscaloosa	Oct. 24
13	Miss. State 10	Tuscaloosa	Oct. 31
31	Penn. State 16	State College (TV)	Nov. 14
28	Auburn 17	Birmingham (TV)	Nov. 28
*12	Texas 14	Cotton Bowl	Jan. 1, 1982
296	151		

1982 — Won 8, Lost 4

45	Georgia Tech 7	Atlanta	Sept. 11
42	Mississippi 14	Jackson	Sept. 18
24	Vanderbilt 21	Tuscaloosa	Sept. 25
34	Arkansas State 7	Birmingham (N)	Oct. 2
42	Penn State 21	Birmingham (TV)	Oct. 9
28	Tennessee 35	Knoxville	Oct. 16
21	Cincinnati 3	Tuscaloosa	Oct. 23
20	Miss. State 12	Jackson	Oct. 30
10	LSU 20	Birmingham	Nov. 6
29	Southern Miss. 38	Tuscaloosa	Nov. 13
22	Auburn 23	Birmingham (TV)	Nov. 27
*21	Illinois 15	Liberty Bowl (N)	Dec. 29
338	216		

COACH RAY PERKINS
1983-1986 — Won 32, Lost 15, Tied 1

1983 — Won 8, Lost 4

20	Georgia Tech 7	Birmingham	Sept. 10
40	Mississippi 0	Tuscaloosa	Sept. 17
44	Vanderbilt 24	Nashville (N)	Sept. 24
44	Memphis State 13	Tuscaloosa	Oct. 1
28	Penn State 34	State College (TV)	Oct. 8
34	Tennessee 41	Birmingham	Oct. 15
35	Miss. State 18	Tuscaloosa	Oct. 29
32	LSU 26	Baton Rouge (TV)	Nov. 5
28	Southern Miss. 16	Birmingham	Nov. 12
13	Boston College 20	Foxboro (TV)	Nov. 25
20	Auburn 23	Birmingham (TV)	Dec. 3
*28	SMU 7	Sun Bowl (TV)	Dec. 24
366	229		

1984 — Won 5, Lost 6

31	Boston College 38	Birmingham (TV)	Sept. 8
6	Georgia Tech 16	Atlanta (TV)	Sept. 15
37	SW Louisiana 14	Tuscaloosa	Sept. 22
21	Vanderbilt 30	Tuscaloosa	Sept. 29
14	Georgia 24	Birmingham (TV)	Oct. 6
6	Penn State 0	Tuscaloosa	Oct. 13
27	Tennessee 28	Knoxville	Oct. 20
24	Miss. State 20	Jackson	Nov. 3
14	LSU 16	Birmingham	Nov. 10
29	Cincinnati 7	Cincinnati	Nov. 17
17	Auburn 15	Birmingham (TV)	Dec. 1
226	208		

1985 — Won 9, Lost 2, Tied 1

20	Georgia 16	Athens (TV)	Sept. 2
23	Texas A&M 10	Birmingham (TV)	Sept. 14
45	Cincinnati 10	Tuscaloosa	Sept. 21
40	Vanderbilt 20	Nashville (TV)	Sept. 28
17	Penn State 19	State College (TV)	Oct. 12
14	Tennessee 16	Birmingham (TV)	Oct. 19
28	Memphis State 9	Memphis	Oct. 26
44	Miss. State 28	Tuscaloosa	Nov. 2
14	LSU 14	Baton Rouge (TV)	Nov. 9
24	Southern Miss. 13	Tuscaloosa	Nov. 16
25	Auburn 23	Birmingham (TV)	Nov. 30
*24	Southern Cal 3	Aloha Bowl (TV)	Dec. 28
318	181		

1986 — Won 10, Lost 3

16	Ohio State 10	E. Rutherford (N) (TV)	Aug. 27
42	Vanderbilt 10	Tuscaloosa (TV)	Sept. 6
31	Southern Miss. 17	Birmingham	Sept. 13
21	Florida 7	Gainesville	Sept. 20
28	Notre Dame 10	Birmingham (TV)	Oct. 4
37	Memphis State 0	Tuscaloosa	Oct. 11
56	Tennessee 28	Knoxville (TV)	Oct. 18
3	Penn State 23	Tuscaloosa (TV)	Oct. 25
38	Miss. State 3	Starkville (TV)	Nov. 1
10	LSU 14	Birmingham (N) (TV)	Nov. 8
24	Temple 14	Tuscaloosa	Nov. 15
17	Auburn 21	Birmingham (TV)	Nov. 29
*28	Washington 6	Sun Bowl (TV)	Dec. 25
351	163		

COACH BILL CURRY
1987-1989 — Won 26, Lost 10

1987 — Won 7, Lost 5

38	Southern Miss 6	Birmingham	Sept. 5
24	Penn State 13	State College (N) (TV)	Sept. 12
14	Florida 23	Birmingham (TV)	Sept. 19
30	Vanderbilt 23	Nashville (N)	Sept. 26
38	SW Louisiana 10	Birmingham	Oct. 3
10	Memphis State 13	Memphis	Oct. 10
41	Tennessee 22	Birmingham (N) (TV)	Oct. 17
21	Miss. State 18	Birmingham (N)	Oct. 31
22	LSU 10	Baton Rouge (N) (TV)	Nov. 7
6	Notre Dame 37	South Bend (TV)	Nov. 14
0	Auburn 10	Birmingham (TV)	Nov. 27
*24	Michigan 28	Hall of Fame (TV)	Jan. 2
268	213		

1988 — Won 9, Lost 3

37	Temple 0	Philadelphia (N)	Sept. 10
44	Vanderbilt 10	Tuscaloosa	Sept. 24
31	Kentucky 27	Lexington (TV)	Oct. 1
12	Mississippi 22	Tuscaloosa (TV)	Oct. 8
28	Tennessee 20	Knoxville	Oct. 15
8	Penn State 3	Birmingham (TV)	Oct. 22
53	Miss. State 34	Starkville	Oct. 29
18	LSU 19	Tuscaloosa (TV)	Nov. 5
17	SW Louisiana 0	Birmingham	Nov. 12
10	Auburn 15	Birmingham (TV) .	Nov. 25
30	Texas A&M 10	College Station (N) (TV)	Dec. 1
*29	Army 28	Sun Bowl (TV)	Dec. 24
297	188		

1989 — Won 10, Lost 2
SEC Champions

35	Memphis State 7	Birmingham	Sept. 16
15	Kentucky 3	Tuscaloosa (TV)	Sept. 23
20	Vanderbilt 14	Nashville (TV)	Sept. 30
62	Mississippi 27	Jackson	Oct. 7
24	SW Louisiana 17	Tuscaloosa	Oct. 14
47	Tennessee 30	Birmingham (TV)	Oct. 21
17	Penn State 16	State College (TV)	Oct. 28
23	Miss. State 10	Birmingham (TV)	Nov. 4
32	LSU 16	Baton Rouge (N) (TV)	Nov. 11
37	Southern Miss 14	Tuscaloosa	Nov. 18
20	Auburn 30	Auburn (TV)	Dec. 2
*25	Miami 33	Sugar Bowl (N) (TV)	Jan. 1
357	217		

Bowl Game
(N)=Night Game
(TV)=Television Game

COACH GENE STALLINGS
1990-1996 — Won 70, Lost 16, Tied 1

1990 — Won 7, Lost 5

24	Southern Miss. 27	Birmingham	Sept. 8
13	Florida 17	Tuscaloosa (TV)	Sept. 15
16	Georgia 17	Athens (TV)	Sept. 22
59	Vanderbilt 28	Tuscaloosa	Sept. 29
25	SW Louisiana 6	Lafayette	Oct. 6
9	Tennessee 6	Knoxville (TV)	Oct. 20
0	Penn State 9	Tuscaloosa (TV)	Oct. 27
22	Miss. State 0	Starkville (TV)	Nov. 3
24	LSU 3	Tuscaloosa	Nov. 10
45	Cincinnati 7	Birmingham	Nov. 17
16	Auburn 7	Birmingham (TV)	Dec. 1
*7	Louisville 34	Fiesta Bowl (TV)	Jan. 1
260	161		

1991 — Won 11, Lost 1

41	Temple 3	Birmingham	Sept. 7
0	Florida 35	Gainesville (N) (TV)	Sept. 14
10	Georgia 0	Tuscaloosa (N) (TV)	Sept. 21
48	Vanderbilt 17	Nashville (N)	Sept. 28
53	UT-Chattanooga 7	Birmingham	Oct. 5
62	Tulane 0	Tuscaloosa	Oct. 12
24	Tennessee 19	Birmingham (TV)	Oct. 19
13	Miss. State 7	Tuscaloosa (TV)	Nov. 2
20	LSU 17	Baton Rouge (TV)	Nov. 9
10	Memphis St. 7	Memphis	Nov. 16
13	Auburn 6	Birmingham (TV)	Nov. 30
*30	Colorado 25	Blockbuster Bowl (TV) Dec. 28	
324	143		

1992 — Won 13, Lost 0
Unanimous National Champions
SEC Champions

25	Vanderbilt 8	Tuscaloosa (TV)	Sept. 5
17	Southern Miss 10	Birmingham	Sept. 12
38	Arkansas 11	Little Rock (N)	Sept. 19
13	Louisiana Tech 0	Birmingham	Sept. 26
48	South Carolina 7	Tuscaloosa	Oct. 3
37	Tulane 0	New Orleans (N)	Oct. 10
17	Tennessee 10	Knoxville (TV)	Oct. 17
31	Ole Miss 10	Tuscaloosa	Oct. 24
31	LSU 11	Baton Rouge (TV)	Nov. 7
30	Miss. State 21	Starkville (N) (TV)	Nov. 14
17	Auburn 0	Birmingham (TV)	Nov. 26
28	Florida 21	Birmingham (TV)	Dec. 5
*34	Miami 13	Sugar Bowl (N) (TV)	Jan . 1
366	122		

1993 — Won 1, Lost 12

%31	Tulane 17	Birmingham	Sept. 4
%17	Vanderbilt 6	Nashville (TV)	Sept. 11
%43	Arkansas 3	Tuscaloosa (TV)	Sept. 18
%56	Louisiana Tech 3	Birmingham	Sept. 25
%17	South Carolina 6	Columbia (N) (TV)	Oct. 2
%17	Tennessee 17	Birmingham (TV)	Oct. 16
%19	Ole Miss 14	Oxford (TV)	Oct. 23
%40	Southern Miss 0	Tuscaloosa	Oct. 30
13	LSU 17	Tuscaloosa (TV)	Nov. 6
%36	Mississippi State 25	Tuscaloosa (TV)	Nov. 13
14	Auburn 22	Auburn	Nov. 20
13	Florida 28	Birmingham (TV)	Dec. 4
*24	North Carolina 10	Gator Bowl (N) (TV)	Dec. 31
316	158		

% Later forfeited by NCAA action

1994 — Won 12, Lost 1

42	UT-Chattanooga 13	Birmingham	Sept. 3
17	Vanderbilt 7	Tuscaloosa (TV)	Sept. 10
13	Arkansas 6	Fayetteville	Sept. 17
20	Tulane 10	Birmingham	Sept. 24
29	Georgia 28	Tuscaloosa (N) (TV)	Oct. 1
14	Southern Miss 6	Tuscaloosa	Oct. 8
17	Tennessee 13	Knoxville (TV)	Oct. 15
21	Ole Miss 10	Tuscaloosa (TV)	Oct. 22
35	LSU 17	Baton Rouge (TV)	Nov. 5
29	Mississippi State 25	Starkville (TV)	Nov. 12
21	Auburn 14	Birmingham (TV)	Nov. 19
23	Florida 24	Atlanta (TV)	Dec. 3
*24	Ohio State 17	Citrus Bowl (TV) Jan. 2, 1995	
305	190		

1995 — Won 8, Lost 3

33	Vanderbilt 25	Nashville	Sept. 3
24	Southern Miss 20	Birmingham	Sept. 9
19	Arkansas 20	Tuscaloosa (TV)	Sept. 16
31	Georgia 0	Athens (TV)	Sept. 30
27	N.C. State 6	Tuscaloosa	Oct. 7
14	Tennessee 41	Birmingham (TV)	Oct. 14
23	Ole Miss 9	Oxford	Oct. 21
38	North Texas 19	Tuscaloosa	Oct. 28
10	LSU 3	Tuscaloosa (TV)	Nov. 4
14	Mississippi St. 9	Tuscaloosa (TV)	Nov. 11
27	Auburn 31	Auburn (N) (TV)	Nov. 18
260	188		

1996 — Won 10, Lost 2

21	Bowling Green 7	Birmingham	Aug. 31
20	Southern Miss 10	Tuscaloosa (TV)	Sept. 7
36	Vanderbilt 26	Tuscaloosa (TV)	Sept. 14
17	Arkansas 7	Little Rock (TV)	Sept. 21
35	Kentucky 7	Tuscaloosa	Oct. 5
24	N.C. State 19	Raleigh (TV)	Oct. 12
37	Ole Miss 0	Tuscaloosa (TV)	Oct. 19
13	Tennessee 20	Knoxville (TV)	Oct. 26
26	LSU 0	Baton Rouge (TV)	Nov. 8
16	Mississippi St. 17	Starkville (TV)	Nov. 15
24	Auburn 23	Birmingham (N) (TV) Nov. 23	
30	Florida 45	Atlanta (TV)	Dec. 7
17	Michigan 14	Outback Bowl (TV) Jan. 1, 1997	
286	143		

COACH MIKE DUBOSE
1997-PRESENT — Won 21, Lost 15

1997 — Won 4, Lost 7

42	Houston 17	Birmingham (TV)	Aug. 30
20	Vanderbilt 0	Nashville (TV)	Sept. 11
16	Arkansas 17	Tuscaloosa (TV)	Sept. 20
27	Southern Miss 14	Birmingham (TV)	Sept. 27
34	Kentucky 40	Lexington (OT) (N)	Oct. 4
21	Tennessee 38	Birmingham (TV)	Oct. 18
29	Ole Miss 20	Oxford (TV)	Oct. 25
20	Louisiana Tech 26	Tuscaloosa	Nov. 1
0	LSU 27	Tuscaloosa (TV)	Nov. 8
20	Mississippi State 32	Tuscaloosa (TV)	Nov. 15
17	Auburn 18	Auburn (TV) (N)	Nov. 22
246	248		

1998 — Won 7, Lost 5

38	Brigham Young 31	Tuscaloosa (TV) (N)	Sept. 5
32	Vanderbilt 7	Birmingham (TV)	Sept. 12
6	Arkansas 42	Fayetteville (TV)	Sept. 26
10	Florida 16	Tuscaloosa (TV)	Oct. 3
20	Ole Miss 17	Tuscaloosa (OT)	Oct. 10
23	East Carolina 22	Birmingham	Oct. 17
18	Tennessee 35	Knoxville (TV)	Oct. 24
30	Southern Miss 20	Tuscaloosa	Oct. 31
22	LSU 16	Baton Rouge (TV)	Nov. 7
14	Mississippi State 26	Starkville (TV)	Nov. 14
31	Auburn 17	Birmingham (N) (TV) Nov. 22	
*7	Virginia Tech 38	Music City (TV) (N)	Dec. 29
251	287		

1999 — Won 10, Lost 3
SEC Champions

28	Vanderbilt 17	Nashville (TV)	Sept. 4
37	Houston 10	Birmingham (TV)	Sept. 11
28	Louisiana Tech 29	Birmingham	Sept. 18
35	Arkansas 28	Tuscaloosa (TV)	Sept. 25
40	Florida 39	Gainesville (OT) (TV) Oct. 2	
30	Ole Miss 24	Oxford (TV)	Oct. 16
7	Tennessee 21	Tuscaloosa (TV)	Oct. 23
35	Southern Miss 14	Tuscaloosa	Oct. 30
23	LSU 17	Tuscaloosa (TV)	Nov. 6
19	Mississippi State 7	Tuscaloosa (TV)	Nov. 13
28	Auburn 17	Auburn (N) (TV)	Nov. 20
34	Florida 7	Atlanta (N) (TV)	Dec. 4
*34	Michigan 35	Orange Bowl (OT) (TV) (N) Jan. 1, 2000	
380	265		

*Bowl Game
(N)=Night Game
(TV)=Television Game
(OT)=Overtime Game

INDEX OF NAMES

PICTURE CREDITS

Photographs reprinted with permission from the following:

Steve Alvis, photographer: 187

AP/Wide World Photos: 108 (Butch Wilson)

The Atlanta Journal/Bud Skinner: 142-143

Bettmann/Corbis: 162-163

The Birmingham News: 66 (chess players), 71 (Bill Lee), 154-155 (photo by Leo Lynch), 166-167

Cliff Byrd, photographer: 176-177

The Dallas Morning News/Tom C. Dillard: 92-93

Dothan Landmarks Foundation: 48, 49 (Johnny Mack Brown at 1926 Rose Bowl)

Faculty Resource Center Imaging Services/UA: 95 (Friedman Hall); 124 (Bryant Hall)

Dixie Fraley: 146

Susan M. Kilgrow: 73 (Ronald Reagan)

Leviton-Atlanta/*Sports Illustrated*: 134

R.D. Moore, photographer: 135

Frank Morgan, photographer: 169

The Tennessean/Frank Empson: 158-159

The Tuscaloosa News: 174-175 (photo by Neil Brake), 182-183 (photo by Billy Mitchell), 184, 185 (photo by Billy Mitchell), 190 (photo by Neil Brake), 200 (photo by Neil Brake), 202 (photo by Neil Brake), 202-203, (photo by Neil Brake), 207 (photo by Neil Brake), 214 (photo by Neil Brake), 215 (photo by Neil Brake), 216 (photo by Neil Brake), 218-219 (photo by Neil Brake), 220-221 (photo by Neil Brake), 222-223 (photo by Jason Harris), 225 (photo by Neil Brake), 228 (photo by Jeannie Compton), 232 (photo by Porfirio Solorzano), 234 (photos by Neil Brake), 236 (photo by Neil Brake), 237 (photo by Porfirio Solorzano), 239 (photo by Neil Brake), 240 (photo by Neil Brake), 240-241 (photo by Porfirio Solorzano), 244 (photo by Neil Brake), 248 (photo by Neil Brake), 249 (photo by Neil Brake), 250-251 (photo by Perry Caldwell)

UA Athletics Media Relations: ii-iii (photo by Kent Gidley/UA), 34, 63 (B.O. House), 64 (Johnny Cain), 70 (Riley Smith), 71 (Don Hutson), 78 (Harry Gilmer action), 96, 111 (Lee Roy Jordan), 116 (Bryant), 122-123, 130 (Wilbur Jackson), 132, 133, 139, 151, 152-153, 154, 156 (Alan McElroy), 170-171 (photo by Kent Gidley/UA), 178-179 (photo by Kent Gidley/UA), 180 (Bill Curry; photo by Barry Fikes), 188, 189 (photo by Kent Gidley/UA), 194-195 (photo by Kent Gidley/UA), 196 (photo by Kent Gidley/UA), 196-197, 198-199 (photo by Kent Gidley/UA), 200-201 (photo by Kent Gidley/UA), 204 (photo by Kent Gidley/UA), 208-209 (photo by Kent Gidley/UA), 210-211 (photo by Kent Gidley/UA), 212-213 (photo by Kent Gidley/UA), 217 (photo by Kent Gidley/UA), 226 (photo by Kent Gidley/UA), 227 (photo by Kent Gidley/UA), 229 (photo by Kent Gidley/UA), 230-231 (photo by Kent Gidley/UA), 233 (photo by Kent Gidley/UA), 234-235 (photo by Kent Gidley/UA), 238-239 (photo by Kent Gidley/UA), 242-243 (photo by Kent Gidley/UA), 245 (photo by Kent Gidley/UA), 246-247 (photo by Kent Gidley/UA)

Photographs provided by the following:

Alabama Heritage: 48, 49 (Johnny Mack Brown at 1926 Rose Bowl)

Birmingham Public Library: 6-7, 10, 10-11

The Paul W. Bryant Museum/UA: All game program covers, vi, 2-3, 8 (photo by Rickey Yanaura/UA), 9, 11 (photo by Rickey Yanaura/UA), 12 (football; photo by Rickey Yanaura/UA), 13 (photo by Rickey Yanaura/UA), 15, 20, 21 (game shot), 22-23, 24 (Turkey Bowman), 24-25, 25, 27, 30 (Frank Thomas), 33, 35, 38-39, 40-41, 42 (Wu Winslett), 43, 44-45, 49 (John Wayne), 50 (pennant; photo by Rickey Yanaura/UA), 51 (train station), 52, 53, 54 (game action), 55, 56, 57, 59, 60 (photo by Rickey Yanaura/UA), 62 (White House), 63 (Thomas & Howell), 64 (Bryant & Hutson), 65, 66 ("Hoochman" Collins), 67, 68 (grass cutters), 69 (photo by Rickey Yanaura/UA), 70 (1934 team), 71, 72 (photo by Rickey Yanaura/UA), 72-73, 73 (movie set), 75 (Bear Bryant in uniform; Charlie Boswell), 76, 78 (young Harry Gilmer), 79, 80, 81, 83 (detail), 84, 85 (Red Drew), 86, 90 (Bobby Marlow), 91, 92, 95 (Hugo Friedman), 97, 99, 100, 101, 102 (Bryant with players), 104, 104-105, 106-107, 107, 108 (Butch Wilson), 109, 114, 117 (Namath), 118-119, 121, 126, 127, 128, 129 (photo by Thomas Kidd), 130 (Pat Dye), 134, 135, 136, 137, 140, 141 (majorette), 142-143, 144-145, 147, 149 (Tony Nathan), 150-151, 154-155, 157, 158-159, 159, 160, 161, 162-163, 164, 165, 166-167, 169, 170-171, 172-173, 174-175, 176, 176-177, 178, 180, 181, 182, 182-183, 184, 185, 186, 187, 190, 190-191, 192-193, 196, 197, 198-199, 199 (photo by Ken Blevins/UA), 200-201, 204, 204-205 (photo by Ken Blevins/UA), 206-207 (photo by Ken Blevins/UA), 207, 230-231, 224

The Cotton Bowl: 92-93 (Tommy Lewis)

William Stanley Hoole Special Collections Library/UA: iv-v, 4, 5, 16 (cheerleaders in car), 21 (George Denny), 24 (Rickwood Field photos), 26, 28-29, 31, 42 (sidelines), 46-47, 58, 73 (Ronald Reagan), 75 (coaching staff), 85 (Legion Field), 87, 89, 94, 98, 102 (Liberty Bowl action), 103, 108 (Sugar Bowl royalty), 110, 111 (Joe Namath), 112 (cheerleaders), 113, 114-115, 116 (drum major), 117 (bonfire), 125, 138, 142

The Orange Bowl: 112 (Shorty Price)

Additional photographs reproduced from:

The Corolla (provided by The Paul W. Bryant Museum): 1, 12 (team shot), 14, 16 (line art), 17, 18, 19, 30 (Xen Scott), 32, 36, 37, 54 (Denny Stadium), 62 (cheerleaders), 68 (1935 Rose Bowl), 74, 77, 90 (Bobby Luna), 124 (Bryant points), 149 (Bryant)

Legend in Crimson: A Photo History of Alabama Football: 51 (Red Brown), 141 (unidentified player), 148, 156 (Vanderbilt game)

ABOUT THE AUTHOR

～

WINSTON GROOM, a graduate of The University of Alabama, is the author of ten books, including the best-selling *Forrest Gump* and *Gump & Co.* He also wrote the acclaimed Vietnam War novel *Better Times Than These,* as well as the prize-winning *As Summers Die,* the prize-winning Civil War history *Shrouds of Glory,* and the Pulitzer Prize nominee *Conversations with the Enemy.* He lives with his wife and daughter in Point Clear, Alabama, and in the mountains of North Carolina.

～